OFFENCES AGAINST THE PERSON

Cavendish Publishing Limited

London • Sydney

OFFENCES AGAINST THE PERSON

Professor Richard Stone, LLB, LLM
Principal of the Inns of Court School of Law

Cavendish
Publishing
Limited

London • Sydney

First published in 1999 by Cavendish Publishing Limited, The Glass House, Wharton Street, London, WC1X 9PX, United Kingdom

Telephone: +44 (0) 171 278 8000 Facsimile: +44 (0) 171 278 8080

E-mail: info@cavendishpublishing.com

Visit our Home Page on http://www.cavendishpublishing.com

Stone, Richard

Offences Against the Person

I. Title

344.10525

ISBN 1 874241 13 9

Printed and bound in Great Britain

PREFACE

All criminal law systems categorise certain types of infringement of a person's bodily integrity by another as offences. This book attempts to provide a guide to this area of English criminal law, commonly referred to as 'offences against the person'. The main discussion of the various offences is contained in Chapters 4–6, which deal in turn with homicide, non-fatal offences and sexual offences. Any consideration of this area, however, needs to take account of some general issues, and these are dealt with in the remaining chapters.

Some preliminary matters and concepts of general application are considered in the first three chapters. Chapter 1 attempts to provide a context for later discussion, by considering the limits of criminality, and noting the rights of both the perpetrator and the victim of violent behaviour in this context. Chapter 2 focuses on the physical and mental elements of offences, dealing with issues which are of general application to many of the specific offences discussed subsequently. Chapter 3 recognises the fact that there may be various degrees of participation in criminal behaviour, and discusses accessorial liability, and the inchoate offences of attempt and conspiracy.

Following the discussion of the offences in Chapters 4–6, Chapter 7 describes the various general defences which may be available. Finally, Chapter 8 outlines the most recent proposals for reform of various areas, including the consultation paper and draft Bill on non-fatal offences issued by the Home Office in February 1998.

Two themes recur at various points throughout the book. The first is the need to recognise the rights of the victim in considering the scope and application of the law. This will become of increasing importance with the incorporation of the European Convention on Human Rights by means of the Human Rights Act 1998. Although the Act will probably not come into force until the year 2000, it is likely that its imminent introduction will start to colour this area from now on. The second, and to some extent related, theme is the significance of the alleged victim's consent (or the defendant's belief in such consent) to actions taken against him or her which would otherwise be criminal. This issue is addressed directly in differing contexts in five of the eight chapters (1, 4, 6, 7 and 8). It has attracted most discussion in recent years as a result of the House of Lords' decision in *Brown* [1993] 2 All ER 75 concerning sado-masochism, but clearly has a wider significance in defining the nature of what behaviour should or should not be treated as criminal, and why.

I hope the book will be of use to students and practitioners in providing a full but manageable account of this area of criminal law. I have tried to state the law as it stood on 1 November 1998.

This book has been a long time in the writing, and I would like to thank the publishing team at Cavendish for their patience in waiting for it. My thanks also go to my wife and four children for their gentle reminders, whenever I appeared to be at a loose end, that there was always a book to be completed.

Richard Stone
Oadby
November 1998

CONTENTS

TABLE OF CASES

TABLE OF STATUTES

TABLE OF EUROPEAN LEGISLATION

CHAPTER 1

INTRODUCTION

This book is concerned with a self-contained, but very important section of the criminal law – offences against the person.

An advantage of this narrow focus is that certain issues which necessarily arise in a more general treatment of the criminal law do not need any, or such detailed, discussion. For example, in looking at the appropriate scope of the use of criminal sanctions, the fact that we are not concerned with offences against property,[1] or the State,[2] or morality[3] simplifies the debate considerably. It does not remove it altogether, as will be seen from subsequent discussions, but it limits the issues which need consideration, since there is general agreement that, for example, deliberate actions which cause physical harm to another person should be subject to criminal sanctions, whereas the question, for example, as to whether the deliberate publication of an obscene article, or the possession of cannabis should be punishable under the criminal law is much more controversial. Nevertheless, rather than relying solely on a perception of what 'everybody agrees', this chapter attempts to explore the reasons why offences against the person are criminal, in order to define the limits on the law in this area. In doing this, it is hoped that it will become clearer why, for example, I do not commit any offence if I deliberately cause myself serious harm (for example, by smashing my foot with a mallet) but, if I ask my friend to do this for me, and he or she does so, a charge of causing grievous bodily harm may be brought against him or her. It will also attempt to shed some light on the issue of why some offences are regarded as more serious than others, and how such grading should take place.

THE NATURE AND EXTENT OF CRIMINALITY

There are many elements which go towards the criminality of an offence against the person. The actions of the perpetrator, the consequences of those actions, the state of mind of perpetrator and victim, the involvement of third parties, the surrounding circumstances may all be relevant. In attempting to unravel the interlinking of these various factors, the approach taken here is to adopt a 'rights' perspective. In other words, the law will be analysed and assessed on the basis of an assumption that its primary purpose is to protect

1 Eg, criminal damage, theft.

2 Eg, treason, sedition.

3 Eg, obscene publications.

individual rights. The framework of rights which will be used will be drawn from the European Convention on Human Rights, which has been used as the basis of the Human Rights Act 1998, and is therefore directly applicable as a standard against which the law of offences against the person can be judged.[4] Such an analysis will not, however, as we shall see, provide a complete picture, and at some points the State assumes the right to intervene to punish behaviour even though the rights of no individual have been infringed. An important question is the extent to which it is justifiable for the State to intervene in this way, and what the limits of any such power to intervene should be. The starting point for discussion, however, will be the rights of the 'victim'. It should be noted at this point that the following convention is adopted throughout this book: the person who has committed, or is alleged to have committed, an offence is referred to as the defendant (D); the person against whom an offence has been committed is referred to as the victim (V). There will also be references at various points to the 'prosecution'. This will generally occur where the discussion relates to technical matters concerning the burden and standard of proof, rather than the rights which have been infringed, or the effect of the defendant's behaviour on the victim.

Following discussion of the victim's rights, this chapter will look at the rights of the defendant. It will then consider the role of the State in defining criminal behaviour which does not involve the infringement of a victim's rights.

The rights of the victim

When one person is struck by another, the most obvious right of the victim (V) which has been infringed is the right to bodily integrity. The individual's right to control his or her own body is fundamental to any free society. The person who infringes such a right by violence will generally be held to have committed a serious offence. It might be thought that in relation to offences against the person, this right would define the extent of liability. As we shall see, however, it is not necessary for there to be an infringement of bodily integrity in order for the criminal law to intervene to protect the victim. The threat of such infringement, which may be conveyed by words, action, or even silence, is sufficient. Clearly then, a broader based right than simply that of bodily integrity is involved. This is to be found in the right to 'privacy', which encompasses bodily integrity, but extends beyond this. 'Privacy' here is used not in the sense of 'confidentiality', but as relating to an individual's private space. The relevant Article in the ECHR is Art 8, which states that:

---

4 For an outline of the ECHR, see Stone, R, *Textbook on Civil Liberties*, 2nd edn, 1997, London: Blackstone, pp 17–29. For detailed discussion, see Harris, D, O'Boyle, K and Warbrick, C, *Law of the European Convention on Human Rights*, 1995, London: Butterworths.

(a) Everyone has the right to respect for his private and family life ...

(b) There shall be no interference by a public authority with the exercise of this right except such as in accordance with the law and is necessary in a democratic society in the interests of national security, public safety or the economic well being of the country, for the prevention of disorder or crime, for the protection of health or morals, or for the protection of the right and freedoms of others.

The right to respect for the individual's private life has been held in several cases under the ECHR to impose a positive duty on Member States to ensure that privacy is protected, as well as dealing with infringements.[5] The leading case for the purposes of discussion of the areas covered by this book is *X and Y v The Netherlands*.[6] Y, a mentally handicapped girl of 16, was sexually assaulted by the D.[7] Y, because of her mental condition, was not competent to sign a complaint against the D, so her father (X) attempted to do so on her behalf. The Netherlands Court of Appeal ruled that the provisions of the relevant Code did not allow for this to happen in such a case (that is, where the complainant was over 16), and therefore there was a gap in the law, which could not be filled by means of a broad interpretation operating to the detriment of the D.[8] The European Court of Human Rights had no doubt that Art 8 of the Convention applied here. The requirement of 'respect' meant that the obligations imposed on a State 'may involve the adoption of measures designed to secure respect for private life even in the sphere of the relations between themselves'.[9] Nor was it sufficient that the V might have a civil law remedy:[10]

> This is a case where fundamental values and essential aspects of private life are at stake. Effective deterrence is indispensable in this area, and it can be achieved only by criminal law provisions.

The argument is thus that the obligation on the State under Art 8 requires it to provide adequate protection from infringement of the rights protected, even by one individual against another. Such protection can only be achieved by effective deterrence: this can only be effected by making the behaviour subject to the criminal law.

This decision of the ECHR, therefore, provides the basis for requiring the criminalisation of all offences against the person, inasmuch as they involve unjustifiable intrusions into the private life of the V. It is quite clear that such intrusions can extend beyond the infringement of the V's bodily integrity.

5 Eg, *Airey v Ireland* (1979–80) 2 EHRR 305.

6 (1986) 8 EHRR 235.

7 Under English law, the offence would almost certainly have been rape.

8 (1986) 8 EHRR 235, p 237, para 12.

9 *Ibid*, pp 239–40, para 23. Cf the similar view taken in the recent Article 3 case, *A v UK* 1998 (unreported) (103/1997/884/1098), discussed below at p 197.

10 *Ibid*, p 241, para 27.

Moreover, the approach rightly places at the centre of the reasons for criminalisation the protection of the rights of the V. Note, however, that the rights guaranteed by Art 8 are not absolute. Various situations are recognised by Art 8(2) in which an infringement of the V's privacy may be justified. Some of these limitations will be considered in more detail in Chapter 7, which is concerned with the defences which may be available to the D.

Before concluding discussion of the ECHR, it should also be noted that Art 2 requires that 'Everyone's right to life shall be protected by law'. This clearly justifies the criminalisation of homicide and, almost certainly, in the light of the statements made in *X and Y v The Netherlands* quoted above, requires States to do so.[11] Thus, in addition to the broad recognition of rights of privacy and bodily integrity under Art 8, there is here a specific obligation imposed on states in relation to situations where the action of one citizen causes the death of another. Once again, due recognition of the rights of the V will generally require the intervention of the criminal law.[12]

The rights of the defendant

A person accused of committing an offence also has rights. These are recognised in Arts 5, 6 and 7, which deal with the standards to be adopted in the investigation and prosecution of offences. Many of these are procedural, and outside the scope of this book,[13] but the following should be noted:

Art 6 (1) In the determination ... of any criminal charge against him, everyone is entitled to a fair and public hearing ...

(2) Everyone charged with a criminal offence shall be presumed innocent until proved guilty according to law.

(3) Everyone charged with a criminal offence has the following minimum rights:

(a) ...

(b) ...

(c) to defend himself in person or through legal assistance of his own choosing ...

(d) to examine or have examined witnesses against him ...

These provisions establish in particular that there must be a proper trial before conviction; that the burden of proof is on the prosecution; and that the D, in defending himself, must be allowed to cross-examine those who give evidence against him.

11 See, eg, the discussion of this provision, *op cit*, Harris, O'Boyle and Warbrick, fn 4, p 38.

12 See, eg, *Widner v Switzerland, No 20527/92* (1993), unreported – noted by Harris, O'Boyle and Warbrick, *op cit*, fn 4, p 38.

13 Eg, the provisions relating to procedure on arrest and to detention before trial.

The enforcement of the D's rights may, at times, run counter to the rights of the V. For example, a D who has committed an offence may escape liability because the prosecution is unable to satisfy the burden of proof. Or, the victim (for example, of a sexual assault) may be unable to face the ordeal of cross-examination. In such cases, a D may escape liability and the infringement of the V's rights will go unacknowledged. Traditionally, treatises on the criminal law have been written from the D's perspective.[14] They have concentrated on what the prosecution has to prove in order to establish a conviction against the D. They have also tended to argue for or against the moral justification for any particular aspect of the criminal law on the basis of how this relates to the moral rights of the D. This has led into issues of 'responsibility' which have focused on the mental state of the D at the time when the offence was committed. Was the D acting intentionally or recklessly? Was he aware of the probable consequences of his actions? All of these issues are important, and will be given due weight in the subsequent chapters of this book. They should not be allowed, however, to obscure the fact that Vs also have rights, and that the law should at times be striking a balance between the rights of the V and the rights of the D. Neither should be regarded as automatically dominant, though the prime function of the law should probably be recognised as the provision of protection to Vs and potential Vs. Giving full recognition to this might lead to an approach which acknowledges the V's rights by finding that an offence has been committed in most situations where an *actus reus* can be proved, and leaves the issue of the D's moral responsibility to be dealt with by discretionary sentencing.

Such an approach would result in a major shift of emphasis, and it is not suggested here that it could easily be adopted across the board. Elements of it can be found, however, in the use of 'diminished responsibility' to reduce murder to manslaughter,[15] thus giving the judge full discretion in sentencing. It also relates to the arguments of those who suggest that the laws concerning sexual offences, rape in particular, do not give proper respect to the rights of the victim. It will be suggested at some points that the law could move further towards this approach, without unduly affecting the rights of the D, and that, at the very least, some aspects of the current law which are difficult to explain logically if looked at from the D's perspective, become much more understandable if the rights of the V are added into the equation. An example is the way in which the seriousness of the offence with which a D may be charged can, in some cases, depend not so much on the nature of the D's behaviour and his state of mind, but on the consequences of that behaviour, which may be beyond the D's control.

14 A notable exception is Lacey, N, Wells, C and Meure, D, *Reconstructing Criminal Law*, 2nd edn, 1998, London: Butterworths, which attempts to place the whole of criminal law in a much broader context.

15 See Chapter 4, pp 82–87.

Consider the situation of the victim of an assault who unexpectedly dies as a result of an allergic reaction to medical treatment: the D will become liable for the offence of manslaughter, rather than simply an assault. From the D's point of view, the approach may seem illogical, since his moral responsibility should be determined by his actions and state of mind, which were the same whether the V lived or died. The approach may be justified, however, as a means of giving proper recognition to the rights of the V, provided that the sentence imposed on the D can take full account of the circumstances in which the offence occurred. These issues will be examined further in the relevant chapters, below.

The interests of the State

Although it has been argued above that the protection of the rights of the V are central to the criminal law concerning offences against the person, it must be recognised that at times the law penalises the D's behaviour even where it seems that the V's rights have not been infringed. If, for example, the D has sexual intercourse with a girl who is under 16, he commits an offence. It is irrelevant whether the girl consented. She may have been a perfectly willing participant, and yet the law deems the D's actions to amount to an offence.[16] Of course, it may be argued that a girl of under 16 is incapable of giving consent. But, this must be an argument based on convention rather than fact. Given that there is a wide range in the speed with which human beings achieve physical and emotional maturity, it is impossible to sustain an argument that the sixteenth birthday produces an automatic change, and that all girls of 15 years and 11 months are incompetent to decide whether or not they wish to use their bodies in a certain way. The argument is even stronger in relation to male homosexual conduct, where the age of consent is 18.[17] Some Vs below the relevant ages may not be consenting, or may be incapable of fully appreciating the consequences of their actions, and therefore need protecting, but this will by no means be true in all cases. An alternative approach would be to require the D to prove that the V was genuinely consenting. As the law stands, it operates to criminalise behaviour where there has been no infringement of the V's rights. The justification is presumably the State's interest in protecting young people from sexual exploitation. However, the same approach is taken in relation to adults and consent to certain types of assault. As we shall see in Chapter 7, concerning defences, a D can be guilty of an offence even where the alleged V is a fully

16 Sexual Offences Act 1956, s 6.

17 Sexual Offences Act 1967, s 1.

competent adult who consented, or possibly even encouraged,[18] the D's actions. The intervention of the criminal law in such a situation is not, therefore, based on the infringement of individual rights. It must be based on a more general interest of the State in discouraging certain types of behaviour which it regards as detrimental to society. Indeed, in intervening in this way, far from protecting the rights of the individual, it may be said that the State is unduly restricting the individual's right to, for example, sexual freedom, under Art 8 of the ECHR.[19] The scope of these arguments and counter-arguments, and their validity, will be considered in more detail in Chapter 7. For the moment, the main point to be noted is that there is this further justification for the intervention of the criminal law, which goes beyond the rights of individuals and operates in the interests of society as a whole. One further point should be noted, however, namely that behaviour which is criminal if committed by the D against the V, will not generally be criminal if committed by the V on herself. The D who beats a consenting V with a whip may be liable for an offence under the Offences Against the Person Act 1861: the V who engages in self-flagellation, or self-mutilation, commits no offence at all (even if the behaviour is serious enough to require medical treatment). Similarly, at the level of termination of life, the V commits no offence by attempting suicide,[20] whereas the D who assists the V in committing suicide, or terminates the V's life at the V's request will be liable to face prosecution. This suggests that it is not the outcome itself which society regards as giving rise to a situation appropriate for the intervention of the criminal law, since this is the same whether the D is involved or whether the V acts on her own. It must be the interrelation between the D and the V which makes the difference.[21] Why this should be so will again be considered further in Chapter 7, but it emphasises the point, already noted above, that we are dealing here with a criminal liability which does not arise out of the infringement of individual rights, but from a decision by the State, on behalf of society, that irrespective of such rights, certain behaviour should be discouraged by the imposition of penalties.

18 In which case, the V may also be liable for aiding and abetting the offence.

19 See, eg, *Brown* [1993] 2 All ER 75. Note, however, that the European Court of Human Rights in *Brown* rejected arguments by the Ds based on Art 8 – *Laskey, Jaggard and Brown v UK* (1997) 24 EHRR 39. They did not consider the V's rights under Art 8.

20 And, as shown by the Court of Appeal decision in *St George's Healthcare National Health Service Trust v S* [1998] 3 All ER 673, a V may also refuse medical treatment which doctors consider is necessary to protect the life of both her and her unborn child. Indeed, doctors who acted without her consent would themselves be committing a criminal offence.

21 Some parallels might be drawn with the law relating to conspiracy, discussed below, p 52, where, in certain circumstances, the agreement to commit acts which if done by an individual would not be criminal, can itself amount to an offence.

CHAPTER 2

ELEMENTS OF OFFENCES

An offence against the person will almost always have two elements commonly described as the *actus reus* and *mens rea*. The rough translation of these Latin tags as 'guilty act' and 'guilty mind', should not be taken as indicating their precise meaning.[1] They are simply a shorthand method of describing two very complex concepts. Nor should it be assumed that they are entirely independent. At times, there is an interrelationship, or a difficulty in drawing a clear line between the two. A person who, as a result of a sudden fit, or seizure, for example, flings out an arm and strikes another, will almost certainly not commit an offence. But is this because of the absence of an *actus reus*, or of *mens rea*, or both? The issue arises because it may be argued that an *actus reus* requires an act that is 'willed' or voluntary. It becomes important in situations where the law refuses to excuse the D even though the prosecution cannot prove the relevant *mens rea* – for example, if this is due to the D's voluntary intoxication.[2] If the defendant can argue that there is no *actus reus*, however, the *mens rea* issue becomes irrelevant. In other offences, the *actus reus* may itself involve a more specific mental element. This is more often the case with offences outside the area of our discussion,[3] but an example which is applicable is the offence of conspiracy. Here, the *actus reus* of the offence is an 'agreement' between two or more parties. Clearly, such an act of agreement implies a conscious decision to make it, and a particular state of mind. The notion of an unconscious agreement is meaningless. Here, then, the determination of the *actus reus* involves at least some consideration of the state of mind of the person concerned.

ACTUS REUS

The definition of the *actus reus* of specific offences may give rise to difficulties as to what precise behaviour is required, as for example, with rape or assault. This section makes only a passing reference to these issues, which are left to the chapters dealing with the particular offences. Here, the focus is on some general matters which arise with all, or a range of, offences against the person.

1 They in fact derive from the longer phrase *actus non facit reum, nisi mens sit rea* (an act does not make a person guilty, unless the mind is guilty).

2 See Chapter 7.

3 See, eg, the offences discussed by Smith, JC and Hogan, B, *Criminal Law Cases and Materials*, 6th edn, 1996, London: Butterworths, Chapter 7.

Many offences against the person are 'result' crimes. In other words, the *actus reus* will consist of behaviour which leads to a particular consequence. Typically for an offence against the person, this might be a violent act which leads to bodily injury on the part of the victim. This connection, whereby an act leads to, or brings about, a result, raises issues of causation. For the *actus reus* to be made out, it must be proved that the behaviour of the D 'caused' an injury to, or had some other effect on, the V. In some situations, this will be unproblematic. If the D slaps the V in the face, thereby breaking her jaw, there is no difficulty in stating that the slap was the 'cause' of the broken jaw. The D has therefore committed the *actus reus* of an assault occasioning actual bodily harm. Similarly, if as a result of the slap the V falls and, hitting her head, suffers a fractured skull, the D's act will be regarded as having caused the injury. There are, however, three particular areas of difficulty, sometimes interrelated, which may arise in relation to causation. The first is where the act and the result are separated by a significant lapse of time; the second is where there may be said to be a number of 'causes' of the result, some of which may pre-date the D's acts, some of which may be subsequent to them; the third is where an injury, or some other relevant consequence, may be said to result from an omission, rather than a positive act on the part of the D.

Lapse of time

Some offences include a time element in their definition. Assault, for example,[4] requires an apprehension by the V of the infliction of *immediate* unlawful violence. The behaviour by the D which is alleged to constitute the *actus reus* must therefore have this effect without significant lapse of time. So, for example, if the D directs a threat at the V, who is asleep at the time, no assault occurs if the V is later, on waking, told of the D's threat by a third party.[5] In such a case, the causation issue is determined simply on the basis of the interpretation of the word 'immediate' (or whatever other specific phrase is used).[6]

Another example of offences including a time element in their definition used to be the requirement that for homicide offences the death of the V must occur within a year and a day. This has, however, been abolished by the Law Reform (Year and a Day Rule) Act 1996.[7] One of the principles which lay behind the former rule, however, may still be said to be of general application. This is that the longer the gap between the D's behaviour and the occurrence

4 As distinct from battery – see Chapter 4, p 103.

5 Cf the similar conclusion reached in relation to s 4 of the Public Order Act 1986, in cases such as *Atkin v DPP* (1989) 89 Cr App R 199, *Horseferry Road Metropolitan Stipendiary Magistrate ex p Siadatan* [1991] 1 All ER 324.

6 This issue as it applies to assault is discussed further in Chapter 5, p 107.

7 See Chapter 4, p 58.

of the result constituting the crime, the more difficult it will be to prove that the behaviour caused the result. Where the definition of the particular offence does not itself impose a specific time limit, this will be the focus of consideration in cases where there is a gap between the two relevant events. It is essentially an evidential issue rather than one of substantive law, and raises similar problems to that discussed in the next section.

Multiple causes

The problem of multiple causes has raised particular difficulties in relation to homicide offences, and the relevant case law will be considered in detail in Chapter 4.[8] There are, however, principles involved which are of general application to all result crimes, and these will be outlined here. First, it is necessary to note the *post hoc, propter hoc* fallacy: that is, because one event occurs after another, the latter was caused by the former. The fact that the D read a certain pornographic publication before committing a rape does not establish that the reading of the publication was a cause of the D's actions. In relation to the issues we are considering, this means that because the behaviour of the D precedes in time the result which forms part of the *actus reus* of the offence it is a necessary condition of D's liability, but not a sufficient one. Furthermore, for the purposes of criminal liability, it is not even sufficient to establish that 'but for' the D's behaviour the result would not have occurred. If a mother tells her child to go to the local supermarket to buy some bread, and on the way the child is attacked by a third party, the mother is not responsible for the assault, even though it would not have occurred 'but for' her telling the child to run the errand. This is so, even if the mother's behaviour may be seen as morally open to criticism, as where the child is deemed to be too young to have been allowed out alone. The issue is easy enough to state, and obvious examples such as those just given do not create problems. Difficulties arise, however, where the V may have reacted in a way which contributed to, or aggravated, the injuries suffered; or where the D's actions affect the V only indirectly; or where the intervention of a third party may not be sufficient to break the chain of causation.

The first situation is exemplified by *Roberts*.[9] The V was given a lift in the D's car. The D stopped the car and tried to remove the V's clothes. She resisted, and eventually tried to get out of the car. As she did so, the D started to move off. The V suffered injuries as a result of jumping from the moving car. It was held that the D's actions had caused her injuries. The V's reaction was a reasonably foreseeable response to the D's initial assault, and the chain of causation was not broken. Only where the V's reaction was not reasonably

8 Chapter 4, pp 58–61.

9 (1971) 56 Cr App R 95.

to be expected would the D escape liability for its consequences. If, however, as Stephenson LJ put it,[10] the reaction was:

> ... so unexpected, not that this particular assailant did not actually foresee it but that no reasonable man could be expected to foresee it, then it is only in a very remote and unreal sense a consequence of his assault, it is really occasioned by a voluntary act on the part of the victim which could not reasonably be foreseen and which breaks the chain of causation between the assault and the harm or injury.[11]

There seems to be a shortage of reported cases where the response of the V has been found to be unreasonable. In part, this is probably due to the fact that such cases do not reach the stage of prosecution, let alone conviction. It is also probably true, however, that the test is a fairly strict one. In other words, the range of reasonable responses to an unlawful attack by the D is wide, and it is only where there is no proportionality between the two that the principle will operate in the D's favour.[12]

The situations just discussed involve an active response by the V. In some cases, however, the V's failure to act may have aggravated the consequences of the D's behaviour. The leading case on this is *Blaue*,[13] which was concerned with a conviction for manslaughter. The V had been stabbed, but the wound would not have been fatal if properly treated. The V, however, was a Jehovah's Witness and, following her religious beliefs, refused to have a blood transfusion. As a result, she died. It was held that her refusal of the standard treatment did not break the chain of causation. The explanation for the decision given by the court was that it was an example of the well established principle of 'taking your victim as you find her'. Thus, in the same way that the D cannot evade responsibility if the consequence of a minor assault turns out to be more serious because the V suffers from brittle bones, so 'taking account of the whole man, not just the physical man',[14] religious beliefs are to be treated in the same way as medical conditions. The difficulty with this approach is to determine whether it should apply to *all* beliefs. Suppose that the reason for refusing the blood transfusion is not religious, but a belief, based on no scientific evidence, that the blood of someone who has eaten beef can transmit BSE. Does this refusal also leave the chain of causation intact? Or, to take another example, suppose that the V, who has suffered a minor wound to the leg insists on treating it with her own herbal remedies, which prove ineffective. If the wound becomes infected and the V's leg has to be

---

10 (1971) 56 Cr App R 95, p 102.

11 Note the similar conclusions reached in the manslaughter cases of *DPP v Daley* [1979] 2 WLR 239, PC; *Mackie* (1973) 57 Cr App R 453, CA; and *Williams and Davis* [1992] 2 All ER 183, CA.

12 Cf the comments of Stuart-Smith LJ, in *Williams and Davis* [1992] 2 All ER 183, p 191.

13 (1975) 61 Cr App R 271, CA.

14 *Ibid*, p 274.

amputated, is the D then liable for inflicting grievous bodily harm? Examples such as these suggest that it might be better to bring these cases within the 'reasonable foresight' principle used in *Roberts*. In other words, if the behaviour of the V is such that it should be reasonably foreseeable, then the D will be responsible for the full extent of the injuries resulting. If, however, it is not reasonably foreseeable, then liability should relate to the injuries of the extent normally to be expected as a consequence of the D's behaviour. Applying this type of test, the result in Blaue would probably be the same. It is well known that certain religious groups will not accept blood transfusions, and this action on the part of the V is therefore reasonably foreseeable. The other examples given would be more difficult to determine, but it is submitted that the D might well be able to argue that neither of these responses was reasonably foreseeable, and that therefore the chain of causation should be deemed to be broken.[15]

A distinction might also be drawn between positive acts on the part of the V and failures to act. It is easier to regard the chain of causation as remaining intact where the end consequences are a 'natural' outcome of the D's original behaviour (as where an untreated wound becomes septic), than where they result from some positive intervention by the V. The most extreme example of such intervention would be where the V's response to the D's behaviour is to commit suicide. In *Dear*,[16] the Court of Appeal took the view that the chain would not be broken if, as was alleged, the V had deliberately reopened wounds caused by the D with the intention of committing suicide, unless this was done for some reason unconnected with the D's attack (for example, remorse for past actions). A hypothetical, but not totally incredible example, falling short of suicide, might arise as follows. Suppose that the D commits a minor assault which will leave a scar on the V's leg. The V belongs to a cult which glorifies perfection and abhors blemishes on a person's body. In accordance with the tenets of this cult, the V amputates his 'disfigured' leg. Is the D to be liable for grievous bodily harm? It is suggested that this is clearly a much weaker case against the D than even the 'herbal remedy' example given above. In this type of situation, it would seem correct to adopt the principle that if a positive intervention by the V (as opposed to a failure to act) exacerbates the effect of the D's behaviour, then the chain of causation is broken, at least unless the response was reasonably foreseeable. On the other hand, the chain will remain intact if the V simply lets events take their natural course, even if such a response may be regarded as unreasonable.[17] As Lawton, LJ put it in *Blaue*:[18]

15 Cf the comments of Ashworth, A, *Principles of Criminal Law*, 2nd edn, 1995, Oxford: Clarendon, pp 128–29, as to what should be regarded as 'abnormal' behaviour.

16 [1996] Crim LR 595.

17 *Ibid*.

18 (1975) 61 Cr App R 271, CA, p 274.

> The question is what caused her death. The answer is the stab wound. The fact that the victim refused to stop this end coming about did not break the causal connection between the act and the death.

The second problem which may arise in relation to multiple causes relates to the situation where the behaviour of the D only indirectly affects the V. There is no doubt that the D can use a third party (T) as an innocent agent of a crime. Suppose that the D wishes to murder the V. He asks the T to take a package, and leave it with the V. The package, unknown to the T, contains a bomb, which explodes, killing the V. The D will be regarded as causing the V's death. The same is true if the D's behaviour causes an involuntary response by the T which results in injury to the V. Suppose that the D deliberately hits the T, who as a result falls against the V; the V is knocked over, bangs her head and suffers serious injuries. Is the D responsible for the injuries to the V? This is an issue which is answered partly by consideration of the D's *mens rea*, and the application of the principle of 'transferred malice'.[19] As far as the *actus reus* is concerned, however, although the direct cause of the V's injuries is the fact that the T fell against her, there is no doubt that the chain of causation will be regarded as intact. This is the conclusion to be drawn from *Mitchell*,[20] in which the facts were virtually identical to the example just given, except that V died from the injuries which she sustained. The charge was therefore one of manslaughter, and D was convicted. The Court of Appeal held that the jury was perfectly entitled to find that D's actions caused V's death.[21] Slightly more difficult is the case where T's behaviour in relation to V is not involuntary, but a conscious response to D. Thus, if D threatens T with serious harm, and T, in running away, pushes V, and V falls suffering injury, are the actions of D, or T (or both), the cause of V's injuries? Combining the principles which have been used in the *Roberts* type of cases, with the approach taken in *Mitchell*, the most likely answer would be that if the T's reaction is reasonably foreseeable, then the D will be regarded as having caused the injuries to the V. It may also be the case, however, that the T will also incur criminal liability if his action in pushing the V can be said to go beyond the unthinking reaction of a person in panic, fleeing threats in the interests of personal safety.

The third type of difficulty which may arise in relation to causation occurs where a third party has intervened, following the D's original behaviour. If the D has assaulted the V and knocked her out, and then the T, finding the V unconscious, inflicts a wound, has the D caused the wound? The principle likely to be applied here is that the T's action is a *novus actus interveniens* ('a new intervening act') which breaks the chain of causation. Much of the case law in this area has arisen in relation to homicide and the question of medical treatment. If the actions of doctors, or other medical staff, can be shown to

19 See below, p 23.

20 (1983) 76 Cr App Rep 293, CA

21 The *mens rea* aspects of this decision are discussed in Chapter 4, p 95.

have aggravated the V's injuries, and perhaps resulted in an avoidable death, does this prevent the D from being liable for the death? Detailed discussion of this particular problem will be left to Chapter 4,[22] but some of the principles involved are sketched here. There are two main factors to be considered. The first is whether the medical treatment was to any degree negligent. If it is not, then there will be no break in the chain of causation. If standard medical procedures have been followed, but have unfortunately resulted in a worsening of the V's condition (as, for example, where the V has an unknown, and unpredictable allergy to a particular drug), the D will remain responsible for the consequences. On the other hand, if the medical treatment can be regarded as incompetent, or grossly negligent, then it is much more likely that the chain of causation will be treated as being broken.

The second factor is whether the injuries inflicted by the D can be said to be a 'substantial and operating cause' of the V's death,[23] or whether they simply form part of the 'history' or 'setting' in which the death occurs.[24] If the V's injuries have virtually healed, for example, and then are treated with an incorrect dose of a drug, which proves fatal, it is unlikely that D will be liable for the V's death.[25] If, however, the original injuries were life-threatening, the fact that the V's life might well have been saved by proper medical treatment will not prevent the D from being liable even where there has been some degree of negligence by medical staff.

Although, on the face of it, the principles being applied in these cases might appear to be based simply on an attempt to operate a logical approach to causation, in fact there is a fairly strong 'moral' element involved. There is a reluctance on the part of the courts to allow the D's responsibility for the consequences of his behaviour to be limited by the fact that someone who was acting with the best of motives, and trying to assist the V, has in fact made matters worse. It is only in the most clear cut of such cases, therefore, that the chain of causation will be held to be broken. This moral element appears more starkly in a decision not concerned with a medical intervention, but with the actions of police officers trying to assist the V. This is the case of *Pagett*,[26] where the V, who was being used as a 'human shield' by the D, was accidentally shot by a police officer. The D was nevertheless held to have 'caused' the V's death. It is by no means clear, however, that the result would have been the same had the V been shot by an accomplice of the D. At the very least, the accomplice would have been jointly liable with the D, whereas the police officer in *Pagett* was absolved of all responsibility. The D's behaviour was treated as being the sole cause of the V's death. Thus, where

22 Chapter 4, p 58.

23 *Smith* [1959] 2 All ER 193.

24 *Jordan* (1956) 40 Cr App R 152.

25 (1956) 40 Cr App R 152.

26 (1983) 76 Cr App R 279.

the intervener is a person who is acting for 'good' motives, and especially if that person is acting in an official capacity as part of his or her job, it is much less likely that their actions will be regarded as a *novus actus* than if they are also acting with the intention of causing harm to the V.

Omissions

The very phrase *actus reus* carries with it the implication of some definite action on the D's part. English law does not generally impose criminal liability on those who fail to act. The classic example,[27] often quoted, is the lack of any legal responsibility on the part of a passer by to assist a person who is drowning and shouting for help. The D, the passer by, will not be guilty of manslaughter if the V drowns, because there is no *actus reus*. Even if the D could easily assist the V without any personal danger, but fails to do so because he wishes the V dead, so that he can inherit under her will, there is still no criminal liability. Some positive act must generally be shown before there can be liability for an offence against the person.

As with most rules, however, there is an exception to this. If the D can be said to be under a duty as regards the V, then a failure to act may give rise to liability. Such a duty may be imposed generally by the law (a 'public duty'), or arise from contract, or even be deemed to exist as a result of past conduct. These will be considered briefly in turn, though further discussion of this issue will be found in subsequent chapters in relation to the discussion of the *actus reus* of particular offences.

Public duty

The most obvious example of this type of duty is that owed by parents to their children. A deliberate failure to act in a situation which leads to injury to the child will render the parent liable to criminal charges. This exception to the general position was recognised by Stephen[27] and has been adopted by the courts in cases such as *Gibbins and Proctor*,[28] and *Downes*.[29] It is also the case that a duty to act will be found as between husband and wife.[30] It is not clear what other family relationships, if any, will give rise to such a duty. It is not even clear, for example, that elderly parents will be owed such a duty by their adult offspring, or whether it exists between siblings.[31] Such possible areas of

27 At least 100 years ago: Stephen, JF, *Digest of the Criminal Law*, 4th edn, 1887, London: Macmillan, Art 212.

28 (1918) 13 Cr App R 134.

29 (1875)) 13 Cox CC 111 – though note that here the duty was held to be imposed by statute, ie, the Poor Law Amendment Act 1868.

30 Eg, *Smith* [1979] Crim LR 251.

31 The case of *William Smith* (1826) 2 C&P 449; 172 ER 203 would suggest that such a duty does not automatically arise, but the decision is only that of a trial judge at assizes.

responsibility will often, in practice, fall within the third category discussed here, that is, a duty derived from past conduct.

A second type of public duty, giving rise to potential criminal liability for a failure to act, is to be found in statutory responsibilities. These arise most commonly in regulatory codes concerning, for example, health and safety at work, and so are outside the scope of this work. An example of a statutory duty, breach of which may lead to consequences similar to an offence against the person, is the offence contained in s 1 of the Children and Young Persons Act 1933. This imposes a duty not to wilfully neglect a child under 16 on a person over 16 having responsibility for the child. The offence is committed where the neglect is 'likely to cause [the child] unnecessary suffering or injury to health'. This is distinguishable from the more general common law duty noted in the previous paragraph, in that there is nothing necessarily to prevent that duty arising in respect of children over the age of 16.[32] Moreover, the statutory duty is clearly most apposite as regards continuing neglect, whereas the common law duty could apply to a single omission.

Police officers are under a public duty to keep the peace and to protect citizens who may be under attack from others.[33] Failure to act in accordance with this duty will constitute the offence of misconduct in a public office,[34] but will not render the officer concerned criminally liable in relation to all the consequences of this omission. Thus, if a police officer stands by while a person is attacked and badly injured, the officer will not be liable for causing grievous bodily harm, or for manslaughter if the victim dies.[35]

Contractual duty

A person's contract of employment may impose upon them an express or implied requirement to act, in situations where a failure to do so may result in harm to others. Obvious examples include firemen or doctors. Failure by such persons to act to prevent harm may lay them open to criminal liability for the consequences. There are relatively few reported cases on this situation, but *Pittwood*[36] is an example often cited. The defendant was a railway gatekeeper. His omission to shut the gate on a particular occasion led to an accident, in which a person was killed. The trial judge, Wright J, ruled that 'a man might incur criminal liability from a duty arising out of contract', and Pittwood was consequently found guilty of manslaughter. As has been noted, a similar contractual duty to act will attach to doctors, and presumably to others

32 But cf *Shepherd* (1862) 9 Cox CC 123 – no duty in the circumstances owed to an 18 year old daughter (who would, of course, have been a minor, the age of majority at that time being 21).

33 *Dytham* [1979] 3 All ER 641.

34 *Ibid.*

35 *Ibid.*

36 (1902) 19 TLR 37.

practising skills allied to medicine (for example, dentists, podiatrists, nurses). In relation to doctors, there is the particular problem of decisions relating to the management of patients who are terminally ill, or in a persistent vegetative state. This area, which concerns liability for homicide, is discussed in Chapter 4.[37] An omission to act to preserve the patient's life has the potential to constitute the *actus reus* of murder or manslaughter, but the question of liability will be affected by the complex moral and medical issues surrounding such cases, including the issue of the patient's consent.[38]

Past conduct

There are two ways in which past conduct can give rise to a duty to act. First, the conduct may indicate the voluntary undertaking of a responsibility towards another, which will then give rise to a duty. Secondly, the conduct may have created a dangerous situation, which the D will have a duty not to ignore.

The concept of the voluntary undertaking towards another is illustrated by the case of *Instan*.[39] The D lived with her elderly aunt. The aunt's money was used to meet the living expenses of both herself and the D. The aunt then became ill, and bedridden. The D, who was well aware of her aunt's condition, failed to provide her with food, or to seek medical help. It was held that her failure to act amounted to the *actus reus* of manslaughter. She was under a moral obligation to look after her aunt. Since the D had not sought other assistance, the responsibility remained on her, and her moral obligation became a legal one. As Lord Coleridge put it:

> It was the clear duty of the prisoner to impart to the deceased so much as was necessary to sustain life of the food ... which was paid for by the deceased's own money ... There was, therefore, a common law duty imposed upon the prisoner which she did not discharge.

A more recent, but distressingly similar, example of the operation of this principle is to be found in *Stone and Dobinson*.[40] The defendants lived together, and took in S's younger sister, V (who was in her sixties) as a lodger. V became both physically and mentally ill. The defendants made some attempts to find V's doctor, and also at one point sought help from a neighbour. They did not, however, pursue this and, for some time, V was left in her bed without adequate food, or other care. She deteriorated and died. S and D were charged with, and convicted of, manslaughter. It was held by the Court of

---

37 See Chapter 4, p 59.

38 See, eg, *St George's Healthcare National Health Service Trust v S* [1998] 3 All ER 673.

39 [1893] 1 QB 450. Though it should be noted that Wright J, in *Pittwood* (1902) 19 TLR 37, regarded it as a case of contractual duty.

40 [1977] 1 QB 354, CA.

Appeal that there was a clear basis on which the jury could have found that the defendants had assumed a responsibility for, and therefore a duty towards, V. They had made some attempts to seek medical help, and to care for her themselves. They were aware of the fact that her condition had deteriorated. The jury:

> ... were entitled to conclude that once Fanny had become helplessly infirm, as she had by 19 July, the appellants were, in the circumstances, obliged either to summon help or else to care for Fanny themselves.

In other words, the Ds' past conduct, in making some attempt to care for V, gave rise to a duty to continue to do so. Their omission to do so was in those circumstances sufficient to constitute the *actus reus* of manslaughter – their failure to seek assistance or care for V themselves could be regarded as causing V's death.

An oddity of this means of establishing the existence of a duty is that it seems to penalise the person who makes a half-hearted attempt at assistance, as against the person who simply refuses to become involved. D1, who is aware that his next door neighbour is ill, and bed-ridden, but simply ignores the fact, may face moral condemnation but not prosecution if and when the neighbour dies. If D2 decides to try to assist, however, and on some occasions provides the neighbour with food, for example, then the position may well be different. There is then at least a risk that a failure to continue such assistance will be regarded as a breach of an assumed duty, and render D2 potentially liable for manslaughter in the event of the neighbour's death. Such considerations may suggest that there is scope for a broader liability for omissions than currently exists under English law, perhaps in the form of specially created offences.[41]

The second type of past conduct which may give rise to liability for a failure to act, is where the D's behaviour has created a dangerous situation. This is best exemplified by the criminal damage case of *Miller*.[42] The D, who had been drinking, went to bed on a mattress. He was smoking a cigarette, and fell asleep while continuing to smoke. He awoke to find the mattress on fire. In his own words, he 'just got up and went into the next room and went back to sleep'.[43] He was subsequently charged with the offence of arson, under s 1(1) and 1(3) of the Criminal Damage Act 1971. His defence was based on the lack of coincidence in time of the *actus reus* and *mens rea* required for the offence.[44] At the time the fire started, accidentally, he was asleep; after he became aware of the fire, his failure to act was an omission which could not be

41 See, eg, Clarkson, CMV and Keating, HM, *Criminal Law: Text and Materials*, 4th edn, 1998, London: Sweet & Maxwell, pp 124–25.

42 [1983] 1 All ER 978, HL

43 *Ibid.*

44 This issue is discussed further below, p 22 *et seq*.

regarded as an *actus reus* which caused the damage resulting from the fire. The House of Lords refused to accept this analysis. They approved the direction given by the trial judge, who had told the jury that the D:

> ... having by his own act started a fire in the mattress which, when he became aware of its existence, presented an obvious risk of damaging the house, became under a duty to take some action to put it out.[45]

Thus, the D's previous behaviour gave rise to a duty to act, so that in those circumstances an omission to do so could constitute the *actus reus* of an offence. Can this principle also apply to offences against the person? There seems no reason why not. If, for example, the fire started by Miller's cigarette had resulted in the death of one or more occupants of the house, then there seems no reason why he should not be liable for manslaughter. As far as offences based on assault are concerned, two authorities are relevant – *Fagan v Metropolitan Police Commissioner*,[46] and *DPP v K*.[47]

In *Fagan*, the D was directed by a police constable to park in a particular place. The D parked his car, whether deliberately or not is uncertain, on the policeman's foot. The D then refused to move the car, and was consequently charged with assaulting a police officer in the execution of his duty.[48] The problem in establishing the offence was essentially the same as that in *Miller* – that is, the need to prove the coincidence in time of *actus reus* and *mens rea*. Assuming that the original parking of the car on the V's foot was accidental, there was no *mens rea* at this time. Once the D became aware that the car was on the V's foot, he did not do anything. He simply allowed his car to remain where it was. Could this failure, or omission, to act amount to an assault? The majority of the Divisional Court[49] held that it could, in that the driving of the car onto the V's foot and then allowing it to remain there was a 'continuing act', so that the *actus reus* of the assault was still in progress when the D realised that the car was where it was, and decided to leave it there. The D could therefore properly be convicted of the offence with which he was charged. The court's decision thus categorises the D's behaviour in leaving the car on the V's foot not as an omission, but as part of an ongoing act. The *ratio* of the case was therefore not based on liability for omissions. Following *Miller*, however, as Lord Diplock implicitly recognised,[50] it is possible to place a different interpretation on *Fagan*. The initial act of driving on to the policeman's foot may be regarded as having created a dangerous situation (that is, one that was likely to cause further injury to the V if action was not

45 [1983] 1 All ER 978, p 983.

46 [1969] 1 QB 439; [1968] 3 All ER 442.

47 [1990] 1 All ER 331.

48 Police Act 1964, s 51; now Police Act 1996, s 89(1).

49 Bridge J dissented, on the basis that there was no act proved which could amount to the *actus reus* of assault.

50 [1983] 1 All ER 978, p 983.

taken). The D, therefore, once he became aware of what had happened, was under a duty to take reasonable steps to remove the danger (that is, by moving his car). His failure or omission to act could therefore constitute the *actus reus* of assault.[51] This interpretation of *Fagan* illustrates the possibility of applying the *Miller* principle to assault offences. A more recent example to the same effect is *DPP v K*.[52]

The facts of *DPP v K* are even more bizarre than *Fagan*. The D was a 15 year old schoolboy who took a test-tube of sulphuric acid into the school toilets, apparently in order to test its effect on some toilet paper. Once in the toilets, he heard someone approaching, and in panic poured the acid into a hot air drier, in order to conceal it. His intention was to return later and wash it out. Unfortunately, before he was able to do so, another pupil used the drier and was squirted with acid, suffering permanent scarring. The D was charged with assault occasioning actual bodily harm. He was acquitted and there was a prosecutor's appeal by way of case stated, which was successful. The main focus of the decision was on the *mens rea* element of the offence, and this is discussed elsewhere.[53] As regards the *actus reus*, however, the court treated this case as analogous to the laying of a trap, as regards which Stephen J, in *Clarence*[54] had said:

> If a man laid a trap for another into which he fell after an interval, the man who laid it would during the interval be guilty of an attempt to assault, and of an actual assault as soon as the man fell in.

Applying this, Parker LJ, in *DPP v K*, felt that 'a defendant who pours a dangerous substance into a machine just as truly assaults the next user of the machine as if he had himself switched the machine on'.[55] It is certainly arguable, however, that this case could have been brought within the *Miller* principle as well. The D, by putting the acid in the machine, had created a dangerous situation. He was therefore under a duty to take reasonable steps to put things right. His failure to do so was an omission which was capable of constituting the *actus reus* of an offence. Assuming the relevant *mens rea* could be proved, therefore, he could be held liable for assault, resulting from his omission to remedy a dangerous situation of his own creation. The need for such an analysis arises from the fact that the initial act (putting the acid into the drier) cannot in itself be classed as an assault. On the other hand, the spraying of the acid in someone's face is clearly the type of act which constitutes an assault. The difficulty in *DPP v K* was that the spraying was carried out as a result of the V's own act in switching on the drier. It cannot be

---

51 Using 'assault' to encompass 'battery' in this context: see Chapter 5, p 103.

52 [1990] 1 All ER 331.

53 See Chapter 5, p 110.

54 (1888) 22 QBD 23, p 45.

55 [1990] 1 All ER 331, p 333.

said that a machine is capable of committing the *actus reus* of assault; nor is it satisfactory to regard it as being carried out by the V against himself. That is why the analysis in terms of an omission to rectify a dangerous situation of the D's own creation is preferable. It also has the advantage that it can be seen as an example of a broader principle of liability for omissions arising from a duty to act, which may be created by a variety of situations. The 'trap' analogy favoured by the court in *DPP v K* is more limited in its scope and applicability.

If the approach outlined in the previous paragraphs is accepted, it becomes clear that the commission of the *actus reus* by omission can be applied to a wide range of offences against the person, including murder, manslaughter, and most offences based on assault or battery. There are, nevertheless, some offences against the person which it is impossible to envisage ever being committed by omission. For example, rape, and other sexual offences, require the D to be present at the time of the *actus reus*, and to be active in committing the offence. These and any other exceptions to the general principles discussed above will be noted at the appropriate point in the discussion of the *actus reus* of the particular offence concerned in later chapters.

MENS REA

In addition to the prosecution having to prove that the D committed the *actus reus* of the offence charged, it also has to prove that this was done with the appropriate state of mind, or *mens rea*. This mental element is part of the definition of the offence, and, as we have seen there must normally be coincidence in time between the *actus reus* and *mens rea*.[56] If the D decides to murder his wife, and puts poison in her tea, he at that point in time has the *mens rea* of murder. His wife, however, may fail to drink the tea, and the D may then have a change of heart, and abandon his plan. If, the next morning, in backing his car out of the garage he accidentally runs over his wife and kills her, he will not be guilty of murder, even if his state of mind on the previous evening can be proved. There is no coincidence between the *actus reus* (causing his wife's death by driving over her) and the *mens rea* (the intention to kill). Even if, after the event, the D expresses the view that he is glad that she is dead, this does not affect his liability, unless it can be shown that his driving into her was done with the required state of mind for either murder or manslaughter.

This requirement can pose problems for the prosecution in some cases, as is shown by *Thabo Meli*.[57] The Ds attacked the V. When they thought the V

56 Some exceptions to this are discussed above in relation to the problems of 'omissions'.
57 [1954] 1 All ER 373.

was dead, they rolled his body over a cliff. In fact, the V was not dead at this point, but died later from exposure. The problem for the prosecution was that it could be argued that at the time of the actions which caused the death (that is, rolling the V over the cliff), the Ds did not have the *mens rea* of murder, because they thought they were dealing with a corpse. The Privy Council, however, rejected this analysis. The actions of the Ds comprised a single 'series' which were all part of the plan to kill the V. Their original intention to kill could be said to have continued to apply even at the stage when the V's body was rolled off the cliff. In this case, the Ds were acting in accordance with a prearranged plan. The same approach, however, has subsequently been taken where the D has assaulted the V, and then, in attempting to conceal his crime, has caused the V's death. In *Church*,[58] the D (like the Ds in *Thabo Meli*) thinking he was dealing with a corpse, threw the V into a canal, where she drowned. In *Le Brun*,[59] the D who had assaulted the V in the street, was trying to move her out of sight when he dropped her, causing fatal injuries. The D could in either case be liable for murder, or manslaughter, depending on his state of mind at the time of the original assault (that is, did the D intend to cause at least serious bodily harm to the V?).[60]

A further way in which the scope of the D's *mens rea* may be extended is through the doctrine of 'transferred malice'. This means that, if the D acts with the relevant *mens rea* against V1, but actually commits the *actus reus* in relation to V2, he will still be liable. The D who sends a letter bomb intended for a member of parliament, will still be liable if it is opened by a secretary, causing her injury. The principle was established in *Latimer*.[61] The D aimed a blow with a belt at X but hit the V, who was standing nearby. Lord Coleridge stated that:

> ... if a person has a malicious intent towards one person, and in carrying into effect that malicious intent he injures another man, he is guilty of what the law considers malice against the person so injured.

The principle has most recently been confirmed by the House of Lords in *Re Attorney General's Reference (No 3 of 1994)*,[62] though the House refused to apply it to the situation before it, where the D attacked a pregnant woman with the result that her child was born prematurely and then died. Although they held that the D could be liable for the manslaughter of the child, this was not on the basis of transferred malice. That concept was appropriate where an action by the D had a direct effect on an unintended victim, as in the examples given above. Here, the effect on the foetus (inducing premature delivery,

58 [1965] 2 All ER 72.

59 [1991] 4 All ER 673.

60 For the *mens rea* of homicide offences, see Chapter 4.

61 (1886) 17 QBD 359.

62 [1994] Crim LR 766; see, also, *Mitchell* [1983] 2 All ER 427, discussed in Chapter 4, p 95.

which in turn contributed to the child's early death) was indirect, and so transferred malice was not applicable.

In relation to some offences, the *mens rea* element is important not only for the purposes of establishing liability, but also to determine the seriousness of the offence. Obvious examples are murder and manslaughter, and the 'grievous bodily harm' offences contained in ss 18 and 20 of the Offences Against the Person Act 1861. As has been noted in Chapter 1, this element, together with the effect on the V of the D's behaviour, and the V's lack of consent to what the D has done, are all important in establishing the D's culpability.

In relation to offences against the person, there are three 'states of mind' which may be relevant. The first two are 'intention' and 'recklessness', and these will be discussed in detail below. The third is 'gross negligence'. This is only relevant to the offence of manslaughter, and is in any case arguably not a 'state of mind' at all, since it can be established by measuring the D's behaviour against that of the reasonable person. For these reasons, discussions of 'gross negligence' will be left to Chapter 4 and consideration of the offence of manslaughter.

Before embarking on a consideration of 'intention' and 'recklessness', we should note that although we are discussing 'states of mind', a court can never have direct evidence of what was going on in somebody's head at a particular moment. It can only rely on evidence of what they said and did before, during, and after the event as a means of drawing conclusions about their mental state at the relevant time.

Intention

In relation to some offences, the prosecution must prove that, at the time he committed the *actus reus*, the D intended to bring about certain consequences (for example, death, or grievous bodily harm). What precisely is meant by this apparently simple statement has exercised the courts greatly over the last 30 years. The problems have arisen mainly in relation to the offence of murder, because it has been found unsatisfactory to rely simply on the common usage of the words 'intend' and 'intention' in order to define what the prosecution has to prove in order to obtain a conviction. This is because the common usage is generally linked to a desired outcome: 'I intend to eat this peach', 'I have the intention of spending the day in Nottingham', 'I intend to pass my examinations'. The speaker of these statements will be taken, in the absence of any indications to the contrary, to be giving expression to a desired outcome – she wants to eat the peach; she wants to spend the day in Nottingham, she wants to pass her examinations. As we shall see, however, this meaning of intention has been found to be too limiting in the criminal law, and a broader definition has come to be used.

Prior to undertaking a detailed consideration of this definition, however, and the case law that has led to it, a related, and sometimes interrelated, issue must be noted. This is the question of how intention is *proved*. As we have noted above, we know that a state of mind can only be evidenced by the words and actions of the person concerned. The question then arises as to the extent that the tribunal of fact is entitled to assume that the D has the foresight and understanding of the reasonable person. If it is the case that, in the situation under consideration, the jury thinks that a reasonable person, acting as the D did, would have foreseen a particular consequence, can they go on to make the assumption that the D did in fact intend that consequence? It was the view of the House of Lords in *DPP v Smith*,[63] a case concerned with the *mens rea* of murder, that they not only could, but must, do so. The House in this case held that there was an irrebuttable presumption of law that a person intends the 'natural consequences' of his actions. By 'natural consequences' is meant those which are 'foreseeable' by the reasonable person. In practice, the decision meant that each member of the jury should decide whether they, in the situation of the D, would have foreseen the consequence which in fact occurred. If they would have done so, then they were obliged to conclude that the D intended the consequence. There was much criticism of this decision on the basis that it in fact used an objective standard of reasonable behaviour, rather than focusing on the actual state of mind of the D at the time of the actions in question. In other words, the test ceased to be one, even in form, of the D's *mens rea*. Subsequently, the law was clarified by s 8 of the Criminal Justice Act 1967. This made it clear that in proving intention (or foresight) as regards consequences, the prosecution had to do more than show that such consequences were the natural result of the D's behaviour. The section reads:

> A court or jury in determining whether a person has committed an offence:
>
> (a) shall not be bound in law to infer that he intended or foresaw a result of his actions by reason only of it being a natural and probable consequence of those actions; but
>
> (b) shall decide whether he did intend or foresee that result by reference to all the evidence drawing such inferences from the evidence as appear proper in the circumstances.

It must be remembered, however, that this section says nothing about *when* intention or foresight must be proved, or the relationship between foresight (as opposed to foreseeability) and intention. Nor does it define 'intention' or 'foresight'. It is only concerned with the way in which these two states of mind may be proved. Further, the section does not preclude (indeed it specifically approves) the drawing of inferences from all the circumstances. One of these circumstances may be the fact that the jury feel that a reasonable person in the position of the D would have either intended, or foreseen, particular consequences of his behaviour. This fact may quite legitimately

63 [1961] AC 290.

form part of the jury's reasons for deciding that the D actually did foresee or intend such consequences.

With this background in mind, we can now turn to the issue of what exactly is meant by 'intention' in the criminal law. We may start by noting that desired consequences which the D is trying to bring about will be regarded as being intended, even if they are unlikely to occur. If I take my driving test, having failed it three times, I intend to pass, even if my instructor thinks it highly unlikely that I shall do so. I am trying my best to pass, and that is the desired consequence. It is therefore clearly 'intended'. Turning to situations of criminality, the D who poisons the V's drink with the desired consequence of killing her, intends V's death, even if the dose of poison used is in fact only sufficient to give her a bad stomach ache. Similarly, the D who fires a gun loaded with blanks at the V's legs, thinking it carries live ammunition, intends to cause grievous bodily harm, even though this outcome is, on the facts, impossible. Such situations do not cause problems as regards the *mens rea* of the D. The difficulties arise with the converse situation – that is, where the consequence is not desired, but is in fact likely to occur. Does the D intend the consequences in this case? Our initial reaction is likely to be 'no'. To use the driving test example given above, it may be that I am very likely to fail my test, but I do not intend to do so. Even if I realise that my chances of passing are very low, it is still my *intention* to pass rather than to fail. This answer to the problem has proved unsatisfactory because it fails to deal in a way which is thought appropriate with situations such as the following 'bomb on a plane' example, which was first used by the Law Commission in its consideration of *DPP v Smith,* and adopted by Lord Hailsham in *Hyam v DPP*:[64]

> ... a man may desire to blow up an aircraft in flight in order to obtain insurance money. But, if any passengers are killed, he is guilty of murder, as their death will be a moral certainty if he carries out his intention. There is no difference between blowing up the aircraft and intending the death of some or all of the passengers.

The *ratio* of *Hyam* incorporated the view, subsequently rejected,[65] that the *mens rea* for murder could be satisfied by proof of something less than 'intention' on the part of the D. Nevertheless, it is clear that in the example given Lord Hailsham was treating the state of mind of the bomber in relation to the death of the passengers as being one of 'intention'. Because the deaths are a 'moral certainty', the bomber can be said to have intended them, even though he does not desire them, and they are not the object of his enterprise. This conclusion is an example of the reasoning which Lord Hailsham notes just before this passage, that a definition of intention in the criminal law which is based on those consequences which the D is trying to bring about, must

---

64 [1974] 2 All ER 41, p 52.

65 See Chapter 4, p 62.

include 'the means as well as the end and the inseparable consequences of the end as well as the means.' This is probably uncontroversial, as long as the consequences are indeed 'inseparable'. It is clear that the D must intend the means by which he proposes to achieve his desired end. If the D wishes to kill the V by shooting him, and so fires a gun at him, the D clearly intends to pull the trigger, he intends that the bullet should be fired from the gun and fly through the air, he intends that it should break the V's skin, and he intends that it should cause serious damage to the V's internal organs. All these things are either the means by which, or the inseparable consequences of, causing the V's death by shooting. The problems start to arise where the consequences are not necessarily inseparable, but are simply very likely, or foreseeable. Another 'bombing' example, adapted from one used by Lord Bridge in *Moloney*[66] will illustrate the point. Suppose that the D is a terrorist who plants a time bomb in a public building, and gives adequate warning to enable the public to be evacuated. The D's intention is not to kill or cause grievous bodily harm, but simply to cause disruption to everyday life, and perhaps to cause damage to property. As the D knew was likely to happen, however, a bomb disposal expert attempts to defuse the bomb. Unfortunately, the expert is unsuccessful in the attempt, the bomb explodes, and the expert is killed. Can the D be said to have intended his death? It cannot be said that the bomber desired the death of the expert, or even that he was trying to bring it about. Nor was it 'morally certain' that anyone would be killed. On most occasions, bomb disposal experts carry out their work successfully, so it cannot be said that death or grievous bodily harm was the most likely outcome of the bomber's actions. Nevertheless, there is a risk that this will happen, and a risk a majority of people would regard as being unacceptable. Unacceptable risk taking which leads to death is normally dealt with as manslaughter, as we shall see. The courts have, however, taken the view that the correct offence for this type of behaviour is murder. There are only two ways of reaching this result. Either the *mens rea* of murder must be defined to include some types of deliberate risk taking, or the definition of intention must be modified to encompass certain situations where the D foresees, but does not desire, the consequences of death or serious injury resulting from his behaviour. As we shall see in Chapter 4, at one time, English law, following the decision in *Hyam*,[67] embraced the first alternative. In *Moloney*, however, the House of Lords insisted that the *mens rea* for murder is only satisfied by proof of an intention on the part of the D to cause death or serious bodily harm. The focus of discussion has thereafter shifted from defining the *mens rea* of murder, to defining what is meant by 'intention'. There are three cases which must be considered: *Moloney* itself, *Hancock and Shankland*,[68] and *Nedrick*.[69] All three

66 [1985] 1 All ER 1025.

67 [1974] 2 All ER 41.

68 [1986] AC 455; 1 All ER 641

69 [1986] 3 All ER 1.

are concerned with murder, but the statements which they contain as to the definition and proof of intention in the criminal law must be taken as being of general application.

The facts of *Moloney* involved a situation where father and son were messing about with guns, and the son shot and fatally wounded his father.[70] It was therefore a case of 'risk taking' resulting in death. If it was accepted that the son had not wished to kill his father, could he nevertheless be held to have intended death or serious harm – as the House of Lords held in this case was necessary for the *mens rea* of murder? Lord Bridge thought that in situations where it was necessary for a jury to consider 'foresight of consequences' in relation to intention,[71] the judge should direct as follows, inviting the jury to consider two questions:[72]

> First, was death or really serious injury in a murder case (or whatever relevant consequence must be proved to have been intended in any other case) a natural consequence of the defendant's voluntary act? Secondly, did the defendant foresee that consequence as being a natural consequence of his act? The jury should then be told that if they answer Yes to both questions it is a proper inference for them to draw that he intended that consequence.

A difficulty with this direction arises from its reference to 'natural consequences'. It is a phrase which is not self-explanatory, and it carries with it echoes of *DPP v Smith*, and the discredited objective test. This cannot be what Lord Bridge meant, and indeed, the rest of his speech suggests that he considered that only those consequences which were likely to follow as a 'moral certainty' should be regarded as 'natural'. Because this was not explicit in the suggested direction, however, the question was left uncertain. The House of Lords thus returned to the issue in *Hancock and Shankland*.

This case arose out of the 1984 miners' strike. Concrete blocks were dropped from a bridge onto the road below, into the path of a taxi carrying a working miner. Unfortunately the block struck the taxi's windscreen, and killed the driver. Those who were responsible for pushing the block from the bridge were charged with murder. The judge directed the jury in the words of Lord Bridge's speech in *Moloney*, and the jury convicted. On appeal, both the Court of Appeal and House of Lords took the view that the direction suggested by Lord Bridge was unsatisfactory, because it did not give any indication of the degree of probability, or likelihood, which had to attach to a foreseen consequence before it would be proper to infer intention. Lord Lane in the Court of Appeal suggested a direction using the phrase 'highly likely'. Lord Scarman, however, delivering the opinion of the House of Lords, preferred not to issue a model direction. He accepted that in cases where it

---

70 See, also, Chapter 4, p 62.

71 And he clearly felt that it would be rare that this would be necessary.

72 [1985] 1 All ER 1025, p 1039.

was necessary to direct a jury on 'intention' (and the present case was such a one), the judge needed to make clear that foresight of the probability of an outcome was very important:[73]

> In a murder case where it is necessary to direct a jury on the issue of intent by reference to foresight of consequences, the probability of death or serious injury resulting from the act done may be critically important. Its importance will depend on the degree of probability: if the likelihood that death or serious injury will result is high, the probability of that result may ... be seen as overwhelming evidence of the existence of the intent to kill or injure.

The *Moloney* guidelines were therefore 'unsafe and misleading':[74]

> They require a reference to probability. They also require an explanation that the greater the probability of a consequence the more likely it is that the consequence was foreseen and, if that consequence was foreseen, the greater the probability is that the consequence was also intended.

Following *Hancock and Shankland*, therefore, the position is that evidence that the D foresaw a consequence as probable may form the basis of an inference that he intended that consequence – with the inference becoming easier to draw the greater the probability of the consequence foreseen.

The Court of Appeal returned in *Nedrick*[75] to the issue of the degree of foresight necessary in order for it to be proper for a jury to infer intention. The approach taken in this case has now been largely approved by the House of Lords in *Woollin*.[76] In *Nedrick*, the D had poured paraffin through the letter box of a house, and set fire to it. His reason for so doing was that he had a grudge against a woman who lived in the house. As a result of the fire, two children who were in the house at the time were killed. The D was charged with murder. He was alleged to have admitted starting the fire, but to have claimed that he only wanted to frighten the woman. The trial took place prior to the publication of the speeches of the House of Lords in *Moloney* and *Hancock*. The judge therefore directed the jury in terms of the law as it stood before those decisions, and suggested that:

> If, when the accused performed the act of setting fire to the house, he knew that it was highly probable that the act would result in serious bodily injury to somebody inside the house, even though he did not desire it, desire to bring that result about, he is guilty of murder.

This was plainly, in the light of the subsequent rulings by the House of Lords, a misdirection.[77] The Court of Appeal noted that in many cases, such as

73 [1986] 1 All ER 641, p 650.

74 *Ibid*, p 651.

75 [1986] 3 All ER 1.

76 (1998) *The Times*, 23 July.

77 A verdict of manslaughter, and a penalty of 15 years imprisonment, was therefore substituted for the murder conviction.

where there is a direct attack by the D on the V, a direction which simply refers to the need to prove an intention to kill or cause serious harm will be sufficient. Where, however, the V dies as a result of a manifestly dangerous act by the D, who did not, however, desire to harm anyone, a more complex direction may be needed. In attempting to 'crystallise' the approach taken by the House of Lords in *Moloney* and *Hancock*, Lord Lane suggested the following steps:

(a) The judge will need to distinguish between 'desire' and 'intention'. In this context. Lord Lane recalled an example of the distinction given by Lord Bridge in *Moloney*:[78]

> A man who, at London Airport, boards a plane which he knows to be bound for Manchester, clearly intends to travel to Manchester, even though Manchester is the last place he wants to be and his motive for boarding the plane is simply to escape pursuit.

This example is not necessarily as clear cut as the courts seem to have assumed in illustrating the distinction between desire and intention. It is at least arguable that the man in Lord Bridge's example does, in the circumstances, 'desire' to go to Manchester, even though he wishes the circumstances were otherwise. Whatever example is used, however, the judge should try to explain that it is not only desired consequences that are, as far as the criminal law is concerned, 'intended'.

(b) The jury should then be asked to consider two questions:

- How probable was the consequence which resulted from the defendant's voluntary act?
- Did he foresee that consequence?'

If the answer to the second question is No, then the D cannot be held to have intended the consequence. If it is Yes, then the degree of probability needs to be considered. The House of Lords in *Woollin* doubted the helpfulness of asking the jury these questions, and suggested that the emphasis should be on the direction set out in (c), below.

(c) As we have seen, in *Moloney*, Lord Bridge referred to 'natural consequences' whereas, in *Hancock and Shankland*, Lord Scarman recognised that degrees of probability of the consequence might affect the likelihood that the D foresaw it, and thus that he could be inferred to have intended it. In *Nedrick*, Lord Lane suggested what appears to be a more rigid approach. He ruled that it is only where a consequence is 'virtually certain' to result that intention should be inferred. The House of Lords in *Woollin* approved the direction suggested by Lord Lane, but found the use

78 [1985] 1 All ER 1025, p 1037.

of words 'to infer' likely to be unhelpful to the jury, and substituted 'to find' in its place. The direction suggested by Lord Lane, as amended by the House of Lords in *Woollin*, is set out in the following passage:

> Where the charge is murder, and in the rare cases where the simple direction is not enough, the jury should be directed that they are not entitled to find the necessary intention unless they feel sure that death or serious bodily harm was a virtual certainty (barring some unforeseen intervention) as a result of the defendant's actions and that the defendant appreciated that such was the case.

Thus, 'degrees of probability' are no longer relevant – it is only where a consequence is virtually certain to occur that intention may be found. This was again confirmed by *Woollin*, where the House of Lords disapproved a direction which had referred to a 'substantial risk' rather than a virtual certainty. The decision in *Walker and Hayles*,[79] where the Court of Appeal approved a direction referring to a 'high probability', must now be regarded as overruled. There is an obvious advantage in having a clear statement of this kind, which has the effect of reducing uncertainty in the law. It would seem, however, that this approach excludes from the definition of intention the state of mind of the 'bomber' in the example used above, who gives a clear warning and expects only property damage, but whose actions result in the death of a bomb disposal expert. It cannot be said that the bomber foresaw death or serious injury as a virtually certain consequence, if he expected, as would generally be the case, that the bomb would be diffused. The most that he could be liable for, therefore, if the *Nedrick* approach is taken, is manslaughter.[80] This may be satisfactory, but it seems unlikely that is a result which the appeal courts would be happy with, given their general approach to 'bombing' cases.

It is probably helpful that the House of Lords in *Woollin* has moved away from the concept of 'inferring' intention developed from *Moloney*, since this has been criticised as an incoherent process because it involves inferring one state of mind from another.[81] An 'inference' is something that can be drawn from a set of facts, but it is said that it makes no sense to state that a jury, satisfied of the fact that a person foresaw a particular consequence as virtually certain, can infer from that that the person concerned had a different state of mind, that is, that they intended the consequence. Why not simply say that facts (for example, what the D said or did) which may be used to infer that the D foresaw a consequence as virtually certain, may, in the alternative, be used to infer (or find) that the D intended the consequence? Is that not the same thing, however, as saying that foreseeing a virtually certain consequence as a

79 (1989) 90 Cr App R 226, CA – attempted murder.

80 This is also the conclusion of Smith, JC and Hogan, B, *Criminal Law Cases and Materials*, 6th edn, 1996, London, Butterworths, p 62.

81 Cf Duff, RA, 'The obscure intentions of the House of Lords' [1986] Crim LR 771.

result of one's behaviour is identical to intending that consequence? The courts have been reluctant to make that connection, even in *Woollin*,[82] and for good reason. A simple example will show that a consequence may very well be seen as virtually certain, and yet not be 'intended':

I am shooting at a target, but I am a very bad shot. The last 99 times I have shot at the target I have missed. I know that it is virtually certain that my next shot will miss. I do not, however, intend to miss. Even though I know that it is virtually certain that I shall miss, my intention is to hit the target. It is therefore perfectly plausible to foresee a consequence as virtually certain and yet not intend it. An analysis of 'intention' which includes within it outcomes which are 'desired', and at the same time equates it with 'foresight of a virtually certain consequence', would in this situation lead to the mutually contradictory statements 'I intend to hit the target' and 'I intend to miss the target' both being true. This cannot be right.

It is probably the fact that the courts have wished to avoid this conclusion that has led them to talk about 'inferring' intention from foresight, and now to 'finding' intention where a result is foreseen as virtually certain. Some of the language may have been inappropriate, but the objective is understandable. The jury must have the opportunity, faced with facts which indicate that a virtually certain consequence was foreseen by the D, of saying that nevertheless the D did not intend that consequence.

Recklessness

The second type of *mens rea* which the prosecution may need to prove to establish criminal liability for an offence against the person is often referred to by the general term 'recklessness'. This is unhelpful because, as will be seen, in terms of its use within the criminal law the word has at least two incompatible definitions, neither of which equates to the meaning which the word has in everyday usage. In fact, there are few occasions on which the statutory definition of an offence against the person uses this word,[83] and it would in many ways be preferable if in discussion of criminal liability the word were to be avoided.[84] It is in such common usage, however, by both the courts and the commentators, that it cannot be ignored, and so an attempt is given here to describe its various meanings.

82 The jury are not obliged to 'find' that the D intended a consequence which he foresaw as virtually certain: this degree of foresight is a necessary, but not necessarily a sufficient, condition for a finding of 'intention'.

83 The offence of rape is a rare example where the word is part of the statutory definition – see below, p 149.

84 As was done, for example, in Public Order Act 1986, s 6.

Cunningham *recklessness*

The decision of the Court of Appeal in *Cunningham*[85] was in fact concerned with the meaning of the word 'maliciously' in s 23 of the Offences Against the Person Act 1861. Cunningham had fractured a gas pipe whilst stealing a gas meter, with the result that a Mrs Wade, who was asleep in an adjoining house, inhaled a quantity of the gas, putting her life in danger. In considering how the judge should have directed the jury on the meaning of the word maliciously, the Court of Appeal approved as accurate the following statement by Professor CS Kenny in his *Outlines of Criminal Law*:[86]

> In any statutory definition of a crime, 'malice' must be taken not in the old vague sense of wickedness in general, but as requiring either (1) an actual intention to do the particular kind of harm that in fact was done, or (2) recklessness as to whether such harm should occur or not (ie, the accused has foreseen that the particular kind of harm might be done, and yet has gone on to take the risk of it).

'Malice' is therefore equated to 'recklessness', which is stated to mean that the D foresees the likely consequences of his actions, and yet goes on to run the risk of them occurring. This has at times been categorised as a 'subjective' test of recklessness, in that it is not enough for the prosecution to prove that a particular consequence was, as a matter of fact, likely to occur, but also that the particular defendant actually foresaw this. This is in contrast to the *Caldwell* test of recklessness, which is said to be 'objective', and is discussed below.

It is of course implicit in this definition of recklessness that the risk taken is unjustifiable. A surgeon may foresee the risk that carrying out a particular operation on a patient may leave that patient permanently paralysed. Nevertheless, if the operation is thought necessary in order to preserve the patient's life, or the risk of paralysis is small whereas the benefits from the operation would be great, we would not wish to categorise the surgeon's action as reckless as regards the undesired consequence. The same argument will apply wherever a risk can be said to be justified. Another example might be the police marksman who shoots at a person holding a hostage, knowing that there is a risk that the hostage will be hit. If this consequence follows, then, quite apart from the issue of causation (which has been discussed in connection with the case of *Pagett*,[87] above) the marksman would not be said to be reckless concerning any injury to the hostage. The risk would be regarded as being justifiable.

The test of justifiability also means that in certain circumstances the foresight of consequences which are as a matter of fact relatively unlikely to

85 [1957] 2 All ER 4120.

86 Kenny, CS, *Outlines of Criminal Law*, 16th edn, 1952, Cambridge: Cambridge UP, p 186.

87 (1983) 76 Cr App R 279, discussed at p 15, above.

occur may still be reckless. If, for example, a person holding a hostage loads a revolver having six chambers with one live round, spins the chamber, points it at the hostage's head, and pulls the trigger, the risk of the live round being fired is only five to one. It is therefore relatively unlikely that the hostage will be injured as a result of this course of action by the criminal. There is little doubt, however, that the criminal's behaviour would be regarded as reckless in relation to the consequence. The likely harm that would be caused if the live round should be fired is so great that the risk is unjustifiable, even though it is more likely than not that the hostage will remain unscathed. (It must be assumed that the criminal could not be regarded as *intending* injury to the hostage, since as we have seen, following *Nedrick*,[88] only consequences which are 'virtually certain' to occur can be held to be intended.)

Cunningham recklessness may therefore be rephrased as the deliberate taking of an unjustifiable risk.

Caldwell ***recklessness***

This type of recklessness derives from the House of Lords' decision in *Caldwell*.[89] This case was concerned with liability under the Criminal Damage Act 1971, and it now seems that it is only to be applied to offences under that Act. It is necessary to discuss it briefly here, however, because certain cases appeared to apply the *Caldwell* test to offences against the person. In particular, it seemed at one point that *Caldwell* recklessness might be sufficient to establish liability for manslaughter. As will be seen in Chapter 4, it now seems that the similar but distinguishable concept of 'gross negligence' is to be preferred to recklessness in relation to this offence. Nevertheless, it is conceivable that at some point the courts might return to the *Caldwell* definition.

It is often overlooked that the context in which the discussion of recklessness took place in *Caldwell*, was an attempted defence based on the intoxication of the defendant. The central issue, therefore, before the House of Lords was whether a defendant who claims that because of self-induced intoxication he did not appreciate the consequences of his actions, or foresee the risks involved, can nevertheless be said to be 'reckless' as regards those consequences. In answering that question in the affirmative, the majority of the House of Lords provided a definition of recklessness which does not depend on the defendant's foresight of consequences. The main speech giving the view of the majority was delivered by Lord Diplock. He took the view that the word 'reckless', which is used in the definition of offences in the Criminal Damage Act 1971, should be given its ordinary meaning, rather than being

88 [1986] 3 All ER 1.

89 [1981] 1 All ER 961.

regarded as a term of legal art. His view was that in ordinary speech the word would be taken as including not only:

> ... deciding to ignore a risk of harmful consequences resulting from one's acts that one has recognised as existing, but also failing to give any thought as to whether or not there is any such risk in circumstances where, if any thought were given to the matter, it would be obvious that there was.[90]

He regarded either of these states of mind as being sufficient to establish recklessness on the part of the defendant. He then gave the following indication of a proper direction to the jury on the issue of recklessness under the Criminal Damage Act:[91]

> ... in my opinion, a person charged with an offence under s 1(1) of the 1971 Act is 'reckless as to whether or not any property would be destroyed or damaged' if (1) he does an act which in fact creates an obvious risk that property will be destroyed or damaged and (2) when he does the act he either has not given any thought to the possibility of there being any such risk or has recognised that there was some risk involved and has nonetheless gone on to do it.

The second part of this test is of course equivalent to the *Cunningham* test of recklessness. The defendant has foreseen the risk of certain consequences following from his conduct, but has nevertheless decided to take that risk. Two further points may be made about this. It must be assumed that when a court is considering whether a risk was 'obvious' for the purposes of this part of the test, it should consider whether it would have been obvious to a person with the knowledge and expertise of the defendant. They would see no reason why a person who recognised a risk because of their special knowledge or expertise should be held to be not reckless simply because such a risk would not have been recognised by an ordinary member of the public. Secondly, it should be noted that the test is whether there was a recognition of 'some' risk. This suggests that it is not necessary for the defendant to foresee the full extent of the risk involved as long as some harmful consequences are recognised as potential outcomes from the defendant's behaviour.

The above test, following as it does the *Cunningham* approach, is not controversial. The first part of the test, however, has been. This is where the defendant is held to be reckless simply through failing to give thought to the possibility of the existence of an obvious risk. At first sight, the test might seem to obviate any need to give consideration to the defendant's state of mind at the time of his actions. All the prosecution appears to need to do is to prove that there was as a matter of fact an obvious risk involved. It is then irrelevant whether the defendant failed to recognise that risk, or recognised it and decided to take it. In either situation, the *Caldwell* test categorises the defendant's state of mind as reckless. There is, however, a third possibility,

90 [1981] 1 All ER 961, p 966.

91 *Ibid*, p 967.

sometimes referred to as the '*Caldwell* gap', which means that some consideration of the mental state of the defendant may be necessary. The *Caldwell* gap arises where there is as a matter of fact an obvious risk, but the particular defendant, having given thought to the matter, has decided that there is no risk. In other words, the defendant does not either deliberately decide to run the risk (because he thinks there is none), nor can he be said to have failed to give thought to the possibility of there being a risk. He has done so, but has come to an incorrect decision as to whether the risk exists. If the court believes that this was the defendant's state of mind when he carried out the acts alleged to amount to an offence then it will be obliged to hold that he was not 'reckless'. It is important to note, however, that this gap will not exist in a situation where the defendant has recognised the possibility of a risk, but thinks that he has taken adequate precautions to avoid the undesired consequences occurring. This is illustrated by *Chief Constable of Avon v Shimmen*.[92] In this case, the defendant who was demonstrating his skills at martial arts to some friends aimed a kick at a plate glass window. His defence was that he believed that he was able to control the kick in a way which would avoid the window being broken. As it turned out he was mistaken and the window was broken. The mistake here, however, was not as to the existence of the risk but as to whether appropriate steps had been taken to eliminate it. The Divisional Court therefore, while recognising the possibility of the *Caldwell* gap, held that it did not apply in this case.[93]

92 (1986) 84 Cr App R 7.

93 See, also, *Reid* (1990) 91 Cr App R 263.

CHAPTER 3

PARTICIPATION IN CRIME

This chapter is concerned with the different ways in which a person may participate in crime. The main focus of the discussion in later chapters will be the commission of an offence by a 'principal' – that is, the person who strikes the blow, uses the knife, has forcible sexual intercourse, etc. There are three other ways, however, in which a person who does not himself complete the *actus reus* of the substantive offence can nevertheless be subject to criminal liability. These are (a) liability as an accessory; (b) attempts; and (c) conspiracy.

As has been noted above, these three topics, which are of general application throughout the criminal law, will here be considered in outline only. Further discussion of particular issues relating to these types of liability as they apply to specific offences against the person will be found at various points in subsequent chapters.

ACCESSORIAL LIABILITY

The legislative framework for accessorial liability is provided by s 8 of the Accessories and Abettors Act 1861. This states that:

> Whosoever shall aid, abet, counsel, or procure the commission of any indictable offence, whether the same be an offence at common law or by virtue of any Act passed or to be passed, shall be liable to be tried, indicted, and punished as a principal offender.

The Act applies to 'indictable' offences. In other words, offences which are triable only summarily are not included. Such offences are, however, dealt with by s 44(1) of the Magistrates' Courts Act 1980, which similarly states that 'a person who aids, abets, counsels or procures the commission by another person of a summary offence shall be guilty of the like offence ...'.

The effect of being found guilty as an accessory is thus that the D is liable to exactly the same punishment as a principal offender:[1] the D is convicted of the offence itself, not of *being an accessory* to the offence. This is of particular importance in relation to murder, since it means that an accessory is subject to the mandatory penalty of life imprisonment, in the same way as the principal offender.

---

1 Note that, in relation to aiding, etc, an offence triable either way, the accessory is also liable for an offence triable either way: Magistrates' Courts Act 1980, s 44(2).

It will be noted that both sections refer to the 'commission' of the offence. It is accepted that this means that at least the *actus reus* of the offence must be committed by D1 before D2 can be liable as an accessory.[2] In general, D1 will be liable as principal. But, if D1 has a defence (such as duress),[3] or cannot be convicted because the prosecution cannot prove the relevant *mens rea*,[4] then D2 can still be liable for aiding, abetting, counselling or procuring the offence. If, however, no *actus reus* is committed, for example, because D1 decides not to go through with the offence, or fails in an attempt to commit it, there can be no accessorial liability. D2 may be liable in such circumstances for some other inchoate offence, such as conspiracy or incitement, but cannot be liable for the substantive offence as an accessory.

The *actus reus* and *mens rea* of accessorial liability will now be outlined. In what follows, 'D1' will be used to refer to the principal offender, and 'D2' to the accessory.

The *actus reus*

It will be seen from the wording of s 8 that there are basically four ways of committing the *actus reus* of being an accessory: aiding, abetting, counselling and procuring. First, however, we should distinguish accessorial liability from liability as a principal. Where, for example, D1 and D2 together beat up the V, both may be liable as joint principals for the offence of, for example, assault occasioning actual bodily harm.[5] Both have committed the *actus reus* of the offence, with the relevant *mens rea*. It is only where D2 does not commit the *actus reus* of the full offence that there is a need for accessorial liability. If, for example, D1 has non-consensual sexual intercourse with the V, who has been lured to the assignation by D2, only D1 commits the *actus reus* of rape. D2 can only be made liable for rape if it can be proved that he has 'aided, abetted counselled, or procured' the commission of the offence by D1.

One further general point needs to be noted. D2's liability as an accessory can only arise out of actions which take place prior to, or during, the commission of the offence by D1. Assistance which is provided to D1 after the event, in order to make good an escape, or conceal evidence, for example, is not within the scope of accessorial liability, though it may in some circumstances constitute some other offence.[6] It does not, however, bring D2

2 See, eg, *Thornton v Mitchell* [1940] 1 All ER 339 – D1 acquitted of 'careless driving'; D2 also acquitted of aiding and abetting – if there was no 'careless driving', there was no *actus reus*.

3 See, eg, *Bourne* (1952) 36 Cr App R 125.

4 See, eg, *Cogan and Leak* [1975] 2 All ER 1059, and *Millward* [1994] Crim LR 527.

5 See Chapter 5, p 114.

6 Eg, Criminal Law Act 1967, s 4 (assisting offenders), s 5 (concealment of evidence); perverting the course of public justice: *R v Vreones* [1891] 1 QB 360; *R v Andrews* [1973] QB 422.

within the scope of s 8 of the 1861 Act. This illustrates the fact that the justification in principle for making D2 liable is that he has contributed in some way to causing the offence.[7] He is thus partly responsible for the infringement of the V's rights which has occurred (whereas the person who assists after the event is not). Indeed, if D2 has been present, and encouraging D1, it may be argued that this in itself indicates a demonstration of disrespect for the V's rights justifying the imposition of liability. It is perhaps this point that Megaw LJ had in mind in *Clarkson*,[8] when he referred to the fact that the presence of D2 at a rape might both encourage D1 and 'discourage the victim'. This does not, of course, apply where the D2 provides assistance prior to the event, of which the V is unaware. Here, D2's contribution to causing the offence is the dominant issue.

As noted above, s 8 identifies four ways of committing the *actus reus* of accessorial liability. It was suggested by the Court of Appeal in *Attorney General's Reference (No 1 of 1975)*[9] that 'each word must be given its ordinary meaning'.[10] In other words, each word should be treated separately, since:

> ... the probability is that there is a difference between each of those four words and the other three, because, if there were no difference, then Parliament would be wasting time in using four words where two or three would do.[11]

This suggests that a precise definition of each method of participation should be possible, and some commentators have attempted this.[12] Although the logic of the Court of Appeal's analysis of the wording of the statute has force, in practice, the courts do not seem to have adopted any consistent definitions. It is probably right, therefore, to conclude, as do Clarkson and Keating,[13] that 'it is almost certain that no real conceptual distinctions can be drawn between most of the terms'. Here, the approach taken is to consider aiding and abetting first, and then counselling and procuring. This is a division used in Archbold, and has its origins in the now defunct distinction in the way in which accessorial liability is applied to felonies as opposed to misdemeanours. It is still justifiable, however, in that aiding and abetting can be taken to describe physical assistance with the offence, provided before or at the time of its commission, whereas counselling and procuring are more apt to describe verbal encouragement provided before the event. The distinction is not rigid, however, as will be seen, and there is an area of overlap between the two

7 Note that this point is not accepted by Smith and Hogan, other than in relation to 'procuring'. But, see the comments of the Court of Appeal in *Calhaem* [1985] 1 QB 808, in relation to counselling, discussed below, p 42.

8 (1971) 55 Cr App R 445, p 450.

9 [1975] 2 All ER 684.

10 *Ibid*, p 686.

11 *Ibid*, p 686

12 See, eg, Smith, JC and Hogan, B, *Criminal Law Cases and Materials*, 6th edn, 1996, London: Butterworths, pp 129–32.

13 Clarkson, CMV and Keating, HM, *Criminal Law: Text and Materials*, 4th edn, 1998, London, Sweet & Maxwell, p 537.

categories. The approach taken here is not that of a comprehensive analysis, but simply the consideration of some examples of behaviour which will fall within each category

Looking first at aiding and abetting before the event, suppose that D1 tells D2 that he is on his way to beat up the V, and asks to borrow D2's baseball bat to use for this purpose. If D2 agrees, and lends the bat, he commits the *actus reus* of accessorial liability, should D1 subsequently attack the V. He has provided one of the means for the commission of the offence, and has a partial responsibility for its causation. The exact offence for which D2 will be liable will depend on what D1 does, and on D2's *mens rea* (which is considered below). Alternatively, the aiding and abetting might take the form of the provision of information to D1 (for example, as to the V's movements, or the effectiveness of particular poisons), which facilitate the commission of an offence.

Assistance at the time of the offence, if active, may easily merge into liability as a joint principal, but there are some cases (as noted above) where the distinction between this, and being an accessory is clear, because D2 does not commit the *actus reus* of the full offence. Thus, the D2 who holds down the V while D1 commits a fatal assault on the V does not commit the *actus reus* of murder, but will almost certainly be liable for that offence as an aider and abettor. Moreover, there is a practical advantage for prosecutors in the overlap between principal and accessorial liability. This arises where it is clear that either D1 or D2 committed an offence against the V, because both were present at the relevant time, but the prosecution does not have sufficient evidence to establish beyond reasonable doubt that either one of them was responsible for the *actus reus* of the offence. Provided that it is provable that either D1 committed the offence, and D2 was an accessory, or vice versa, then both can be convicted. Without this possibility *neither* could be convicted.

An issue which has at times troubled the courts in relation to aiding and abetting is the degree of participation required from D2 who is present at the commission of an offence in order to render him liable as an accessory. Is, for example, the silent observer of an assault which takes place in the street, and which D2 happens upon, guilty of any offence? To find so would run counter to the general rules about liability for omissions (discussed in Chapter 2),[14] which suggest that criminal liability should only be imposed for inaction where there is a duty to intervene. Two cases concerning offences against the person require consideration: *Coney*[15] and *Clarkson*.[16] *Coney* was concerned with the liability of spectators at an unlawful prize fight for the offences of battery committed by the participants. Did their voluntary presence amount

14 Above, p 16.

15 (1882) 8 QBD 534.

16 [1971] 3 All ER 344.

to 'aiding and abetting'? The trial judge's summing up had been ambiguous as to the need for active encouragement from D2 (one of the spectators) in order to render him liable, and D2 was convicted. On appeal, the conviction was quashed because of the ambiguity in the summing up. As Cave J, who delivered the leading judgment, put it:[17]

> It [the summing up] may mean either that mere presence unexplained is evidence of encouragement, and so of guilt, or that mere presence unexplained is conclusive proof of encouragement, and so of guilt. If the former is the correct meaning I concur in the law so laid down; if the latter, I am unable to do so.

The conclusion is, then, that voluntary presence may be evidence to support a charge of aiding and abetting, but is not conclusive of the fact. The key word appears to be 'encouragement'. This is picked up in *Clarkson*. The evidence in this case was that D2, with two others, entered a room from which he had heard the sounds of a rape taking place. He remained present during the rape of the V. He did not intervene, but nor was there any evidence that he took any physical action to assist, or even gave verbal encouragement to D1. D2 was convicted of aiding and abetting the rape. On appeal, it was held that his conviction should be quashed. The court noted the *dictum* of Hawkins J in *Coney* to the effect that: 'It is no criminal offence to stand by, a mere passive spectator of a crime, even of a murder. Non-interference to prevent a crime is not itself a crime.' What is needed for liability as an accessory is 'wilful encouragement'. The element of wilfulness will be left to the next section, which discusses *mens rea*. Here it is sufficient to note that the Court of Appeal in *Clarkson* regarded encouragement as the necessary *actus reus*.[18] It was a matter of evidence as to whether D2's behaviour had this effect, but it was possible for it to result from D2's presence: '... his presence and the presence of others might in fact encourage the rapers or discourage the victim.'[19]

The *actus reus* of aiding and abetting may therefore be summarised as behaviour which provides D1 with assistance before the offence, or with assistance or encouragement at the time of the offence.[20]

Turning to 'counselling and procuring', the *actus reus* of this mode of liability will always take place prior to the commission of the offence. 'Counselling' involves encouragement to commit the offence, and has close links with both conspiracy and incitement. The provision of advice as to the best method of committing an offence, or simply support for the actions being

---

17 (1882) 8 QBD 534, p 543.

18 See, also, *Allan* [1965] 1 QB 130, p 138, relied on in *Clarkson* [1971] 3 All ER 344, where it is made clear that actual encouragement of D1 is necessary.

19 [1971] 3 All ER 344, p 347. See, also, *Tait* [1993] Crim LR 538.

20 Note, also, the discussion of joint enterprise liability, below, p 45.

proposed by D1 may be sufficient to amount to 'counselling'. In *Calhaem*,[21] it was accepted by the Court of Appeal that the ordinary meaning of the word is '"advise", "solicit", or something of that sort'.[22] In that case, D2 had instructed D1 to murder a woman who was having an affair with D2's solicitor (with whom D2 had become infatuated). D1 had killed the V, but at his trial alleged that he had not intended to go through with the plan, until the V screamed, at which point D1 'went berserk' and killed the V. D2 argued that this meant that her 'counselling' was not a substantial cause of the murder. The Court of Appeal, however, said that all that was required was 'first, contact between the parties, and, second, a connection between the counselling and the murder'.[23] It was only where the D1 committed the offence completely independently of his 'authority' as indicated by the counselling, for example, by fortuitously killing the intended V in the course of some other action, that D2 would be able to escape liability.

The word 'procuring' seems to carry with it the implication that D2 is likely to be more involved with a desire to bring about the offence, and may even take the initiative towards its commission. The actions of D1 may well be undertaken to fulfil the objectives of D2. This can also be the case with counselling, as is shown by *Calhaem*, but it is most clearly present in procuring. This is confirmed by the statement in *Attorney General's Reference (No 1 of 1975)*[24] that 'to procure means to produce by endeavour'.[25] That case concerned the 'spiking' of a drink consumed by D1 who was subsequently convicted of driving with excess alcohol in his blood. D2, who had put the alcohol into the drink, was convicted as an accessory, for having procured the offence (assuming that D2 knew that D1 was intending to drive).[26] This type of scenario, involving D1 being liable for a strict liability offence, and therefore possibly unaware that he is committing it, is unlikely to occur in most of the situations under consideration in this book. It might apply, however, where D2 arranged for D1 to have sexual intercourse with a girl under the age of 16, having told D1 that she was over 16.[27] D2 could no doubt be guilty as an accessory, having procured the commission of the offence. These examples emphasise the fact that procuring is probably the most appropriate word to use where D2 has taken the initiative in encouraging D1 to commit the offence, perhaps overcoming D1's reluctance. It is also clear that the need for a causal link between the behaviour of D2 and the offence is most obvious in

---

21 [1985] 1 QB 808.

22 *Ibid*, p 813.

23 *Ibid*, p 813.

24 [1975] 2 All ER 684.

25 *Ibid*, p 686.

26 Cf *Blakely, Sutton* [1991] Crim LR 763, where the D2 having laced D1's drink with alcohol, hoped to prevent his driving.

27 So that D1 commits an offence under Sexual Offences Act 1956, s 6; see Chapter 6, p 156.

relation to this form of accessorial liability.[28] As has been argued above, however, the view taken here is that causation is relevant to all types of such liability.

The *mens rea*

The state of mind which the prosecution has to prove on the part of D2 in order to establish liability will be linked to, but not necessarily coterminous with the state of mind to be proved against D1. It is, of course, necessary to prove that the assistance provided by D2 was not inadvertent. That is why in relation to aiding or abetting by being present at the commission of the offence, it has been held that wilful encouragement of the D1 is necessary.[29] It is not enough that D2's behaviour has this effect, in fact, if D2 does not intend it to do so. Thus, a voyeur at a rape is not necessarily liable as an accessory:[30]

> While his presence ... might in fact encourage the rapers or discourage the victim, he, himself, enjoying the scene or at least standing by assenting, might not intend that his presence should offer encouragement to rapers and would-be rapers or discouragement to the victim ... while encouragement there might be, it would not be a case in which ... the accused person 'wilfully encouraged'.

Beyond this, the mental element required for aiding and abetting has been described by Archbold as being not an intention or recklessness as to the commission of the offence but 'an intention to render assistance to another in the realisation that that other may' commit the offence (having the relevant state of mind).[31] In other words, D2's state of mind as regards D1's plans must be that he knows, or, more precisely believes, that D1 is going to commit an offence. It is not necessary, however, that D2 should know the precise offence which is planned, or which occurs. The leading authorities on this issue are *Bainbridge*,[32] and *Maxwell v DPP for Northern Ireland*.[33] The approach taken by the Court of Appeal in *Bainbridge* was to suggest that 'it is not enough that it should be shown that a man knows that some illegal venture is intended.' On the other hand, 'it is unnecessary that knowledge of the particular crime [for example, on a particular date and particular premises] which was in fact committed should be shown to his knowledge to have been intended.'[34] As the trial judge had made clear in his direction, 'there must be not merely suspicion but knowledge that a crime of the type in question was intended,'

28 *Attorney General's Reference (No 1 of 1975)* [1975] 2 All ER 684, p 687.

29 See, eg, *Clarkson* [1971] 3 All ER 344.

30 *Ibid*, p 347.

31 Archbold, *Criminal Evidence, Pleading and Practice*, 1998, London, Sweet & Maxwell, para 17-67.

32 [1960] 1 QB 129.

33 [1978] 3 All ER 1140.

34 [1960] 1 QB 129, p 133.

and the assistance must be provided with that in view.[35] Thus, D2 who lends D1 his baseball bat, realising the possibility that D1 may at some point in the future hit someone with it, will not be liable as an accessory. D2 must believe that D1 has some assault offence in mind at the time the bat is handed over. He does not need to know, however, the precise victim, the date of the proposed attack, or even the level of assault proposed. If D1 subsequently commits an offence, from battery, up to causing grievous bodily harm,[36] D2 will be liable as an accessory. This approach, based on belief as to the type of offence intended by D2, although easier to state than to apply, was confirmed by the House of Lords in *Maxwell v DPP for Northern Ireland*. The D2 in this case had guided a car, which he believed to be involved in a terrorist attack. He did not know, however, the form which the attack would take. In fact, D1 had a bomb, which he threw into a public house. D2 was convicted as an accessory to offences under the Explosive Substances Act 1883. He appealed, on the basis that he had no knowledge of the type of offence intended, which might have been, for example, a shooting, or other assault, or arson. The House of Lords approved the speech of Lowry LCJ in the Northern Ireland Court of Criminal Appeal, in which he stated that where a D2 realises that D1 may have a number of different offences in mind:

> ... his [D2's] guilt springs from the fact that he contemplates the commission of one (or more) of a number of crimes by the principal [that is, D1] and he intentionally lends his assistance in order that such a crime will be committed. In other words, he knows that the principal is committing or about to commit one of a number of specified illegal acts and with that knowledge he helps him to do so.[37]

Lord Scarman, in the House of Lords, pointed out that the merit of this approach was that it concentrated on the state of mind of D2, focusing on 'not what he ought to have in contemplation, but what he did have'.[38] D2 may have one offence in contemplation, or several. In the latter case, the D2 who leaves the choice to the D1 will be liable for whatever offence is committed, 'provided always the choice is made from the range of offences from which the accessory contemplates the choice will be made'.[39] What the prosecution has to prove, therefore, is that the offence in fact committed by D1 was among those which D2 realised at the time of providing assistance that D1 might commit. There are further complications in this area, however, in relation to the issue of 'joint enterprise' liability. This topic is discussed separately below.[40]

---

35 [1960] 1 QB 129.

36 See OAPA 1861, s 18: see Chapter 5, p 125.

37 [1978] 3 All ER 1151n, p 1162.

38 [1978] 3 All ER 1140, p 1151.

39 *Ibid.*

40 See p 45.

In relation to counselling and procuring, the position is more straightforward, in that D2 is much more likely to have a specific offence in mind. Indeed, in relation to procuring, D2 will be trying to bring about the commission of a particular offence. What the prosecution will need to prove in these cases is that D2 acted with the intention that the full offence should be carried out, and the expectation, or desire, that it would be carried out by D1. The Court of Appeal in *Blakely, Sutton*[41] accepted the possibility that recklessness as to the commission of the offence by D1 might be sufficient to satisfy the *mens rea* of procuring. The court did not decide the issue, but made it clear that if recklessness was to be sufficient, it would have to be 'advertent' (that is, *Cunningham*)[42] recklessness, not simply the failure to recognise an obvious risk that the D1 would commit the offence. The court also noted, however, that:

> ... it may be, as the judgment of Lord Goddard CJ in *Ferguson v Weaving* [1951] 1 KB 814, p 819 would permit and as the judgment of Lord Widgery CJ in *Attorney General's Reference (No 1 of 1975)* [1975] RTR 473, p 477H-J strongly suggests, that it is necessary to prove that the accused intended to bring about the principal offence.

The issue is therefore open, but the balance of opinion seems to be towards requiring the prosecution to prove intention, rather than even advertent recklessness, where D2 is alleged to have procured the commission of the offence by D1.

Joint enterprise liability

The courts have at times found particular difficulty in dealing with cases where D1 and D2 are engaged on a joint criminal enterprise, but events take a turn which D2 claims was unexpected. They set out, for example, to commit robbery, or to beat someone up, and in the course of this D1 kills the V. In what circumstances will D2 be liable for murder or manslaughter? The relevant principles are to be found in *Anderson and Morris*,[43] *Chan Wing Siu*[44] and *Powell*.[45] The problem which was raised was whether, if the offence which D1 committed was one which required the proof of intention, such as murder, or s 18 of the OAPA (wounding or causing grievous bodily harm with intent to cause grievous bodily harm),[46] the prosecution needed to prove a similar intention in relation to D2. The answer given by the Court of Appeal

41 [1991] Crim LR 763.

42 See Chapter 2, p 33.

43 [1966] 2 QB 110.

44 [1984] 3 All ER 877, PC.

45 [1997] 4 All ER 545. See, also, *Hyde* [1990] 3 All ER 892 and *Hui Chi-ming* [1991] 3 All ER 897.

46 See Chapter 5, p 125.

in *Anderson and Morris*, the Privy Council in *Chan Wing Siu*, and the House of Lords in *Powell*, is that this is not necessary. In *Anderson and Morris*, this was based to some extent on the concept that D2 was in 'tacit agreement' with D1's actions as part of their joint venture. The later cases, however, preferred to put the emphasis on D2's 'foresight' of what D1 might do, rather than his agreement to it, holding that this approach may also be found in *Anderson and Morris*. All that is required, therefore, is that the D2 foresees the risk that D1 will commit the relevant acts with the relevant intention. In *Chan Wing Siu*, Sir Robin Cooke identified a principle:

> ... whereby a secondary party is criminally liable for acts by the primary offender of a type which the former foresees but does not necessarily intend. That there is such a principle is not in doubt. It turns on contemplation or, putting the same idea in other words, authorisation, which may be expressed but is more usually implied. It meets the case of a crime foreseen as a possible incident of the common unlawful enterprise. The criminal culpability lies in participating in the venture with that foresight.[47]

Moreover, this foresight does not have to be of a high level of probability:[48]

> Where a man lends himself to a criminal enterprise knowing that potentially murderous weapons are to be carried, and in the event they are in fact used by his partner with intent sufficient for murder, he should not escape the consequences by reliance on a nuance of prior assessment, only too likely to have been optimistic.

As Lord Hutton put it in *Powell*, agreeing with the approach of the Privy Council in *Chan Wing Siu*:[49]

> [D2] is subject to criminal liability if he contemplated the act causing the death as a possible incident of the joint venture, unless the risk was so remote that the jury take the view that the secondary party genuinely dismissed it as altogether negligible.

It is only the foresight of the D2 which is relevant here, and the prosecution does not have to prove that D1 had a similar foresight at the start of the enterprise.[50] Indeed, the liability of the D2 is sufficiently independent of the D1 that it is possible for the D2 to be convicted of murder, even though the D1 was only convicted of manslaughter,[51] and vice versa.[52]

The application of these principles to attempted murder was considered by the Court of Appeal in *O'Brien*.[53] The judge had directed the jury in

---

47 [1984] 3 All ER 877, pp 880–81.

48 *Ibid*, p 882.

49 [1997] 4 All ER 545, p 566.

50 *Hui Chi-ming* [1991] 3 All ER 897.

51 *Ibid*.

52 *Stewart and Schofield* [1995] 1 Cr App R 441.

53 [1995] Crim LR 734.

relation to joint enterprise on the basis that it must be proved that D2 anticipated that D1 *would* shoot to kill if the need arose, before he could be liable for attempted murder. The Court of Appeal, however, confirmed that the necessary state of mind was the same whether D1 was liable for murder or attempted murder. In either case, it was enough to prove that D2 foresaw that D1 might act against the V with intent to kill. If the attempt was successful, and D1 was liable for murder, then D2 would also be liable for murder if he foresaw that D1 might intentionally use grievous bodily harm against the V.

In *Powell*, the House of Lords also considered the principles that should apply where the D1 foresees a particular outcome, but not the manner in which it occurs. This issue was raised by the facts of *English*, which was heard together with *Powell*. In this case, D1 and D2 had together attacked a police officer with wooden posts. In the course of the attack D1 used a knife with which he stabbed the officer to death. The trial judge directed the jury that they could convict D2 of murder if they thought he realised that there was a substantial risk D1 might in the course of their attack kill or at least cause some really serious injury to the police officer. The House of Lords, however, again relying on principles drawn from *Anderson and Morris*, held that this was a misdirection. The relevant passage from Lord Parker's judgment in *Anderson and Morris* is as follows:[54]

> It seems to this court that to say that adventurers are guilty of manslaughter when one of them had departed completely from the concerted action of the common design and has suddenly formed an intent to kill and has used a weapon and acted in a way which no party to that common design could suspect is something which would revolt the conscience of people today.

Applying this to the *English* case, the trial judge's direction was inadequate because it did not allow the jury to consider whether or not D2 had foreseen the possibility that D1 would use a knife as part of their attack. Thus, where the lethal act of D1 is fundamentally different from the acts foreseen by the D2 then D2 should not be liable for murder. The difficulty of applying this test in practice, however, is made clear by Lord Hutton's diffidence about trying to formulate a precise rule to cover this situation, and by his comment that the use of a different, but equally dangerous, weapon (such as a knife instead of a gun) should not in itself allow D2 to escape liability.[55]

The distinction of 'joint enterprise' liability from the general liability of 'aiders and abettors' has been criticised by Smith and Hogan,[56] but it has clearly become accepted by all the appellate courts, as well as by the Law Commission.[57]

---

54 [1966] 2 QB 110, p 120.

55 [1997] 4 All ER 545, p 566. Note the application of the approach taken in *Powell* in the subsequent cases of *Uddin* [1998] 2 All ER 744 and *Greatrex* [1998] Crim LR 733

56 *Op cit*, Smith and Hogan, fn 12, p 147.

57 Consultation Paper No 131, *Assisting and Encouraging Crime.*

Withdrawal from participation

D2, who in the course of a criminal enterprise, has a change of heart, and wishes to withdraw from participation, will have to take very clear steps to do so. In *Becerra*,[58] D2 was taking part in a violent burglary when he and his fellow burglars were disturbed by the V. D2 shouted out 'Come on, let's go', and left the building. D1 remained, and stabbed the V (with a knife which had been given to him by D2), killing him. D2 was convicted of murder, but appealed on the basis that he had withdrawn his participation before the killing. The Court of Appeal refused to set down any firm rules as to what was required for withdrawal, but recognised the possibility that in some cases physical action to prevent D1 committing the offence might be necessary. On the facts, however, taking into account D2's prior actions, if he wanted to withdraw:

> ... he would have to 'countermand', to use the word that is used in some of the cases or 'repent' to use another word so used, in some manner vastly different and vastly more effective than merely to say 'Come on, let's go' and go out through the window.

The *Becerra* approach has been approved in *Rook*,[59] which held that a silent withdrawal and absence from the planned crime was insufficient, since it had not been made clear to the other participants. Clearly, the issue will be affected by the stage which the offence has reached. At the planning stage, it may be enough for the D2 to state that he wants no further part in the enterprise, and encourage the others to desist.[60] Once the criminal enterprise is underway, however, it will be very difficult for D2 to do enough to convince a jury that he had effectively withdrawn.

Attempts

The basic elements of the offence of attempting to commit a crime are set out in s 1(1) of the Criminal Attempts Act 1981:

> If, with intent to commit an offence to which this section applies, a person does an act which is more than merely preparatory to the commission of an offence, he is guilty of attempting to commit the offence.

It should be noted that the offence of attempt does not apply to every criminal offence. Section 1(4) provides that s 1(1) only applies to indictable offences, and even then not to conspiracies, liability as an accessory, and certain offences under the Criminal Law Act 1977.[61] This means that offences triable

58 (1975) 62 Cr App R 212.

59 [1993] 2 All ER 955.

60 See, eg, *Grundy* [1977] Crim LR 543.

61 The Criminal Law Act 1977, s 4(1) (assisting offenders) and s 5(1) (accepting or agreeing to accept consideration for not disclosing information about an arrestable offence).

only summarily are not included – it is not an offence to attempt to commit such an offence. This limitation is of little consequence in relation to the offences considered in this book, since virtually all of them are triable either on indictment, or either way.

The rationale for liability for attempts is difficult to base on the infringement of the V's rights, since, as will be seen, the *actus reus* of an attempt can be committed without any such infringement. The justification must be based primarily on the 'interests of the State'. As far as the D is concerned there will often be little moral distinction between the person who has made an unsuccessful attempt, and one who has succeeded in his enterprise, and so it is justifiable to bring this category of person within the scope of the criminal law.

The *actus reus* and *mens rea* of attempts will now be considered.

Actus reus

The *actus reus* of attempt is indicated by the phrase used in s 1 of the 1981 Act requiring that the D has done an act which is 'more than merely preparatory to the commission of an offence'. This phrase is a modification of the pre-Act case law on attempts, when this type of liability was defined solely by the common law. The Court of Appeal has, however, in *Gullefer*[62] and *Jones*,[63] expressed the view that it is unnecessary to consider the old cases (which were not consistent) in interpreting the Act. The courts should concentrate on the 'natural meaning of the statutory words'. What, then, is the meaning of 'more than merely preparatory'? There are two types of situation to consider where a charge of attempt may be appropriate. The first is where the D has tried to go through with the offence, but for some reason has failed. The assassin who shoots at the intended V, but misses, has clearly done an act that is more than merely preparatory, and can be charged with attempted murder. This type of situation creates little difficulty. The second type involves the situation where the D has gone some way towards the commission of the offence, but then has stopped. The reason for this may be discovery, problems with the proposed plan of action, or a change of mind on the D's part. At what stage in the series of actions leading up to the offence can the D's behaviour be said to be more than merely preparatory? Consider the situation where the D decides to assault the V. He forms a plan as to how to carry out the assault without being detected, and writes this down. He lies in wait for the V. As she arrives at the point the D has selected for the assault, the D slips out behind her intending to attack her from the rear. At that point, the D sees a policeman approaching, and abandons his plan. Has the D, at any stage, committed an act which is more than merely preparatory to his intended assault? If, for

62 [1990] 3 All ER 882.

63 [1990] 3 All ER 886.

example, the police were to find the plan which he has written, would that be enough to form the basis of a charge of attempted assault? Would it do so if combined with evidence of his behaviour, as observed by the policeman, of slipping from his hiding place to follow the V? The question is ultimately one of fact for the jury in a particular case, but the judge has to decide whether there is sufficient evidence for the jury to consider it. A relevant decision is that of *Jones*.[64] The V was having an affair with the D's wife. The D armed himself with a shotgun, and got into the rear seat of the V's car. He pointed the gun at the V, and said: 'You are not going to like this.' At this point, the V managed to wrestle the gun away from the D and escape. The D was convicted of attempted murder. On appeal, it was argued that he had not committed the *actus reus* of this offence, because there were still several actions which he would have needed to take before shooting the V. At the time the gun was pointed at the V, the safety catch was still on. The D would therefore have had to release this, put his finger on the trigger, and pull it. The Court of Appeal rejected the argument that the test used in some pre-Act cases of whether the act of the D was the 'last act' necessary before the commission of the offence was appropriate. It approved the approach taken by the court in *Gullefer*,[65] where Lord Lane CJ had referred to the test being whether the D has embarked on the crime proper. In relation to D's behaviour in this case:[66]

> Clearly, his actions in obtaining the gun, in shortening it, in loading it, in putting on his disguise and in going to the school could only be regarded as preparatory acts. But, in our judgment, once he had got into the car, taken out the loaded gun and pointed it at the victim with the intention of killing him there was sufficient evidence for the consideration of the jury on the charge of attempted murder.

Applying this approach to the assault example used above, it is clear that the D will not have committed the *actus reus* of attempt at any point prior to slipping from his hiding place. Everything up to that point must be regarded as merely preparatory. There is no certainty however that even at the final point he has done enough. The question is whether he has 'embarked on the crime proper'. In *Campbell*,[67] for example, the D who planned to rob a post office, was arrested as he approached his target, and was one yard from the door, wearing a disguise, and with an imitation firearm in his pocket. The Court of Appeal held that this was insufficient to amount to an attempt to rob the post office. He could not be said to have done more than merely preparatory acts. It would presumably only be when he had entered the post office, and approached the counter, and issued some threat, that he could be said to have embarked on the crime proper. On the other hand, it has also

64 [1990] 3 All ER 886

65 [1990] 3 All ER 882

66 [1990] 3 All ER 886, pp 890–91.

67 [1991] Crim LR 268.

been held by the Court of Appeal, applying the same test, that it is not necessary for the offence of attempted rape that there should be an attempt to penetrate the V's vagina.[68] It is hard to disagree with the conclusion of Clarkson and Keating that 'It is almost impossible to extract any clear principles from the cases interpreting s 1(1)' of the 1981 Act.[69] Returning to our hypothetical attempted assault, however, it is suggested that if it could be said that the D was approaching the V with the intention of carrying out the assault at the time he saw the policeman, he would have 'embarked on the crime proper', and an attempt charge could appropriately be left to the jury. Anything less than that, however, would fall outside the scope of s 1(1).

Mens rea

The *mens rea* of attempts is more straightforward, in that s 1(1) of the 1981 Act makes it clear that what is required is an *intention* to commit the *actus reus* of the full offence. This confirms the common law position as stated in *Whybrow*.[70] Thus, in relation to offences for which the *mens rea* may be satisfied by proof of either intention or recklessness as to an outcome, the D may only be convicted of an attempt if the prosecution proves that he *intended* that outcome:[71] recklessness is not enough.[72] Moreover, in relation to murder, an intention to *kill* must be proved, even though the full offence may be committed with an intention to cause grievous bodily harm.[73] This is because the *actus reus* of murder is only satisfied where the V dies: it is that *actus reus* that the D must intend in order to be liable for an attempt to murder the V.

Finally, the Act makes clear, by virtue of s 1(2) and (3) that the D may be liable even though the outcome intended is impossible. This may be because the means used by the D are inadequate (s 1(2)) or because the circumstances are not as the D thinks they are (s 1(3)). Thus, the person who attempts to shoot the V at long range may be guilty of attempted murder, even though the weapon he is using could never fire a bullet the required distance. The same will be true where the D attacks a tailor's dummy, thinking it to be the V. His intention is to cause harm to the V, and the fact that the V is not there makes

---

68 *Attorney General's Reference (No 1 of 1992)* (1992) 96 Cr App R 298. This case is discussed further in Chapter 6, p 152. Cf also *Griffin* [1995] Crim LR 515.

69 *Op cit*, Clarkson and Keating, fn 13, p 493.

70 (1951) 35 Cr App R 141.

71 The meaning of intention is discussed in detail in Chapter 2.

72 But, note the decision in *Khan* [1990] 2 All ER 783, where the Court of Appeal held that recklessness as to circumstances may be sufficient as regards attempted rape. This is discussed further in Chapter 6, p 154. See, also, *Attorney General's Reference (No 3 of 1992)* [1994] Crim LR 348; Criminal Damage Act 1971, s 1(2).

73 See Chapter 4, p 61. Cf *Walker and Hayles* (1990) 90 Cr App R 226.

no difference, provided that the D has done acts which are more than merely preparatory towards the commission of the offence.[74]

Conspiracy

The law relating to the offence of conspiracy is governed by ss 1–5 of the Criminal Law Act 1977. Section 1(1) provides that:

> Subject to the following provisions of this Part of this Act, if a person agrees with any other person or persons that a course of conduct shall be pursued which, if the agreement is carried out in accordance with their intentions, either:
>
> (a) will necessarily amount to or involve the commission of any offence or offences by one or more of the parties to the agreement; or
>
> (b) would do so but for the existence of facts which render the commission of the offence or any of the offences impossible,
>
> he is guilty of conspiracy to commit the offence or offences in question.

The essence of conspiracy is an agreement between the D and one or more others to commit a criminal offence.[75] It is irrelevant whether or not the full offence is committed. Once again, therefore, the rationale for this type of criminal liability cannot be based on the infringement of the V's rights, since none may occur. As with attempts, it must be based on the interests of the State. These must be taken to be that there is a danger to society in people agreeing to commit offences, which is greater than the danger threatened by one person who plans to commit an offence.

Note that in contrast to the position in relation to attempts, it is an offence to conspire to commit a summary offence.

Actus reus

The *actus reus* of conspiracy is the agreement. No other behaviour need be proved. It is not necessary here to show that the parties to the agreement took any steps towards the commission of the offence. D1 and D2 who agree to kill the V at that point may be guilty of conspiracy to murder, even though they never take any steps towards putting their plan into effect. In practice, of course, the fact that an agreement has been made may well need to be proved by implication from other behaviour of the Ds.[76]

---

74 *Shivpuri* [1986] 2 All ER 334.

75 There can also be a conspiracy to defraud, or a conspiracy to corrupt public morals, neither of which need involve a plan to commit acts which would be criminal if done by one person, but this is outside the scope of this book: Criminal Law Act 1977, s 5.

76 *Op cit*, Smith and Hogan, fn 12, p 304; Archbold, fn 31, para 33-11.

There must be at least two people involved, though there may be more. Where this is the case, there is no requirement that they should all be in touch with each other. A conspiracy can consist of a 'wheel' (D1 makes separate agreements with D2, D3, D4 ...) or a 'chain' (D1 makes an agreement with D2, D2 makes an agreement with D3, etc).[77] It need take no particular form,[78] as long as it demonstrates the common intention between the parties.

Because of the nature of the offence of conspiracy, issues relating to the *actus reus* are times difficult to separate from those concerning the *mens rea*. Discussion of the precise nature of the agreement required is left to the latter heading, to which we now turn

Mens rea

The *mens rea* for a criminal conspiracy is indicated by s 1(1) of the 1977 Act, as set out above. What is needed is an intention to pursue a course of conduct which will necessarily amount to or involve the commission of a criminal offence. A number of points arise from this.

First, the requirement is of 'intention'. No form of 'recklessness' will suffice. Secondly, the phrase 'course of conduct' must be taken to include the consequences of such conduct. D1 and D2 may conspire to cause V serious injury, and agree to tamper with the brakes on her car in order to achieve this. The 'course of conduct' is, of course, in one sense the tampering with the brakes, but there is no doubt that D1 and D2 are liable for conspiracy to cause grievous bodily harm even if the V notices the problem with the brakes while driving slowly, and so manages to avoid an accident. Thirdly, the phrase 'necessarily result' is qualified by the subsequent clause 'if carried out with in accordance with their intentions'. Once again, the *intended* result, not the *actual* result is what is important. In the previous example, it is clear that tampering with the brakes will not necessarily result in injury to the V. Nevertheless, if the plan proceeded according to the Ds intentions, the V would have an accident, and be seriously injured. This consequence necessarily results in an offence under s 18 of the OAPA 1861. The Ds can therefore be liable for conspiracy to commit this offence. Equally, if the end result which they wished to achieve was the death of the V, they could be liable for conspiracy to murder. Note that the emphasis on intention means that there can only be liability for conspiracy to commit offences where liability for the substantive offence can be based on proving an intention in relation to consequences or circumstances. There cannot, for example, be a conspiracy to commit manslaughter: either death is intended, in which case the conspiracy is to

77 *Meyrick* (1929) 21 Cr App R 94.

78 It does not, for example, need to be a 'contract' according to civil law: *Anderson* [1986] 1 AC 27.

murder, or it is not, in which case the conspiracy will at most be to commit an offence under s 18 of the OAPA.

It will be seen from s 1(1)(b) of the Criminal Law Act 1977 that there can be a conspiracy to commit an offence which is in fact impossible of completion. An agreement to kill the V is still a conspiracy to murder, whether or not the V is alive at the time of the agreement, or at the time of the planned offence. The same will be true of a conspiracy to rape where the intended V is in fact keen to have intercourse with the Ds, and will consent to its taking place.

On the other hand, there is no room for strict liability in relation to conspiracy. Section 1(2) states that:

> Where liability for an offence may be incurred without knowledge on the part of the person committing it of any particular fact of circumstance necessary for the commission of the offence, a person shall nevertheless not be guilty of conspiracy to commit that offence ... unless he and at least one other party to the agreement intend or know that that fact or circumstance shall or will exist at the time when the conduct constituting the offence is to take place.

Thus, an agreement to have sexual intercourse with the V, whom all the Ds think is over 16, will not amount to a conspiracy to commit an offence under s 6 of the Sexual Offences Act 1956, even though the V is in fact only 15.

The word of s 1(2) is perhaps not very apt, as has been frequently pointed out, since 'intention' is more appropriately used in relation to consequences, rather than facts or circumstances, and one can never 'know' that a circumstance will exist at some point in the future. 'Belief' in the existence of the fact or circumstance is what it is universally assumed is meant by the sub-section.

CHAPTER 4

HOMICIDE

The most serious interference that there can be with a person's bodily integrity is the termination of life itself. It follows that the most serious offences against the person under the English law are those which result in the death of the victim. All of the offences which are considered in this chapter are, therefore, result crimes – that is, the consequence (that is, the death of the victim) is an integral part of the offence.

English law recognises two main homicide offences – murder and manslaughter. These are distinguished purely by the state of mind of the A. The external elements (*actus reus*) of the offence are identical in each case. In addition, there are some special statutory offences, such as causing death by dangerous driving and infanticide, which will be considered separately at the end of the chapter. Both murder and manslaughter are common law offences. Although the Homicide Act 1957 contains provisions which are relevant to them, it does not define either offence. Indeed, the precise scope of each offence has been the subject of debate in a number of appeals to the House of Lords in the past 10 years. It reflects little credit on English criminal law that the definition of two of its most serious offences is surrounded by such uncertainty. Proposals for reform of manslaughter are discussed in Chapter 8.

Before moving to a consideration of the elements of homicide under English law, it should be noted that Art 2 of the European Convention on Human Rights states that 'Everyone's right to life shall be protected by law'. This Article is, of course, incorporated into English law by the Human Rights Act 1988. It imposes an obligation on the government to provide laws against homicide, though the Article recognises certain situations where killing is permissible (for example, capital punishment) or excusable (for example, self-defence). The obligation becomes more direct where members of the police or security services are involved in the killing. Thus, there have been challenges to the UK under this Article in relation to the activities of the security services in Northern Ireland, or in relation to suspected terrorists.[1] There is no doubt, however, that the general law of murder and manslaughter would be regarded as fulfilling the UK's obligations under Art 2.

1 Eg, *Ireland v UK* (1972) 15 Yearbook of the ECHR 92; *Kelly v UK* (1993) 16 EHRR CD 20; *McCann v UK* (1996) 21 EHRR 97.

ACTUS REUS OF HOMICIDE OFFENCES

For the D to be convicted of either murder or manslaughter, it must be proved that the D caused or accelerated the death of another person. Until recently that death had to take place within a year and a day,[2] but, as we shall see, that rule has now been abolished, and the question is simply whether the D's acts (or possibly omissions) meet the 'causation' requirements for the offence.

The actions of the D must 'cause or accelerate' death. Since none of us is immortal, 'accelerate' is probably the more appropriate verb in all cases. However, the commonly used phrase emphasises the fact that a homicide offence can result not only where the V was, prior to the D's actions, in the best of health, but also where the V had in any case only a short time to live. The fact that the V is suffering from a terminal illness, or has, prior to the D's actions been wounded by someone else in a way which might well prove fatal, does not prevent the D being liable for the V's death. It may become crucial, therefore, to determine at what point death occurs, even though the year and a day rule no longer operates. If the D has violently attacked what is in legal terms a corpse, then there will be no liability. If, however, the V is on the point of death, but not actually dead at the time of the attack, the D can be liable for murder or manslaughter. The English courts have been hesitant about laying down firm rules as to the legal definition of death. The judges have tended to prefer to follow the lead of the medical profession in this area. Thus the current position is probably accurately stated by Lord Goff in *Airedale NHS Trust v Bland*,[3] which concerned the legality of a proposed withdrawal of treatment from a young man who was in a 'persistent vegetative state'. Lord Goff commented as follows:

> I start with the simple fact that, in law, Anthony is still alive. It is true that his condition is such that it can be described as a living death; but he is nevertheless still alive. This is because, as a result of developments in modern medical technology, doctors no longer associate death exclusively with breathing and heart beat, and it has come to be accepted that death occurs when the brain, and in particular the brain stem, has been destroyed.

In support of this view, Lord Goff cited a chapter by Ian Kennedy in *Treat Me Right*, where he describes the concept 'brain death' in the following terms:[4]

---

2 This was part of Coke's classic definition of murder (3 Inst 47):

> Murder is when a man of sound memory, and of the age of discretion, unlawfully killeth within any county of the realm any reasonable creature in rerum natura under the king's peace, with malice aforethought, either expressed by the party or implied by law, so as the party wounded, or hurt, etc die of the wound or hurt, etc, within a year and a day after the same.

3 [1993] 1 All ER 821, p 865.

4 Kennedy, I, 'Switching off life-support machines: the legal implications', in *Treat Me Right, Essays in Medical Law and Ethics*, 1988, Oxford: Clarendon, pp 349, 351. This chapter is a revised version of an article by Kennedy first published in the *Criminal Law Review* ([1977] Crim LR 443).

> A person will not breathe, nor will his heart beat, without a functioning brain-stem; and if this is destroyed, he will never recover the ability to do so, since, once destroyed, brain cells do not regenerate. A machine may well perform these tasks for him for some considerable period of time, but it has come to be accepted that once the brain can be shown to be dead, the machine is not keeping the patient 'alive' in any accepted sense of the word; it is merely ventilating a corpse.

The acceptance by the medical profession of brain-stem death as the operating concept for identifying the termination of life dates from the 1976 report of the medical Royal Colleges and their faculties.[5] This also included a code of practice, setting out procedures for establishing brain-stem death. These need not concern us here, but a description of the kind of process involved may be found in the report of *Re A*.[6]

Lords Keith and Browne-Wilkinson agreed with Lord Goff in *Airedale NHS Trust v Bland* that brain-stem death constituted the legal as well the medical definition of death. Whether this view was *obiter* (as Card suggests[7]), or part of the *ratio* (as argued by Kennedy and Grubb),[8] is probably of little practical consequence. There is no serious alternative legal definition of death being promoted, and we may take it that for the foreseeable future, the courts will treat brain-stem death as the relevant concept. The implications of this for issues such as the switching-off of life-support machines are considered elsewhere.[9]

The limitation that the D cannot commit murder or manslaughter in relation to a corpse is, of course, also expressed in the requirement that the V must be a 'person'. This requirement has relevance to the question of when these offences can be committed against a V at the other end of human existence. That is, at what stage after conception does a 'person' come into existence as a potential victim of murder or manslaughter. The current rule is that this stage is reached only after a live birth, when the baby has an existence independent of his or her mother.[10] The killing of a foetus in the womb is, if a crime at all, an illegal abortion, which may amount to an offence under s 58 of the OAPA 1861. It has recently been held by the House of Lords, however, that an attack on a pregnant woman who then gives birth, may lead to a charge of manslaughter against the D, if the child then dies.[11] The difficult issues surrounding the questions of possible offences committed at or around

5 (1976) 2 BMJ 1187.

6 [1992] 3 Med LR 303.

7 Card, Cross and Jones, *Criminal Law*, 14th edn, 1998, London: Butterworths, p 170.

8 Kennedy, I, and Grubb, A, *Medical Law*, 2nd edn, 1994, London: Butterworths, p 1395.

9 See, below, p 59.

10 *Poulton* (1832) 5 C&P 329; *Enoch* (1833) 5 C&P 539; *Handley* (1874) 13 Cox CC 79 – all these authorities consist of rulings by the trial judge.

11 *Attorney General's Reference (No 3 of 1994)*, discussed above in Chapter 2, p 23.

the time of birth are considered further below, in the section of this chapter concerned with infanticide.

There are two other categories of people who are incapable of being the victims of murder or manslaughter. First, there are those who are under lawful sentence of death. The killing of such a person by execution is by definition lawful, and so cannot constitute an offence. It seems, however, that an offence may be committed if the *manner* of the killing is unauthorised (either in relation to the way in which it is carried out, or the person who does it).[12] The point is unlikely to arise in an English court, given the recent abolition of the death penalty for all offences.[13] The second category comprises those who are not 'under the Queen's peace'.[14] No example of such a person seems to exist, however, apart from an enemy alien, killed in the heat of battle.[15]

The next issue to be considered is that of causation – did the actions of the D cause the death? We have already discussed some general issues of causation in Chapter 2. Here, the focus is on the way in which the principles discussed there apply to the homicide offences. Some issues are clear. The actions of the D must, as a matter of fact, precede the death of the V, whatever the D's view of the matter. There is no homicide offence in throwing a corpse into a river, even if the D thinks that the V is still alive at the time, and intends that she will drown.[16] (If the D has made the opposite mistake, however, assuming that a person still alive is in fact already dead, there may be liability for manslaughter.)[17] The V's death does not have to follow within any particular period, however. The long standing rule that death must occur within 'a year and a day' of the actions alleged to have caused it,[18] was abolished by the Law Reform (Year and a Day Rule) Act 1996. The rule clearly had a practical basis in the fact that it may well be difficult, if not impossible, to establish a clear causal link between action and death if the time lapse is too great. A simple rule cutting off the possibility of a homicide trial after a year has some sense in this context. It also avoids the situation where D is held in 'limbo', while the prosecution waits to see whether death will follow, or whether the D should be charged simply with a serious assault,[19] or attempted murder. These considerations have been overridden, however, by

---

12 *Hale*, 1 PC 433.

13 As regards high treason (Treason Act 1814, s 1) and piracy with violence (Piracy Act 1837, s 2) the penalty was abolished by the Crime and Disorder Act 1998, s 36.

14 This again is derived from Coke's definition – *op cit*, fn 2.

15 This example is given by *Hale*, 1 PC 433, and has been cited by virtually all commentators since.

16 The D's actions may, however, constitute attempted murder – see Chapter 5, p 127.

17 See *Church* [1965] 2 All ER 72, below, p 93.

18 This is traceable at least back to Coke's definition – *op cit*, fn 2; see, also, the Statute of Gloucester 1278.

19 Most likely, OAPA, s 18 – Chapter 5, p 125.

the concern that advances in medical science may have resulted in too great a risk that those responsible for causing death will not be able to be charged with a homicide offence. It is now possible for those who have suffered very serious, life threatening injuries to be kept alive, even if in a coma. Indeed, it may be regarded as desirable, if not a requirement of medical ethics, that life support systems should not be switched off until a considerable period has passed,[20] and it can be established, for example, that the victim is in a 'persistent vegetative state' (PVS).

When it is decided that a victim is in a PVS, and that no chance of recovery is possible, the removal of life support systems will not be regarded as a *novus actus interveniens* breaking the chain of causation. The issue was considered by the Court of Appeal in *Malcherek and Steel*.[21] In *Malcherek*, the V had been stabbed nine times in the abdomen with a kitchen knife; in Steel the V had been beaten about the head with a heavy stone. Both victims were placed on a ventilator while in hospital; in both cases the ventilator was withdrawn when it appeared that the V had suffered irreversible brain damage, and would not recover. At the (separate) trials of the assailants, the judge withdrew the issue of causation from the jury, which in each case found the D guilty of murder. The Court of Appeal held that the judge was right not to leave causation to the jury. In reaching this conclusion, it was clearly influenced by the common sense view that:[22]

> Whatever the strict logic of the matter may be, it is perhaps somewhat bizarre to suggest ... that where a doctor tries his conscientious best to save the life of a patient brought to hospital in extremis, skilfully using sophisticated methods, drugs and machinery to do so, but fails in his attempt and therefore discontinues treatment, he can be said to have caused the death of the patient.

The legal reasoning which supported this common sense conclusion was that there was no evidence that the original injuries were not, in each case, a continuing, operating and substantial cause of the death of the V. Although the issue of causation is one of fact for the jury, if there is no conflict of evidence, the judge is entitled to tell the jury how the law applies to the admitted facts – for example, by directing them that the injuries inflicted by the D are to be regarded as an operative cause of the death of the V.[23] In reaching its conclusion, the court relied on the earlier decision of the Courts-Martial Appeal Court in *Smith*.[24] In this case, the V had received two bayonet wounds, one of which was more serious than was realised at the time. The person who was carrying the V to the medical station dropped him twice.

20 BMA guidelines suggest that artificial feeding should not be withdrawn for at least a year.

21 [1981] 2 All ER 422.

22 *Ibid*, p 429.

23 *Blaue* [1975] 3 All ER 446, p 450.

24 [1959] 2 All ER 193.

Once there, because the seriousness of the wound was not appreciated, the V received treatment which was inadequate and 'thoroughly bad'.[25] The V died two hours after arriving at the medical station. Although it was accepted that, if the V had received immediate and more appropriate treatment, he might well have survived, nevertheless, the cause of death was haemorrhaging from a punctured lung, resulting from the original stabbing. The events which occurred between the stabbing and the death were not sufficient to break the chain of causation. The principle which the court applied was expressed in the following terms:

> If at the time of death the original wound is still an operating cause and a substantial cause, then the death can properly be said to be the result of the wound, albeit that some other cause of death is also operating. Only if it can be said that the original wounding is merely the setting in which another cause operates can it be said that the death does not result from the wound. Putting it another way, only if the second cause is so overwhelming as to make the original wound merely part of the history can it be said that the death does not flow from the wound ...

This is a stringent test. It had, however, been satisfied, so the court thought, in the earlier case of *Jordan*.[26] This again involved a serious stab wound, which had pierced the V's intestine. The V was, in this case, however, treated properly up to the point where the wound had almost healed. At this stage, to avoid infection, he was given a drug to which he turned out to be intolerant. Nevertheless, treatment with this drug continued, and was followed by other 'palpably wrong' procedures, which caused pneumonia. The V died. The evidence concerning the wrong treatment was not presented at the trial, and the jury convicted. The Court of Appeal had no doubt, however, that had they heard the evidence they 'would have felt precluded from saying that they were satisfied that the death was caused by stab wound'.[27] To use the terminology adopted in *Smith*, the wound had become merely part of the history, and was no longer an operating or substantial cause of the death.

The Court of Appeal returned to the issue of defective medical treatment in *Cheshire*.[28] This case may be said to fall in between *Jordan* and *Smith* in that the treatment was negligent, but not as 'palpably wrong' as in *Jordan*. Moreover, it seemed that the original wounds were no longer life-threatening at the time of death. The V had been shot by the D, and was being treated in hospital. One of the wounds was to his abdomen and he was for several weeks fitted with a tracheotomy tube to aid breathing. About two months after the original wound had been inflicted, the V had serious trouble with his breathing, and died from 'cardio-respiratory arrest'. It transpired that the

25 See [1959] 2 All ER 193, *per* Lord Parker CJ, p 198.

26 (1956) 40 Crim App Rep 152.

27 *Ibid*, p 158.

28 [1991] 3 All ER 670.

cause of the breathing difficulties was the narrowing of the windpipe near the site of the tracheotomy scar – a rare, but not unknown consequence of this procedure. There was evidence at the trial that the failure of the medical staff to identify the cause of the breathing difficulties could be regarded as negligent. The judge directed the jury, however, that they should only find the chain of causation broken if the medical treatment was 'reckless'. The jury convicted of murder. On appeal, the Court of Appeal held that the judge had misdirected the jury in referring to recklessness. This directed attention to the blame-worthiness of those treating the V, rather than the causative effect of the treatment. The court was clear, however, that treatment which simply fell below the standard of care and skill to be expected of the competent medical practitioner would not of itself break the chain of causation. This would only occur where the treatment could be said to be 'so independent of the acts of the accused that it could be regarded in law as the cause of the victim's death to the exclusion of the accused's acts'.[29] The jury should be directed that the Crown had to prove that the D's acts, though not necessarily the 'sole cause or even the main cause of death' nevertheless contributed significantly to that result. It was only where later negligent treatment was 'so independent of (the D's) acts, and in itself so potent in causing death, that they regard the contribution made by his acts as insignificant' that the jury should find that the chain of causation is broken.

The test from *Cheshire* is thus one of 'a significant cause'. It is not clear that this is any different from the 'operating and substantial' cause referred to in *Smith*. If anything, the *Cheshire* test requires a lesser contribution from the D's acts than that used in *Smith*. Both tests suffer, however, from requiring the jury to embark on the somewhat circular process of deciding a 'causation' issue by means of a test which itself uses 'cause' as a part of its definition. To that extent, the references to whether the original wound had become 'part of the history', or whether the later treatment was 'independent' of the D's acts, may in practice be more helpful as a guide to the jury.

MURDER

Mens rea

The state of mind which the prosecution must prove in relation to murder has traditionally been referred to as 'malice aforethought'.[30] This is unhelpful, in that, as has often been pointed out, neither 'malice' (at least in the popular sense of the word), nor 'forethought' is in fact required in order to establish

29 [1991] 3 All ER 670, p 677.

30 See, eg, *op cit*, Coke, fn 2.

the relevant *mens rea*. Unfortunately, the phrase has statutory recognition by virtue of s 1 of the Homicide Act 1957:

> Where a person kills in the course or furtherance of some other offence, the killing shall not amount to murder unless done with the same malice aforethought (express or implied) as is required for a killing to amount to murder when not done in the course or furtherance of another offence.

The main object of this section was to abolish 'constructive malice', whereby, if a death occurred during the commission of some other serious offence, the D was automatically guilty of murder. The section, however, is exclusive in its effect, and does not give any positive indication as to what state of mind will amount to malice aforethought. The issue has therefore remained to be determined by the courts. The current position derives from the House of Lords decision in *Moloney*,[31] where it was held that the prosecution must prove that the D intended to kill or cause 'grievous bodily harm', meaning really serious bodily harm.[32] The definition of 'intention' has been considered at length in Chapter 2, and there in no need to repeat that discussion here – particularly since virtually all the authorities dealt with relate to homicides. It should be noted, however, that the decision in *Moloney* involved a rejection of the suggestion that something less than intention (for example, some degree of 'recklessness') would suffice as the *mens rea* of murder.[33] The earlier decision of the House of Lords in *Hyam*[34] had left this point uncertain. The case involved a D who set fire to a house, with the result that two children were killed. She claimed that her intention was simply to frighten the occupier of the house, of whom she was jealous, into leaving the neighbourhood. The House of Lords held that she was rightly convicted of murder if the jury was convinced that she foresaw death or serious injury as a 'highly probable' (or possibly even simply a 'probable') consequence of her actions. It was unclear, however, whether this was on the basis that such foresight amounted to 'intention', or was simply an alternative form of 'malice aforethought'. In any case, the House of Lords in *Moloney* took a different view. As we have seen,[35] it held that foresight, even of a virtually certain consequence, is not the equivalent of intention. It also held that 'malice aforethought' is only established by proof of 'intention'. Thus, in the subsequent case of *Nedrick*,[36] which had facts almost identical to those which occurred in *Hyam*,[37] the Court

---

31 [1985] 1 All ER 1025.

32 Though a direction in terms of 'serious bodily harm', omitting the 'really', may be acceptable where for example the circumstances make it implausible that anything less than really serious harm can have been intended: *Janjua* [1998] Crim LR 675.

33 See, however, the discussion in Chapter 2 as the ways in which 'foresight of consequences' may none the less be relevant to establishing 'intention'.

34 [1974] 2 All ER 41.

35 Chapter 2, pp 26–32.

36 [1986] 3 All ER 1.

37 See Chapter 2, p 29.

of Appeal held that the appropriate offence was manslaughter rather than murder, unless the intention to kill or cause serious bodily harm was established.

This brings us to consideration of the consequences which must be intended. Once something other than an intention to kill is held to be sufficient, the question arises as to where the line should be drawn. In *Hyam*, for example, Lord Diplock and Lord Kilbrandon supported the view that only where the intended act was recognised by the D as likely to endanger life, should the mens rea of murder be satisfied.[38] Alternatively, it might be argued that only where death is, as a matter of fact, likely to follow from the intended acts should the D be guilty (whether or not the D himself recognised the risk). In *Cunningham*,[39] however, the House of Lords confirmed the view expressed by the Court of Appeal in the pre-*Hyam* case of *Vickers*,[40] that an intention to cause serious bodily harm was in itself sufficient, and no foreseeable risk of death was necessary. It is this type of *mens rea* that is probably meant by the reference in s 1(1) of the Homicide Act to 'implied' malice: but, as Smith and Hogan point out, this phrase is misleading, and is fortunately not in common use. The effect of the current law is thus that a D who intentionally breaks a V's leg will be guilty of murder if the V, as a result of an unpredictable reaction to standard medical treatment, dies.[41] This seems harsh. Even if it is felt that the law should give proper recognition to the absolute infringement of the V's rights which has occurred, a verdict of manslaughter would probably be sufficient for this purpose. The majority of appellate judges, however, seem prepared to accept the present position, or view it as a matter which only parliament can properly change. If and when such parliamentary intervention does take place, it seems almost certain that the position will change, since all recent recommendations for reform of the law in this area have advocated that an intention to cause serious bodily harm should only suffice as the mens rea for murder where the D has also recognised that death is a real risk of his actions.[42]

Defences to murder

General discussion of defences available in relation to offences against the person is contained in Chapter 7. Here, however, note is made of some variations in the standard position as regards the way in which these defences

38 This was not accepted by the majority, two of whom felt that this limitation was unnecessary, and one failed to express an opinion.

39 [1981] 2 All ER 863.

40 [1957] 2 All ER 741.

41 Cf the example used by Lord Edmund-Davies, in *Cunningham* [1981] 2 All ER 863, p 871.

42 See, eg, *Report of the House of Lords Select Committee on Murder and Life Imprisonment*, HL Paper No 78–1 (1989).

apply in relation to murder. There is also discussion of four defences which only apply to murder, and which have the effect, if successful, of not producing a complete acquittal, but simply reducing the offence to manslaughter. These are the defences of provocation, diminished responsibility, infanticide and suicide pact.

Self-defence and prevention of crime[43]

These defences are available in the normal way to a charge of murder. A person who uses lethal force in order to avoid being killed himself by an attacker, or as the only means of preventing the commission of a serious offence against a third party, is entitled to be found not guilty of murder. If, however, excessive force (defined according to the principles discussed in Chapter 7) is used, then the defences will be unavailable. A strong attempt was made in *Clegg*[44] to argue that in certain situations the use of excessive force should reduce the charge to manslaughter. C was a soldier serving in Northern Ireland who, at his trial,[45] was found to have fatally wounded the V who was in a car which had passed through a road block. He argued that he had shot in defence of himself and a fellow soldier. The judge at his trial[46] held that the fourth shot which C had fired, and which had contributed to the V's death, was unnecessary, and that therefore the defence of self-defence failed. On appeal to the House of Lords, it was argued that this was a case of the mistaken use of excessive force, which, while not resulting in an acquittal, should have the effect of reducing the offence to manslaughter. This argument was rejected, the House of Lords expressing the view that if a change in the law was required, then this was a matter for parliament, not the courts. The House of Lords took the same view of issue of whether there should be a special rule applying to members of the police, or armed services, acting in the course of duty. It noted that there may be special problems as to measuring the degree of force where a soldier is faced with the options of firing his weapon at a suspect, or doing nothing, and allowing the suspect to commit an offence, or evade arrest. If he fires and hits, he is almost certain to cause serious injury, and thus be potentially liable for murder – there are no 'degrees of force' available in such circumstances. Nevertheless, the House of Lords did not feel it appropriate to intervene to change the law on this issue. Nor was there any defence of 'superior orders' known to English Law. C's conviction for murder was thus confirmed.

---

43 See Chapter 7, p 172.

44 [1995] 1 AC 482.

45 Later investigations have raised doubts as to whether the shots fired by C were the cause of death and a retrial has been ordered.

46 Which, being held in Northern Ireland, took place in a so called 'Diplock Court', where a judge sits without a jury as the sole arbiter of fact as well as law.

It should also be noted here that the use of lethal force in the prevention of crime may amount to a breach of Art 2 of the ECHR. As we have seen, this Article states that 'Everyone's right to life shall be protected by law'. The situations where deprivation of life will not, however, be treated as amounting to a breach of this provision are set out in Art 2(2). They arise where no more force than is 'absolutely necessary' is used:

(a) in defence of any person from unlawful violence;

(b) in order to effect a lawful arrest or to prevent the escape of a person lawfully detained;

(c) in action lawfully taken for the purpose of quelling a riot or insurrection.

It will be noted that, although this covers self-defence, defence of third parties, or arrest, it does not include the possible defence based on 'prevention of crime' which appears in s 3(1) of the Criminal Law Act 1967.[47] The issue has not been addressed directly in any case before the European Commission or Court of Human Rights, but the Commission in *Kelly v UK*[48] recognised that 'prevention of crime' does not appear as a justification under Art 2(2). The Commission did not pursue this point, however, since it was able to find that in the circumstances before it,[49] the actions alleged to amount to a breach of Art 2 could be said to have taken place in the context of an attempt to make a lawful arrest.

In *McCann v United Kingdom*,[50] the British Government was found by the court to be in breach of Art 2, in relation to an operation by the security services in Gibraltar, which resulted in three suspected terrorists (who were at the time unarmed) being shot dead. They were suspected of being about to discharge a bomb. While the action of the individual soldiers concerned in the shooting were not condemned (since they had acted in accordance with information which, if true, would have justified the use of lethal force), the conduct of the operation as a whole meant that the killings could not be said to have been 'absolutely necessary'. There were other ways in which the suspected terrorist attack could have been prevented. This decision, while very significant for those concerned with anti-terrorism measures, does not, however, challenge any of the general principles of English law relating to self-defence and prevention of crime. It does, however, impose a high standard as to what may be regarded as 'necessary' in such situations.

47 Discussed in more detail in Chapter 7, p 172.

48 (1993) 16 EHRR CD 20.

49 The applicant's son, who was joyriding in Belfast, and tried to evade a roadblock was shot by soldiers, who claimed that they believed that the occupants of the car were terrorists.

50 (1994) 21 EHRR 97. See, also, *Andronicou and Constantinou v Cyprus* (1998) 25 EHRR 491.

Duress or necessity

Being compelled to commit a crime as a result of threats from another, or, in certain situations, by force of circumstances ('necessity'), is generally a complete defence under English law.[51] This is not the case, however, in relation to murder. In *Howe*,[52] the D had taken part in a serious assault on the V, which resulted in the V's death. The D's defence was that he took part in the attack only because he believed he would receive the same treatment as the V if he refused. In other words, he claimed that he acted under duress. The House of Lords, however, rejected this as a defence to murder. Lord Mackay noted that English law had, in the famous case of *Dudley and Stephens*,[53] rejected a plea of necessity as a justification of murder. That case had involved shipwrecked sailors killing and eating a cabin boy to ensure their own survival. The court had refused to accept this as a valid defence to murder. Lord Mackay considered that the same approach should be taken to the plea of duress in the present case. The reason for such an approach was primarily the status accorded to the need to protect human life:[54]

> It seems plain to me that the reason that it was for so long stated by writers of authority that the defence of duress was not available in a charge of murder was because of the supreme importance that the law afforded to the protection of human life and that it seemed repugnant that the law should recognise in any individual in any circumstance, however extreme, the right to choose that one innocent person should be killed rather than another.

The defence of duress, it was therefore confirmed, is not available to a charge of murder. The House of Lords in *Howe* stated that this rule also applies to those charged as accessories to murder, thus reversing the approach taken by the House of Lords in the earlier case of *Lynch v DPP for Northern Ireland*.[55] A suggestion that duress might have the effect of reducing a charge of murder to manslaughter was also rejected, as being inconsistent with the general principle that duress, where available, entitles the D to a full acquittal.[56]

This approach also means that to kill on the basis that it is 'necessary' in order to relieve the suffering of the V, who is afflicted with a serious illness, provides no defence to a charge of murder.[57] It seems, however, that it is permissible to administer large doses of pain killers or sedatives in order to

51 See Chapter 7, p 187.

52 [1987] 1 All ER 771.

53 (1884) 14 QBD 273.

54 [1987] 1 All ER 771, p 798.

55 [1975] 1 All ER 913.

56 See, eg, Lord Hailsham's comments [1987] 1 All ER 782, p 782b–f.

57 Cf *Bodkin Adams* [1957] Crim LR 365; *Cox* (1992) 12 BMLR 38.

relieve suffering, even though the incidental, but inevitable, consequence of this is to shorten life.[58]

Consent

The defence of consent is problematic throughout the area of offences against the person.[59] The problem is chiefly that of where to draw the line as regards the level of injury to which the V may, by consenting to its infliction, relieve the D of liability. There is no doubt, however, that termination of life will currently be regarded as falling outside the scope of the defence. Although it is no longer an offence for an individual to attempt suicide, it is an offence to encourage or assist such an attempt,[60] and, moreover, taking active steps to shorten the V's life at her request will amount to murder. In other words, the V's consent to the actions which the D carries out is irrelevant to the D's liability if they result in V's death. The only exception to this is where the killing is in the course of a suicide pact, which is discussed below, p 89.

It will be argued, in Chapter 7, that the current English law on consent is incoherent. In line with one of the guiding themes of this book, it will be argued that, in general, the D should not be criminally liable for doing something to the V at the V's request, or with the V's consent, if the V could have lawfully done that thing to herself. This follows from the concept of the criminal law concerning offences against the person having as one of its founding principles the need to recognise and protect the infringement of the V's personal rights which results from the offence. Where the V has requested or consented to the D's behaviour, there is no infringement of personal rights, and thus the need to impose criminal liability becomes questionable. Applying these principles, the conclusion is that it should not constitute any offence, let alone the offence of murder, to terminate or shorten a person's life at his or her own request.

There is, however, one practical difficulty in this area concerning the way in which consent may be proved. Since the V is by definition dead in such cases, she is not available to testify as to whether she did consent or request the D to shorten her life. There may, of course, be written evidence, or support from third parties. But in the absence of a recording, at the time when the D acted, of the V asking him to do so, and indicating an awareness of the consequences of this, it may simply be too risky to accept that the V did freely consent to being killed. In the case of severely ill Vs, it may well be that the request to shorten life is made at an earlier stage in the progression of the

58 The defence of 'necessity' is discussed further in Chapter 7, p 194.

59 See Chapter 7, p 178.

60 Suicide Act 1961, s 2, which created the offence of 'aiding, abetting, counselling or procuring the suicide of another or an attempt by another to commit suicide'. Mere advice as to methods which might be used is not necssarily an offence: *Attorney General v Able* [1984] 1 All ER 277.

illness. At the time when the D finally acts, the V may be incapable of giving consent. Is the court entitled to assume that the V had not changed her mind in the meantime? It may be dangerous to do so. For these practical reasons, if for no other, it may be desirable to continue to retain some criminal liability in relation to the D in such circumstances. It is submitted, however, that while the mandatory penalty for murder remains, it would be more appropriate for the offence to be that of manslaughter, thus allowing full sentencing discretion to the judge, who will be able to take into account the particular circumstances in which the death occurred. This is the effect of the special rules applying to suicide pacts, mentioned above.[61]

This is another area where Art 2 of the ECHR may be relevant, though no case has as yet gone to the court on the issue of euthanasia. The European Commission of Human Rights has, however, ruled that withdrawal of treatment, which results in the death of the V, is not required to be a crime by virtue of Art 2.[62] It is difficult to see that active euthanasia would breach Art 2 either, assuming that the V's consent was established, for there would be no infringement of the V's rights. Indeed, to prevent euthanasia in such circumstances might be held to infringe the V's 'privacy' rights under Art 8 of the ECHR.

Provocation

The defence of provocation is a common law concept and, if successful, reduces what would otherwise (in terms of *actus reus* and *mens rea*) amount to the offence of murder to manslaughter. The operation of the defence has been affected by statutory intervention, but the burden of proof remains on the prosecution to rebut it, once some evidence on which the defence might be based has arisen. In certain circumstances, the judge will have a duty to direct the jury on provocation, even if the defence has not specifically raised the issue,[63] provided that relevant evidence is before the court (even if tenuous).[64]

The statutory intervention appears in s 3 of the Homicide Act 1957, which states:

> Where on a charge of murder there is evidence on which the jury can find that the person charged was provoked (whether by things done or by things said or by both together) to lose his self-control, the question whether the provocation was enough to make a reasonable man do as he did shall be left to be determined by the jury; and in determining that question the jury shall take into account everything both done and said according to the effect which, in their opinion, it would have on the reasonable man.

61 They are discussed below, p 89.

62 *Widner v Switzerland No 20527/92* (1993), unreported.

63 This may happen if, eg, the defence is relying on self-defence which if successful will result in an acquittal, rather than a conviction of manslaughter. Cf *Rossiter* [1994] 2 All ER 752 (self-defence or accident); *Stewart* [1995] 4 All ER 999 (defence of 'accident').

64 *Mancini v DPP* [1941] 3 All ER 272; *Rossiter* [1994] 2 All ER 752.

The following elements of the defence of provocation appear explicitly or implicitly from this provision:

(a) there must have been some 'provoking' words or actions;

(b) the D must have, as a result, lost his self-control (the 'subjective element');

(c) the actions which the D took, having lost self-control, must be within the range of responses to be expected of a reasonable person in that situation (the 'objective element').

The role of the judge in relation to these elements is limited to deciding whether there is any evidence of the first two. The defence will not be put to the jury if the judge decides that there is no evidence of any provoking words or action, or that there is no evidence that the D lost his self-control. Thus, in *Cocker*,[65] the D's killing of his terminally ill wife could not be said to be result of 'provocation', despite the fact that she had entreated him to end her life,[66] since there was no evidence that the D had lost his self-control. Conversely, it was held in *Acott*[67] that, although there was some evidence that the D had lost his temper, there was no evidence of any provocative conduct which had caused this. There was therefore no need for the judge to leave the defence to the jury.

Once the judge has decided that there is the evidential basis on which the issue should be considered, the jury has two tasks. First it must decide whether the provocative behaviour did cause the D to lose his self-control. This is described as the subjective test, since it looks solely at the effect of the words and behaviour on the D himself. It is irrelevant whether the behaviour would have provoked a reasonable person to lose his self-control. The fact that the D is particularly irascible or particularly phlegmatic may effect whether self-control was lost. The jury must concentrate simply on the fact of the loss, however, and must ignore the fact that they do not think that a reasonable person would have lost his self-control. Similarly, the fact that the jury feel that a reasonable person would have lost his self-control must be ignored, if it appears that the D was in fact unmoved. If the jury's view is that the D did not lose his self-control, then the defence falls at that point. If it thinks that he did, then it must go on to consider the second question.

The second question the jury must ask is whether the provocation would have caused a reasonable person to do what the D did (that is, take the deliberate actions which led to the death of the V). This is referred to as the 'objective' question, since the D's actual state of mind is now irrelevant, and the jury need only to consider the likely response of the reasonable person to the provocative behaviour.

65 [1989] Crim LR 740.

66 Which could no doubt amount to relevant 'words or action'.

67 [1996] 4 All ER 443.

Although the division of the jury's tasks into these two questions in theory applies to every case, in practice, it is only where the D is unusually resistant to provocation that the subjective question will have any effect on the verdict. If the jury decides that, despite great provocation, which might well have produced a violent reaction in the reasonable man, the D remained calm, and acted with cool deliberation, the verdict will be murder. If, however, the jury decides that the D was provoked, it must then, as we have seen, ask whether the D's response was reasonable. It is hard to see a jury concluding that, although it was unreasonable for the D to lose his self-control, it was nevertheless reasonable for him to inflict lethal force on the V. In other words, the subjective test will always work against the D whose response to provocation falls outside that of the reasonable man. If the D is unusually calm, then he will lose the benefit of the defence; if he is unusually irascible, he is likely to be found to have reacted disproportionately to the provocation. The main effect of the subjective element is thus to prevent an unusually calm D from taking advantage of the defence, when he had not in fact lost his self-control, even though a reasonable person might well have been provoked to violence.

The three elements of the defence outlined above will now be considered further, in the light of the case law attaching to them:

(a) There must have been some 'provoking' words or actions.

Prior to 1957, the only relevant provocative behaviour was actions taken by the V, and directed towards the D.[68] The case law on the 1957 Act has, however, extended the range of provocation to cover not only words uttered by the V, but also words and behaviour of third parties.[69] It seems that provided there is some evidence that the words or actions of some other person caused the D to lose his self-control, the defence should be left to the jury, no matter who is the source. There is no requirement that the behaviour should have been intended to provoke, or that it should have been directed at the D. Thus, in *Doughty*,[70] the alleged provocation was the persistent crying of the D's baby. It was held that this fell within the scope of 'things said or done', and that if there was evidence on which the jury might find that the crying had caused the D to lose his self-control, then the defence of provocation should be left. It follows from this that behaviour which is directed towards a third party may also amount to provocation. This was confirmed in *Pearson*,[71] where part of the alleged provocation involved mistreatment handed out by the V to the D's brother. Events which do not have a particular human source will not,

68 *Duffy* [1949] 1 All ER 932n.

69 *Davies* [1975] 1 All ER 890; *Twine* [1967] Crim LR 710.

70 (1986) 83 Cr App Rep 319.

71 [1992] Crim LR 193.

however, be relevant. A person who goes into a rage as a result of failing to win the National Lottery, will not even pass the first hurdle towards establishing the defence. Nor, it seems will the person who loses control following a natural disaster, such as freak storm which blows the roof off his house. As Smith and Hogan point out,[72] given the broad definition now given to provocation, this particular exclusion does not seem to have much logic to it. Nevertheless, the clear reference in s 1 to things 'done or said' seems to require a human agent for the provocation.

(b) The D must have lost his self-control (the 'subjective element').

This element has been the cause of some controversy in recent years, in the context of reactions to domestic abuse, in particular of wives by their husbands. Case law prior to 1957 established that the defence was only available if the D had lost his self-control at the time when the fatal attack took place. The classic statement appears in the direction given by Devlin J in *Duffy*,[73] in the context of the need to distinguish a provoked, and uncontrolled, attack from planned revenge:

> Indeed, circumstances which induce a desire for revenge are inconsistent with provocation, since the conscious formulation of a desire for revenge means that a person has had time to think, to reflect, and that would negative a sudden temporary loss of self-control, which is of the essence of provocation.

Although this remains the law, as has been confirmed in a number of recent cases,[74] there has been some relaxation in the way in which it has been applied. Devlin's direction implicitly suggests the instant, unthinking, reaction to a particular event as the typical model: as where a husband or wife discovers their partner in the act of adultery. It follows from this that a person who has been provoked, but has 'cooled-down' before reacting, will not be able to claim the defence. Thus, in *Ibrams and Gregory*,[75] there was a gap of five days between the last 'provocation' and the attack on the V, during which the Ds formulated a plan to trap the V. The Court of Appeal held that the judge had been right to withdraw the defence from the jury. Subsequently, however, it has been recognised that the requirement in s 3 to take account of everything said or done, means that the existence of a gap between the last provocative act and the fatal attack should not automatically rule out the defence. It is simply a question of whether the D had lost control at the relevant time. It was recognised in *Ahluwalia* that the 'slow-burn' reaction of a woman subjected to abuse over a period of time may still be regarded as 'sudden'.[76] Thus,

72 Smith, JC and Hogan, B, *Criminal Law Cases and Materials*, 6th edn, 1996, London: Butterworths, p 363.

73 [1919] 1 All ER 932n.

74 Eg, *Thornton* [1992] 1 All ER 306; *Alhuwalia* [1992] 4 All ER 889.

75 (1982) 74 Cr App Rep 154.

76 [1992] 4 All ER 889.

the person who broods on provocation for a time and then suddenly explodes into violence will not, it seems, be prevented from raising the defence. The longer the delay, however, the less likely it is that the jury will believe that the D had lost self-control at the relevant time, and the easier it will be for the prosecution to negative the defence.[77] The recognition that a delay between the provocation and the attack does not necessarily rule out the defence would not, of course, have assisted the Ds in *Ibrams*, where there was not only delay, but also an agreed plan of attack. Such planning is clearly inconsistent with the idea of a loss of self-control.

Connected with the above issue is the recognition that a course of conduct over a number of years, rather than a particular event, may form the basis of the defence, provided that at the end of the conduct there is a 'sudden and temporary loss of self-control'[78] A good example of the way in which various strands of provocation can work together is to be found in *Humphreys*.[79] In the summer of 1994, H, who was at the time aged 16 and working as a prostitute, was picked up by A, who took her to live with him. He was jealous and possessive. While continuing to allow H to work as a prostitute, he started to beat her up. The beatings continued, combined with encouragement to prostitution. While H was on remand in relation to two incidents around Christmas and New Year 1985, A took in another younger girl. When H was conditionally discharged she returned to live with A. H also had a history of attempted suicides, involving the slashing of her wrists. One evening in February 1985, while they were at a bar, A threatened H with a 'gang-bang' that night. Later that evening when they had returned home, H slashed her wrists. A, who had gone out again, returned and undressed, apparently, as H thought, seeking sex with her. A then taunted H about the fact that she had not made a very good job of her wrist slashing. At this point, H stabbed A with a knife which she had in her hand at the time. A plea of provocation failed at the trial. In the Court of Appeal, however, it was held that the judge's summing up had been inadequate, in that it simply gave a history of the events, without analysing the various strands which could have contributed to the provocation. As Hirst LJ put it:[80]

> This tempestuous relationship was a complex story with several distinct and cumulative strands of potentially provocative conduct building up until the final encounter.
>
> Over the long term, there was the continuing cruelty, represented by the beatings and the continued encouragement of prostitution and by the breakdown of the sexual relationship.

77 [1992] 4 All ER 889 76.

78 *Pearson* [1992] Crim LR 193.

79 [1995] 4 All ER 1008.

80 *Ibid*, pp 1023–24.

> On the first part of the night in question there was the threatened 'gang-bang' and the drunkenness. Immediately before the killing, quite apart from the wounding verbal taunt, there was his appearance in an undressed state, posing a threat of sex which she did not want and which he must have known she did not want ... Finally, of course, there is the taunt itself ...

All these various strands could have contributed to the provocation, and it was incumbent on the judge to give the jury guidance on them, so that it could understand their potential significance.

In considering whether the D was suffering from a loss of self-control at the relevant time, therefore, every factor which might be relevant, either in itself, or in conjunction with others, must be left to the jury. Moreover, the judge has a duty to give guidance to the jury on the issue, particularly where a number of different factors may have operated together to produce a loss of self-control.

The loss of control does not have to be complete.[81] Indeed, such a loss, so that the D was unaware of what he was doing might provide a defence on a different basis, in that the prosecution would have failed to prove that the D had, at the time of the killing, the relevant mental state for a charge of murder. For the defence of provocation it is sufficient if the D, while aware of what he is doing, is simply unable to control himself.

(c) The actions which the D took, having lost self-control, must be within the range of responses to be expected of a reasonable person in that situation (the 'objective element').

As we have seen, s 3 requires the jury to consider whether the provocation would have led the 'reasonable man' to 'do as [the D] did'. In deciding this, the jury must 'take into account everything both done and said according to the effect which, in their opinion, it would have on the reasonable man.' As has often been pointed out, this is a strange task, since the jury is asked to apply a test of 'reasonableness' to a person who has by definition 'lost control' of himself, and so might well be thought to be acting 'without reason'. In practice, however, the test is focusing not on 'reasonableness', in the sense of 'rationality', but in the sense of 'normal', or 'to be expected', or 'not out of the ordinary'.[82] It has links with such concepts as a 'reasonable price' (a fair price), or a 'reasonable amount' (not exceptional), or a 'reasonable request' (to be expected). The issue might therefore be better expressed as asking whether the response to the provocation is itself 'reasonable' in these senses, rather than whether it is the response of a *reasonable man*. The statutory wording, however, requires the courts to consider the 'reasonable man', and the difficulty of operating this concept in practice has generated a considerable case law, as we shall see below.

81 *Richens* [1993] 4 All ER 877.

82 See the comments of Lord Goff on this issue, in *Morhall* [1995] 3 All ER 659, pp 665–66.

Whether the focus is on the *reasonable response* or the *reasonable man*, the level of retaliation to the provocation is a relevant consideration. Prior to the 1957 Act, there was authority that, as a matter of law, the D's response must relate to the nature of the provocative act.[83] Thus, an unarmed attack on the D would not justify the use of a knife against the V.[84] 'Fists may be answered with fists, but not with a deadly weapon.'[85] The House of Lords in *Camplin*[86] indicated that under the Act, there could be no rule of law of this kind. The issue must be left to the jury to decide. This does not mean that the level of retaliation is irrelevant; simply that the judge cannot direct the jury that a particular response is, or is not, reasonable. No doubt the jury itself will nevertheless be much influenced by the relationship between the provocation and the D's reaction, and also by the surrounding circumstances. As the Privy Council noted in *Phillips v R*:[87]

> The average man reacts to provocation according to its degree with angry words, with a blow of the hand, possibly, if the provocation is gross and there is a dangerous weapon to hand, with that weapon.

The second part of this quotation indicates why it is difficult to provide hard and fast rules as to the reasonable level of retaliation. If, for example, a wife is told by her husband that he has been sexually abusing their children, the level of her response may depend on whether she is at the time in the kitchen, with a carving knife or rolling pin to hand,[88] or in the bedroom with no comparable weapon available. The fact that in the latter case she might attack her husband simply with blows from hands and feet, does not mean that in the former case a lethal attack with knife or rolling pin should be regarded as unreasonable. All the circumstances may need to be considered.

Much of the case law on s 3 has concerned the issue of the characteristics to be attached to the 'reasonable man' or 'reasonable person'. Prior to the 1957 Act, the decision in *Bedder v DPP*[89] had laid down that the 'reasonable man' standard was to be applied uniformly in every case, and should ignore any special characteristics possessed by the D. Thus, in *Bedder* itself, the fact that the D was impotent was to be ignored, despite the fact that the V, a prostitute, had apparently taunted him about this. The jury was required in every case to consider the likely response of the reasonable, sober, adult, having no unusual characteristics. The unreality of this approach was finally recognised in *DPP v Camplin*.[90] The D was a 15 year old boy, who had been buggered, against his

83 *Mancini v DPP* [1941] 3 All ER 272.

84 *Ibid*.

85 *Duffy* [1949] 1 All ER 932n.

86 [1978] 2 All ER 168.

87 [1969] 2 AC 130, p 137.

88 Cf the facts of *Rossiter* [1994] 2 All ER 752.

89 [1954] 2 All ER 801.

90 [1978] 2 All ER 168.

will, by the V. The V had then laughed at him. The D claimed that he then lost control, and hit the V with a heavy pan. The judge had directed the jury that they should ignore the D's age, and consider simply whether a reasonable adult man would have reacted as the D did. The House of Lords[91] held that this was a misdirection. The introduction of the possibility by virtue of s 3 of the Homicide Act 1957 that words can amount to provocation meant that it was no longer correct to ignore all personal characteristics of the D. As Lord Morris pointed out:[92]

> If the accused is of particular colour or particular ethnic origin and things are said which to him are grossly insulting it would be utterly unreal if the jury had to consider whether the words would have provoked a man of different colour or ethnic origin, or to consider how such a man would have acted or reacted.

In the present case, the age of the D was a relevant factor, which the jury should have been left to take into account. The *ratio* of *Camplin* has been taken to be best expressed in the following quotation from Lord Diplock's speech:[93]

> The judge should state what the question is, using the very terms of the section. He should then explain to them that the reasonable man referred to in the question is a person of the sex and age of the accused, but in other respects sharing such of the accused's characteristics as they think would affect the gravity of the provocation to him, and that the question is not merely whether such a person would in like circumstances be provoked to lose his self-control but also would react to the provocation as the accused did.

This test seems to recognise two types of characteristic. First, age and sex are always to be considered when assessing the D's response to the provocation. It is legitimate to take the view, for example, that a young person may more easily lose self-control than an adult. As regards other characteristics, however, only those which 'affect the gravity of the provocation' should be taken into account. This has particular application to the situation where the provocation is by words. Clearly if, for example, a person has a glass eye, this is irrelevant if they are taunted with impotence. The characteristic of being blind in one eye has no effect on the gravity of the provocation. It would be otherwise if they were jeered at for being 'blind'. Simple examples of this kind create no problems. The issue of which characteristics are relevant to provocation has been problematic, however, and has led to many appellate decisions over the past 20 years. There is general agreement that certain temporary characteristics, such as drunkenness, should not be taken into account. But, does this apply to all temporary states? What about illnesses, particularly mental illnesses? Can these ever be taken into account in

91 Affirming the decision of the Court of Appeal: [1978] 1 All ER 218.

92 [1978] 2 All ER 168, p 177.

93 *Ibid*, p 175.

assessing the effects of provocation? It will be useful to consider in outline the development of this case law, before the current position is assessed.

The first case to consider the issue following *Camplin* was *Newell*.[94] The D here was an alcoholic, who at the time of the offence was depressed about the fact that his girlfriend had left him, and had been drinking heavily. He reacted with violence against the V, who had made disparaging comments about the D's girlfriend, and had made a homosexual advance to him. In trying to determine the meaning of the word 'characteristics' as used in *Camplin*, the Court of Appeal relied heavily on the judgment of North J in the New Zealand case of *McGregor*.[95] In interpreting the relevant New Zealand statute,[96] which is not in identical terms to the Homicide Act 1957, but which includes a reference to the 'characteristics of the offender', North J commented:

> It is not every trait or disposition of the offender that can be invoked to modify the concept of the ordinary man. The characteristic must be something definite and of sufficient significance to make the offender a different person from the ordinary run of mankind, and have also a sufficient degree of permanence to warrant its being regarded as something constituting part of the individual's character or personality.

Transitory states such as moods of depression, excitability or irascibility, or a state induced by intoxication, would not be 'characteristics'. In addition, there had to be a 'real connection' between the nature of the provocation and the particular characteristic by which it was sought to modify the reasonable man. Applying this approach to the case before it, the Court of Appeal concluded that the only alleged 'characteristic' which was sufficiently permanent to satisfy this part of the criterion was the D's alcoholism. This, however, had no connection with the alleged provocation, and so the judge had been correct in not leaving the defence to the jury.

In *Morhall*,[97] the House of Lords agreed with the Court of Appeal's decision in *Newell*, on the facts, but warned against reliance on North J's analysis of 'characteristics', since he was concerned with the interpretation of a specific statutory phrase, and in any case, strong reservations about this judgment had been expressed by the New Zealand Court of Appeal in *McCarthy*.[98] The Court of Appeal in *Morhall* had held that an addiction to 'glue-sniffing' was not a characteristic which could be taken into account, because it was repugnant to the concept of the reasonable man. The House of Lords disagreed. Although it was correct that the simple fact that the D was intoxicated (whether by drink, drugs, or glue) at the time of the offence could

94 (1980) 71 Cr App Rep 331.

95 [1962] NZLR 1069.

96 Ie, New Zealand Crimes Act 1961, s 169.

97 [1995] 3 All ER 659.

98 [1992] NZLR 550.

not, as a matter of policy, be taken into account, the position was different where, as was the case in *Morhall*, the D was taunted about his addiction. In such a circumstance, although the condition may be 'discreditable', it can be considered, because it goes to the gravity of the provocation. The same would apply where the provocation related to, for example, the fact that the D had previously been convicted of a sexual offence.

As regards the requirement of 'permanence', the House of Lords did not consider this a necessary attribute of a relevant 'characteristic'. As Lord Goff pointed out, some physical conditions, such as eczema, may be transitory in nature, but, if the subject of taunts, should be taken into account.[99] The exclusion of drunkenness from consideration was a matter of policy, not related to the fact that it was a transitory state.

The House of Lords also pointed out that other circumstances, apart from the D's own characteristics, which might affect the gravity of the provocation may need to considered. Lord Goff refers to 'the defendant's history or the circumstances in which he is placed at the relevant time'.[100] It is this broadening of the approach which has allowed the Court of Appeal in some recent cases to give weight in this context to a history of mistreatment, particularly of wives by their husbands – sometimes referred to as 'battered wife syndrome' or 'BWS' – as well as certain other psychological conditions. Four cases must be considered – *Ahluwalia*,[101] *Dryden*,[102] *Humphreys*[103] and *Thornton (No 2)*[104] – though as we shall see come doubt has been cast on these decisions by a later Privy Council opinion – *Luc Thiet Thuan v R*.[105]

In *Ahluwalia* (which pre-dates the decision in *Morhall*), 'BWS' was raised in the Court of Appeal as a possible 'characteristic' affecting provocation. The D had suffered many years of violence and abuse from the V, her husband, including threats to kill her. After an argument in which the V threatened to beat the D the following morning if she did not give him £200, the V went to bed. The D threw petrol and a lighted stick into the V's bedroom. The V died from his burns. At the D's trial, the defence of provocation was raised, but the jury convicted of murder. On appeal, it was argued that the judge should have directed the jury more specifically on the issue of BWS, as being a 'characteristic' possessed by the D, which might have affected the gravity of the provocation. It was argued that the treatment she had suffered had affected her personality so as to produce a state of 'learnt helplessness'.[106] The

99 [1995] 3 All ER 659, p 667.

100 *Ibid*, p 666.

101 [1992] 4 All ER 889.

102 [1995] 4 All ER 987.

103 [1995] 4 All ER 1008.

104 [1996] 2 All ER 1023.

105 [1996] 2 All ER 1033.

106 [1992] 4 All ER 889, p 897.

Court of Appeal rejected the criticism of the judge's summing up, since there was no evidence before him that the D was suffering from any specific disorder or condition, such as BWS, which would indicate that she was different from the ordinary run of women. The court, however, commented that:[107]

> Had the evidence which has now been put before this court been adduced before the trial judge, different considerations may have applied.

Although *obiter*, this statement clearly indicated that the court accepted the possibility that, if appropriate evidence was available, BWS would be a possible 'characteristic' affecting the gravity of the provocation.[108] A similar line was taken in relation to a different type of characteristic in *Dryden*.[109] Here, there was medical evidence relating to the D's obsessiveness and eccentric character, which the Court of Appeal (without referring to *Ahluwalia*, though Lord Taylor, LCJ, delivered the judgment in both cases) again considered could be regarded as relevant 'characteristics' to be left to the jury.[110] Similarly, in *Humphreys*,[111] the facts of which have been discussed above,[112] it was held, by a differently constituted Court of Appeal, that the D's attention-seeking behaviour, manifested in part by her wrist-slashing, could be regarded as a psychological illness or disorder. As such, it was a 'characteristic' which, together with the D's immaturity, should have been left to the jury to consider in relation to the defence of provocation. Finally, in *Thornton (No 2)*,[113] the Court of Appeal returned to the issue of BWS. The D had suffered violence at the hands of the V, her husband. Eventually she had killed him by stabbing him with a bread knife, which she had apparently sharpened for the purpose. She was convicted of murder, and an initial appeal failed.[114] Further medical evidence was produced, however, and the case was referred back by the Home Secretary to the Court of Appeal. Lord Taylor took the opportunity to state the principles which applied to a plea of provocation based on BWS. He started by making clear that it is essential that the jury believe that the D 'suffered or may have suffered a sudden and temporary loss of self-control' at the relevant time. Subject to that, BWS may be relevant in two ways:[115]

> First, it may form an important background to the *actus reus*. A jury may more readily find there was a sudden loss of control triggered by even a minor

107 [1992] 4 All ER 889, p 898.

108 Note that the appeal was allowed on other grounds.

109 [1995] 4 All ER 987.

110 Though the appeal failed, because of the lack of evidence that the D had lost self-control at the relevant time.

111 [1995] 4 All ER 1008.

112 See above, p 72.

113 [1996] 2 All ER 1023.

114 [1992] 1 All ER 306.

115 [1996] 2 All ER 1023, p 1030.

> incident, if the defendant has endured abuse over a period, on the 'last straw' basis. Secondly, depending on the medical evidence, the syndrome may have affected the defendant's personality so as to constitute a significant characteristic relevant ... to the second question the jury has to consider in regard to provocation.

On this basis, therefore, BWS may be relevant to both the 'subjective' and 'objective' issues which the jury must consider.

Turning to the case before it, the court noted that, in *Morhall*, the House of Lords had indicated that in considering the D's characteristics, mental as well as physical characteristics, should be taken into account, and that the judge should give the jury directions as to what, on the evidence, is capable of amounting to a relevant characteristic. Here, there was new evidence relating to the D's personality disorder, and the effect on her of prolonged abuse by the V. If this had been before the judge, he should and would have given the jury directions in relation to these. The verdict was therefore unsafe and unsatisfactory, and a new trial was ordered.[116]

This series of decisions by the Court of Appeal has thus suggested a broad range of factors which may justifiably be regarded as 'characteristics' of the D which should be grafted on to the 'reasonable person' in assessing his or her reaction to the provocation. As we have noted, the House of Lords decision in *Morhall* has had a role in encouraging this trend. A warning note has, however, been sounded by the Privy Council in *Luc Thiet Thuan*.[117] Although a Privy Council decision is, of course, only of persuasive authority in English courts, it is significant that the opinion of the majority was delivered by Lord Goff, who also gave the main speech in the unanimous decision of the House of Lords in *Morhall*. On the other hand, as Smith and Hogan point out,[118] the Judicial Committee on this occasion contained only two members of the House of Lords, one of whom (Lord Steyn), dissented. In these circumstances, it is perhaps not surprising that the Court of Appeal, in *Smith (Morgan James)*[119] has refused to follow the majority view in *Luc Thiet Thuan*, preferring to accept the earlier decisions of the Court of Appeal as binding on it. The opinions in *Luc Thiet Thuan* are nevertheless worth examining in some detail, since they may well form the basis for future consideration of this area by the House of Lords, if and when a case is appealed that far.

The problem identified by Lord Goff in this case, which was an appeal from the Hong Kong Court of Appeal, related to the extent to which a characteristic may only be taken into account if it affects the 'gravity of the

116 At the retrial, the D was convicted of manslaughter, and sentenced to five years imprisonment.

117 [1996] 2 All ER 1033.

118 *Op cit*, Smith and Hogan, fn 72, p 370.

119 [1998] 4 All ER 387.

provocation'. In the case before it, there was evidence that the D suffered from brain damage, though the expert witnesses were not unanimous as to any effect that this would have on his behaviour. The alleged provocation by the V, the D's former girlfriend, consisted of taunts about the V's new boyfriend, and about the D's sexual inadequacy. The judge refused to refer to the D's brain damage when directing the jury on provocation. The majority of the Privy Council agreed with the Hong Kong Court of Appeal, that the judge had been correct to direct in the way he did.

In coming to this conclusion, Lord Goff conducted a careful analysis of *Camplin* and the subsequent case law. As he had done in *Morhall*, he warned against reliance on the judgment of North J in the New Zealand case of *McGregor*,[120] pointing out at some length that that decision was concerned with a differently worded statutory provision, that it had probably been influenced by the lack of a defence of 'diminished responsibility' in New Zealand, and that it had subsequently been severely criticised even in that jurisdiction.[121] He emphasised that the test laid down in *Camplin* is whether the alleged 'characteristic' affects the 'gravity of the provocation'. In this context, he approved the statement by Ashworth, writing pre-Camplin, that, in assessing whether the D has reacted in the way of a 'reasonable person':[122]

> The proper distinction ... is that individual peculiarities which bear on the gravity of the provocation should be taken into account, whereas individual peculiarities bearing on the accused's level of self-control should not.

Thus, the broad approach to what can amount to 'characteristics' taken in *Morhall*, in that they do not need to be permanent, or morally reputable, must be limited by the fact that they will only be relevant in applying the test under s 3 of the Homicide Act, if they are related in some way to the provocative behaviour. That is what is meant by the requirement that the characteristic must be one which affects the gravity of the provocation. The fact that the D is suffering from a mental infirmity which affects his self-control cannot, therefore, in itself be regarded as a relevant characteristic. On the other hand:[123]

> It is, of course, consistent with Lord Diplock's analysis in *Camplin*, and indeed with the decision of the House of Lords in *Morhall*, that mental infirmity of the defendant, *if itself the subject of taunts by the deceased*, may be taken into account as going to the gravity of the provocation as applied to the defendant ... But this is a far cry from the appellant's submission that the mental infirmity of the defendant, impairing his power of self-control, *should as such be attributed to the reasonable man for the purposes of the objective test* (emphasis added).

120 [1962] NZLR 1069.

121 Ie, in *McCarthy* [1992] 2 NZLR 550.

122 Ashworth, A, 'The doctrine of provocation' [1976] CLJ 292, p 300.

123 [1996] 2 All ER 1033, p 1046.

This does not mean, however, that the provocation must be *directed* towards this mental infirmity, or other characteristic (though it often will be). As long as the existence of the characteristic makes the provocation more serious, then it can be taken into account. The fact that a remark is made by the V in innocence of the D's characteristic, does not prevent the D relying on it in those circumstances.[124] Thus, a callous, and unthinking, remark about epilepsy to someone who, unknown to the person making the remark, suffers from that condition, must be considered as to its effect on the reasonable person who suffers from epilepsy. Indeed, as long as the D thinks (presumably with some reason, such as previous circumstances) that a comment relates to some characteristic of his, then the characteristic may be taken into account.[125]

As has been noted above, Lord Steyn delivered a dissenting opinion in *Luc Thiet Thuan*. He accepted the decisions in *Ahluwalia*, etc, outlined above, as involving legitimate applications of the principles to be derived from *Camplin*. Given that that decision allowed the age of the D to be considered, and that this characteristic was not in itself related to the provocative behaviour, but rather to the degree of self-control to be reasonably expected of the D, it followed that other 'infirmities' such as mental abnormality should similarly be allowed to be considered by the jury in applying the objective test. In reaching this conclusion Lord Steyn appears to be interpreting the phrase 'characteristics which affect the gravity of the provocation' as meaning characteristics (other than drunkenness or irascibility) which will affect the D's reaction to the provocation, whether or not the provocative behaviour had any particular relationship to the characteristic. Thus, a D having a mental age below his actual age,[126] or suffering from BWS, or from some other condition which is likely to lead to more violent reaction to provocation than would be expected from a reasonable person without that characteristic, is entitled to have the jury consider this in applying the objective test. Lord Steyn also pointed out that such an approach would avoid the difficult task of directing a jury that certain characteristics could be relevant in deciding 'did the D lose self-control', but should then be disregarded in deciding whether a reasonable person would have done as the D did.

Lord Steyn's opinion was not followed by the other members of the Judicial Committee. We must therefore consider what the effect of the majority opinion may be on the operation of the defence, should it be adopted by the House of Lords. It would certainly have the effect of reducing the use which can be made of characteristics which may form an important backdrop to the provocation, but which cannot in themselves be said to have affected its 'gravity'. Given that Lord Goff specifically doubted the approach taken in

124 [1996] 2 All ER 1033, p 1048.

125 *Ibid*.

126 As in *Raven* [1982] Crim LR 51.

Ahluwalia, *Dryden* and *Humphreys*, it would seem that to be suffering from BWS, an obsessive personality, or an attention-seeking proclivity to attempt suicide,[127] would not in themselves be factors which should be considered in applying the standard of the reasonable person. The decision in *Thornton (No 2)* would also have to be regarded as of doubtful authority, in its acceptance of BWS and the D's personality disorder as 'characteristics' relevant to the objective test.

Given that the opinion of the majority in *Luc Thiet Thuan* represented an attempt to reverse an orthodoxy which had become established in the Court of Appeal, and has subsequently been reaffirmed by that court,[128] in what direction should the law now develop? There is logic to support the arguments of both Lord Goff, and Lord Steyn. Nor does there seem to be much profit if further attempts to analyse what precisely was meant by the framers of the 1957 legislation, or the House of Lords in *Camplin*. The issue is rather that of the breadth to be allowed, as a matter of policy, to the defence of provocation. As long as the mandatory life sentence for murder remains, there will be pressure to increase its scope. The position arrived at in *Thornton (No 2)* is one that was arrived at incrementally, and in the context of much discussion of the issues both by the courts, and more generally. It might well be argued that that decision, and Lord Steyn's dissent in *Luc Thiet Thuan*, represent a policy which currently has wider general acceptance than that propounded by Lord Goff. That certainly seems to be the view of the Court of Appeal as expressed in *Smith (Morgan James)*.[129] The matter must await further consideration by the House of Lords. In the meantime, BWS and other similar conditions should continue to be taken into account in assessing a D's reaction to provocation, whether or not the provocative behaviour related specifically to that condition.

Diminished responsibility

The fifth defence differs from the others so far considered in this section in that the burden of proof lies on the defence, on the balance of probabilities. The defence is statutory, and is set out in s 2 of the Homicide Act 1957:

> (1) Where a person kills or is party to the killing of another, he shall not be convicted of murder if he was suffering from such abnormality of mind (whether arising from a condition of arrested or retarded development of mind or any inherent causes or induced by disease or injury) as

---

127 To the extent that the provocation in *Humphreys* related to the D's habit of slashing her wrists it would presumably, even under Lord Goff's approach, still be legitimate to consider it as a factor affecting the gravity of the provocation.

128 Ie, in *Smith (Morgan James)* [1998] 4 All ER 387.

129 *Ibid*.

> substantially impaired his mental responsibility for his acts and omissions in doing or being a party to the killing.

Section 2(2) places the burden of proof on the defence, and s 2(3) provides that, if successful, the D who would otherwise be convicted of murder,[130] will be convicted of manslaughter.

It is generally up to the defence to raise the issue of diminished responsibility, though the prosecution may raise it if the defence has in some other way put the D's mental state in issue, for example, by pleading insanity,[131] or automatism. In this case, the prosecution will have to prove beyond reasonable doubt that the D was suffering from diminished responsibility. Where the defence raises the issue, on the other hand, the prosecution may, agree to accept a plea of guilty to manslaughter on this ground. Such an agreement may be vetoed by the judge, as was done in the case of the trial of the so called 'Yorkshire Ripper', Peter Sutcliffe.[132] Unlike the position in relation to provocation, there is no obligation on the judge to direct the jury on the defence if it has not been specifically raised. Moreover, the D who takes a deliberate decision not to rely on diminished responsibility at trial, may be prevented from raising it on appeal.[133]

As will be seen from the definition contained in s 2, there are two main elements to the defence: abnormality of mind, and substantial impairment of mental responsibility. These will now be considered in turn.

Abnormality of mind

The list of possible causes of abnormality contained in s 2 indicates the breadth of the concept. It can be a result of an inherent mental defect, such as a low mental age, disease, or injury. The abnormality may therefore be one which the D has had since birth, or it may have developed subsequently. Can it be a temporary abnormality? There is nothing in the wording of the s to prevent this, though the issue does not seem to have been addressed directly in any appellate decisions. The relevant issue, however, is whether, *at the time of the killing*, the D was suffering from the abnormality. Thus a psychiatric illness from which the D subsequently makes a full recovery may clearly

130 In other words, the prosecution must prove the *actus reus* and *mens rea* of murder, to the usual standard. If it does not prove either of these, then the D will of course be entitled to an acquittal, and diminished responsibility will be irrelevant.

131 Criminal Procedure (Insanity) Act 1964, s 6.

132 Lacey, N, Wells, C and Meure, D, *Reconstructing Criminal Law*, 2nd edn, 1998, London: Butterworths, pp 585–86.

133 *Straw* [1995] 1 All ER 187.

provide evidence of abnormality.[134] Similarly, the acceptance of a plea of diminished responsibility in relation to mercy killings shows that the courts are prepared to accept temporary states of mind as falling within the scope of the defence. The defence is heavily dependant on medical evidence, however. An attempt was made in *Dix*[135] to run the defence without such evidence, relying simply on evidence of the D's conduct at the time of the killing, together with information about the surrounding circumstances and relevant history. The Court of Appeal confirmed that the trial judge had been correct to refuse to allow the defence to go to the jury on that basis. Scientific evidence of a medical kind is required to establish the cause of any abnormality of mind, and its effect on the D's mental responsibility:

> Thus, while the sub-section does not in terms require that medical evidence be adduced in support of a defence of diminished responsibility, it makes it a practical necessity if that defence is to begin to run at all.[136]

This is particularly so, given that the burden of proof is on the D.

One type of temporary state which will not support the defence is one voluntarily induced by drugs or alcohol. Of course, if the D is so intoxicated that he fails to form the intent to kill or cause grievous bodily harm,[137] then diminished responsibility is in any case irrelevant, since it is only if the D would otherwise be guilty of murder that the defence can be used. Murder being a specific intent offence[138] will, if the accused, through voluntary intoxication, failed to form the relevant intention, for this reason be reduced to manslaughter. If the intoxication is not at this level, however, then it cannot be used to support a plea of diminished responsibility. This can lead to the need to draw fine distinctions, however, where there is evidence that the D is addicted to drugs or alcohol. Such addiction, as opposed to intoxication on a particular occasion, might, if supported by medical evidence, provide the basis for the defence. The difficulties which this poses are illustrated by *Tandy*.[139] The D, who was an alcoholic, strangled the V, her 11 year old daughter. There was evidence that this was precipitated by the D's belief that her husband, the V's stepfather, had been sexually abusing the V. Her defence was based on diminished responsibility, as a result of her alcoholism. On the day of the killing, it appeared that she had consumed almost a whole bottle of vodka, rather than her customary vermouth or barley wine. The D was convicted. The issue on appeal was the relationship between her alcoholism in general, and her drinking on the day of the killing in particular. The Court of

134 Cf the consideration of 'Othello Syndrome' in *Vinagre* (1979) 69 Cr App R 104 – though the Court of Appeal appeared sceptical of the evidence in this case.

135 (1982) 74 Cr App R 306.

136 *Ibid*, p 311.

137 See Chapter 7, p 204.

138 For the meaning of 'specific intent' in this context, see Chapter 7, p 206.

139 [1989] 1 All ER 267.

Appeal accepted that chronic alcoholism, by impairing a person's judgment and emotional responses, could produce an abnormality of mind sufficient for the defence. If, however, the D had been voluntarily drinking on the day in question, and it was this intoxication which produced the abnormality, then the defence would fail. The crucial question was therefore whether the D, in starting to drink alcohol that day, had simply given in to an impulse to drink, or had been compelled to do so by an irresistible craving. Since there was evidence that the D had been in control of her drinking on the day in question, and the judge had correctly directed the jury on the issue of whether the D's drinking was involuntary or not, the appeal was dismissed.[140]

The case is illustrative of the somewhat artificial distinctions that the jury may be required to make as a result of the fact that intoxication does not provide a defence, while alcoholism may. A similar problem arises in relation to other types of abnormality where there is also evidence that the D has been drinking or taking drugs prior to the killing. The jury must put aside the intoxication caused by the voluntary consumption of drink and drugs, and try to decide whether, without this factor, the abnormality of mind from which the D suffered would have sufficiently affected his mental responsibility to allow the defence of diminished responsibility to succeed. As Lord Lane put it in *Gittens*,[141] approving the decision in *Fenton*:[142]

> The jury should be directed to disregard what, in their view, the effect of the alcohol or drugs on the defendant was, since abnormality of mind induced by alcohol or drugs is not, generally speaking, due to inherent causes ... Then the jury should consider whether the combined effect of the other matters which do fall within the section amounted to such abnormality of mind as substantially impaired the defendant's mental responsibility.

Where there is a basis for saying that the D was suffering from an 'abnormality' resulting from disease, there is clearly a potential overlap with the defence of insanity. As we shall see, that defence is available where the D was suffering from a 'defect of reason, due to disease of the mind'.[143] A disease of the mind may also provide the basis for a defence of diminished responsibility. Which of the two defences is appropriate will depend on the effect of the disease on the D's mental processes, and this is what we must now turn to consider, in looking at the second main element of the defence of diminished responsibility.

---

140 *Op cit*, Lacey, Wells and Meure, fn 132, p 587, point out that the Court of Appeal in this case appeared to have little appreciation of the effect that the discovery of the sexual abuse of her daughter by her current husband might have had on the D.

141 [1984] 3 All ER 252, p 256.

142 (1975) 61 Cr App R 261.

143 See Chapter 7, p 200.

Substantial impairment of mental responsibility

Whether a particular abnormality supports a defence of diminished responsibility depends in part on its effect. Only if it has the effect of substantially impairing the D's mental responsibility at the relevant time will it reduce the offence to manslaughter. Unfortunately, the concept of 'substantial impairment of mental responsibility' is not easy to understand, nor to explain to a jury. Clearly, it does not mean that the D was unaware of what he was doing. If that was the case, the plea would either be one of total innocence (because no relevant *mens rea* had been formed), or of insanity under the *M'Naghten* rules.[144] The D is aware that he is killing, or causing serious bodily harm to the V, and intends to do so, but the abnormality reduces his mental responsibility. One clear example of the required effect is where the abnormality produces an 'irresistible impulse' to carry out the attack on the V. This was confirmed early in the history of the defence by the decision in *Byrne*.[145]

The D, who had strangled and mutilated the V, was, according to the medical evidence, a sexual psychopath, suffering from violent and perverted sexual desires which he found it difficult or impossible to control. At his trial, the judge directed the jury that the consequent impulse or urge to kill did not 'constitute such abnormality of mind as substantially to impair a man's mental responsibility for his acts.'[146] The Court of Appeal ruled that this was a misdirection. In its view, the phrase 'abnormality of mind' is:

> ... wide enough to cover the mind's activities in all its aspects, not only the perception of physical acts and matters and the ability to form a rational judgment whether an act is right or wrong, but also the ability to exercise will-power to control physical acts in accordance with that rational judgment. The expression 'mental responsibility for his acts' points to a consideration of the extent to which the accused's mind is answerable for his physical acts which must include a consideration of the extent of his ability to exercise will-power to control his physical acts.

The defence of 'irresistible impulse', provided that it is based on an abnormality of mind,[147] will therefore be available as part of 'diminished responsibility'. This includes acts which the D is unable to exercise the will-power to control, and may include those which the D finds difficult to control (depending on the degree of difficulty).[148]

144 See Chapter 7, p 197

145 [1960] 3 All ER 1.

146 *Ibid*, p 4.

147 This may be thought to involve a circular argument, in that evidence that the D suffers from 'irresistible impulses' may be taken to be evidence of 'abnormality'.

148 [1960] 3 All ER 1, p 5.

Apart from 'irresistible impulse', which is a fairly clear form of 'lack of mental responsibility', it is difficult to categorise other effects which fall within this concept. It has been argued, by Griew,[149] that the reference to impairment of mental responsibility is 'improperly elliptical', in that what is meant is impairment to the D's capacity (for example, of perception, judgment, feeling, control), which reduces his culpability, and therefore his liability.[150] Similarly, the Butler Committee on Mentally Abnormal Offenders,[151] found the phrase mental responsibility difficult in that it was either a concept of law or a concept of morality, rather than a clinical fact susceptible to being established by expert medical evidence. The Committee suggested that 'moral issues do not normally enter into the definition of a crime'.[152] Nevertheless, in essence, it is a moral question that in practice the jury is likely to be asking itself: 'Does the abnormality from which the D was suffering mean that it would be morally wrong to convict him of murder?'

Despite the difficulties of definition, particularly in relation to the second issue, the defence has survived for nearly 30 years, and has been extensively used throughout that period. Its nebulousness, resulting in flexibility, may well be its strength, in fact. It has allowed the defence to be used as the courts, and in particular juries, have felt appropriate. Thus, it has been used at different times to cover, for example, the clinically depressed, the alcoholic, the sufferer from pre-menstrual syndrome, the mercy-killer, and the battered wife. Moreover, the fact that sentencing is at large means that the judge, as well as the jury, is able to 'let the punishment fit the crime.' Thus, Byrne, the sexual psychopath, received a life sentence (the same as he had been given for murder), despite the success of his appeal. Some mercy-killers, or battered wives, on the other hand, have been given sentences of probation, or, where successful on appeal against murder, prison sentences which allow their immediate release.[153] A further sentencing possibility is the making of a hospital order under s 37 of the Mental Health Act 1983. This may be appropriate where the 'mental abnormality' is of a continuing kind, and there is therefore the possibility of further offending if the condition is not treated.

Infanticide

One particular type of 'diminished responsibility' predates the Homicide Act 1957. This is the partial defence of 'infanticide' contained in s 1 of the Infanticide Act 1938. The section applies where a mother kills her child when it is under 12 months old, and she would otherwise be guilty of murder. If the

149 Griew, E, 'The future of diminished responsibility' [1988] Crim LR 75.

150 *Ibid*, pp 81–82.

151 1975, Cmnd 6244, London: HMSO.

152 *Ibid*, para 19.5.

153 Eg, the outcome of the retrial following *Ahluwalia* [1992] 4 All ER 889.

D has been charged with murder, and wishes to plead infanticide, she will have to satisfy an evidential burden to the effect that:

> ... the balance of her mind was disturbed by reason of her not having fully recovered from the effect of giving birth to the child or by reason of the effect of lactation consequent upon the birth of the child.

Alternatively, it is possible for the D to be charged initially with infanticide, in which case the burden of proof, including the proof of mental disturbance, is entirely on the prosecution. It appears that it is this possibility,[154] which avoids the mother being charged with murder, which is one of the principal reasons for the retention of the defence alongside that of diminished responsibility.[155] The Criminal Law Revision Committee has noted, however, that by no means all infanticide cases involve mental disturbance of a kind which would support a defence of diminished responsibility.[156] Given that there might well be a reluctance amongst juries to convict mothers who have killed their young children of murder, the result of abolition of infanticide could lead to a stretching of the concept of diminished responsibility. This process (that is, juries refusing to convict of murder) apparently lay behind the original enactment of this defence.[157]

The effect of a successful defence under the 1938 Act is a conviction for 'infanticide', which s 1 states is to be dealt with in the same way as regards penalty as a conviction for manslaughter. Thus, the maximum penalty is life imprisonment. In practice, however, probation is a much more likely sentence.[158]

The defence has been the subject of criticism on a number of grounds. One is that its basis is false. Mothers of new-born children may, as a result of a variety of pressures, some of them social, be led to treat their children violently. It does not necessarily follow that they are mentally disturbed. A successful use of the Act, however, requires such a finding. Moreover, the implication (reinforced by the reference to lactation) that this attributable to physical causes is particularly unhelpful. The defence has also been criticised in that it is not available to men, who may also suffer from similar social and psychological pressures following the birth of a child.[159] A final criticism is that, if the mother has more than one child, it may not be the new arrival who is on the receiving end of any violent behaviour. If the V is over 12 months

154 *Op cit*, Smith and Hogan, fn 72, p 395.

155 Manslaughter by virtue of diminished responsibility cannot be charged – though, as we have seen, a plea to this effect may be accepted prior to trial.

156 See, also, Mackay (Lord), 'The consequences of killing very young children' [1993] Crim LR 21.

157 In 1922: at that time, the mandatory penalty for murder was death, which gave additional force to the reluctance to convict, even though the penalty would almost certainly be commuted.

158 *Ibid*, Mackay.

159 Eg, *Doughty* (1986) 83 Cr App R 319.

old, however, the defence of infanticide is unavailable, and the charge must be murder.[160] A possible answer to this point is hinted at in the list, reproduced by Smith and Hogan, of the reasons advanced prior the 1922 Act.[161] The first of these is that 'the injury to the child was less, for it was incapable of the kind of suffering which might be undergone by the adult victim of murder'. This argument is, of course, relevant to one of the themes underlying this book, that the rights of the V are a relevant factor in determining criminal liability, alongside the moral responsibility of the D. Here, the suggestion is that the infant V is less capable of suffering than a person more fully grown, and that the infringement of his or her rights is therefore less serious. It is clearly an argument which would have been more easily accepted at a time when children, and their rights, were regarded with less respect than is the case in our society at present. The general view nowadays appears to be that children need more, rather than less, protection than adults. An argument based on the V's rights might therefore suggest that infanticide should always be murder. A further difficulty in accepting the opposite view is, of course, that it could be argued to apply to all killings of young children, whoever the perpetrator. In the end it seems that this is a case where the determining factor is the view taken of the moral responsibility of the mother, and the sympathy likely to be felt generally, and in particular by juries, towards a woman who, while distressed, kills her own young child.

Suicide pact

A 'suicide pact' is defined in s 4(3) of the Homicide Act 1957 as:

> ... a common agreement between two or more persons having for its object the death of all of them, whether or not each is to take his own life ...

The wording of this provision is slightly odd, given the context, since there is no obvious reason for including the phrase 'whether or not each is to take his own life'. If the pact involves each member taking his own life then there could be no liability for homicide anyway.[162] The inclusion of the phrase thus appears otiose. The situation which the section is most obviously intended to cover is where the D and the V agree to end their lives with the D killing the V, and then himself. If the D, in line with this agreement, kills the V, and then fails to kill himself (either by 'chickening out', or by using inadequate means), he would, in the absence of s 4 of the Homicide Act be guilty of murder. Section 4(1), however, provides that:

> It shall be manslaughter, and shall not be murder, for a person acting in pursuance of a suicide pact between him and another to kill the other party ...

160 Though, of course, it may be possible on appropriate facts to run a defence of provocation (*Doughty*), or diminished responsibility.

161 *Op cit*, Smith and Hogan, fn 72, p 394.

162 Criminal liability for suicide was removed by the Suicide Act 1961, s 1.

The same dispensation applies to the D who assists X to kill the V in connection with a suicide pact to which the D (though not necessarily X) is a party. In such a situation, the D would otherwise be liable for murder as an accessory.[163]

The burden of proof in relation the existence of the pact, and the fact that the D killed the V as part of it, lies on the defence.[164] It is not enough merely to prove that a pact was made. It must also be shown that at the time he killed the V, the D had 'the settled intention of dying in pursuance of the pact'.[165]

The rationale for this defence is unclear, given that, as we have seen, in general the V's consent or willingness to die will not reduce murder to manslaughter.[166] It could be taken to constitute a specific type of 'diminished responsibility', in the sense that those who agree to end their lives must be considered to be acting in a way that indicates that the balance of their minds may be disturbed.[167] If that is the case, however, it is difficult to see why it was not simply subsumed within the defence of diminished responsibility, particularly since it was the same Act (that is, the Homicide Act 1957) which introduced both defences to English law.

It should also be noted here, for the sake of completeness, that a D who assists in a V's suicide (for example, by knowingly providing the means), but does not actually cause the V's death, may be charged with an offence under s 2 of the Suicide Act 1961. This makes it an indictable offence, punishable with up to 14 years imprisonment, to aid, abet, counsel or procure 'the suicide of another or an attempt by another to commit suicide'. This offence covers both the well intentioned friend who assists a V to her death, and the D who encourages a V to kill herself for purely personal motives (for example, financial gain).[168] There is perhaps an anomaly here, in that the D in the latter case runs the risk of a maximum of 14 years imprisonment, whereas the D who is the participant in an unsuccessful suicide pact may be sentenced to life imprisonment.[169]

163 See the discussion of accessorial liability in Chapter 3, p 37 *et seq*.

164 Homicide Act 1957, s 4(2).

165 *Ibid*, s 4(3).

166 *Ibid*, s 4(3).

167 See, further, on this issue, Clarkson, CMV and Keating, HM, *Criminal Law: Text and Materials*, 4th edn, 1998, London: Sweet & Maxwell, pp 709–10.

168 Eg, *McShane* (1977) 66 Cr App R 97: the D here was convicted of an attempt to counsel or procure the V's suicide.

169 See the comments of Ashworth, A, *Principles of Criminal Law*, 2nd edn, 1995, Oxford: Clarendon, p 284, and *ibid*, Clarkson and Keating, p 668.

Involuntary manslaughter

Involuntary manslaughter arises where the D's actions cause a V's death, but the D does not have the *mens rea* for murder. It is often contrasted with 'voluntary manslaughter' which covers killings affected by provocation,[170] or diminished responsibility,[171] or which take place as part of a suicide pact.[172] In these three situations, the D has the *mens rea* of murder, but the offence is reduced to manslaughter by reason of one of the mitigating factors.

There are two main categories of involuntary manslaughter. The first arises where the D has committed some unlawful and dangerous act which has resulted in the V's death. This is sometimes referred to as 'constructive manslaughter'. The second category arises where the D has acted with such a degree of negligence or recklessness in causing the V's death that it is appropriate to make him criminally liable. In relation to both categories, it must be assumed that the prosecution is unable to prove that the D acted with an intention to kill or cause grievous bodily harm. Such an intention, if proved, would, of course, turn the offence into murder. A conviction for manslaughter may result from a murder charge, where the prosecution fail to prove the relevant intention. The offence can, however, also be charged in its own right. The two categories must now be considered in more detail.

Unlawful and dangerous act

'Unlawful' in this context means criminal. It is not enough that the act would give rise to civil liability (for example, for the tort of negligence). This was the view taken by the trial judge in *Franklin*,[173] where the D had thrown a box from a pier into the sea, hitting the V and causing his death. The throwing of the box was an act which might have amounted to the tort of trespass,[174] but it did not constitute a criminal offence. Field J ruled that the D could not be guilty of unlawful act manslaughter, though he might be guilty of reckless manslaughter.[175] This approach has been confirmed by subsequent appellate decisions. In *Lamb*,[176] the D and the V were playing with a loaded revolver, which the D pointed at the V. The D was aware that the revolver had two bullets in the chamber, but did not understand the mechanism of the gun, whereby the chamber moved as the trigger was pulled. The D, still in jest,

---

170 Above, p 68.

171 Above, p 82.

172 Above, p 89.

173 (1883) 15 Cox CC 163.

174 In modern tort law, it would almost certainly constitute negligence.

175 The jury found the D guilty of manslaughter, presumably on this basis.

176 [1967] 2 All ER 1282.

pulled the trigger. This moved a bullet into the firing position, and the D shot and fatally wounded the V. The judge refused to direct the jury on 'the niceties of the question whether or not' the action of the D 'did constitute or did not constitute an assault'. The Court of Appeal held that this was a misdirection, since 'it is long settled that it is not in point to consider whether an act is unlawful merely from the angle of civil liabilities'.[177] Criminal unlawfulness is therefore required for this species of manslaughter. The decision in *Cato*,[178] which seems to accept that this criminality can exist without the need to identify a specific offence, must be regarded as of dubious authority. The D injected the V with heroin, which resulted in the V's death. The Court of Appeal was prepared to treat the unlawful act as 'injecting [the V] with a mixture of heroin and water which at the time of the injection [the D] had unlawfully taken into his possession'.[179] This decision was unnecessary, however, since the court also found that the D was guilty of an offence under s 23 of the Offences Against the Person Act 1861.[180] Although Smith and Hogan find a similar lack of a specified offence in *Newbury*,[181] where the Ds threw a paving stone from the parapet of a bridge, and killed the guard on a train passing underneath, there was surely here an offence under s 1 of the Criminal Damage Act 1971. As will be seen below, there is no reason why an offence against property should not constitute the unlawful act.[182] Assuming that *Cato* goes further than is acceptable, however, some specific offence must be identified. Moreover, the criminality must not simply arise from the fact that an otherwise lawful act is carried out without proper care. The best example of this relates to driving, which becomes unlawful if carried out 'dangerously' or 'without due care and attention'.[183] As was made clear by Lord Atkin in *Andrews v DPP*,[184] criminality arising from such carelessness is not sufficient for the purposes of this type of manslaughter. It follows from this that a negligent omission such as might constitute the wilful neglect of a child under s 1(1) of the Children and Young Persons Act 1933, will not carry sufficient criminality to sustain a charge of unlawful act manslaughter. This was the view of the Court of Appeal in *Lowe*,[185] which expressed the view that this would also be the case even if the omission was deliberate. The

177 [1967] 2 All ER 1282, p 1284.

178 [1976] 1 All ER 260.

179 *Ibid*, p 267.

180 'Administering a noxious thing.'

181 [1976] 2 All ER 365.

182 Smith and Hogan find this 'objectionable' (*op cit*, fn 72, p 379), but it is not clear why. Section 1 of the Criminal Damage Act itself contains a recognition that, in certain circumstances, such damage can endanger life; so why should it not, therefore, form the basis of a manslaughter charge?

183 Road Traffic Act 1988, ss 2, 3. Note, however, the specific offences of causing death by dangerous or careless driving, considered below, p 99.

184 [1937] 2 All ER 552, p 555.

185 [1973] 1 All ER 805.

House of Lords in *Sheppard*, however, disapproved the interpretation of the 1933 Act used in *Lowe*, though not the specific point with which we are concerned here. It has been suggested by Smith and Hogan,[186] that the Court of Appeal's approach in *Lowe* should not extend to deliberate omissions (for example, to summon medical help),[187] and this point of view has much sense. Indeed, Ashworth has described the distinction between acts and omissions which seems to follow from *Lowe* as 'morally untenable'.[188] Nevertheless, it seems that the current position is that omissions, of whatever kind, are not sufficient to sustain a charge of unlawful act manslaughter.

The requirement of criminality means, of course, that if the D would have a defence to the criminal offence concerned, then there will also be a defence to manslaughter.[189] Thus, the jury, in considering whether the D who has hit the V, with the result that the V has fallen, hit her head, and died, is liable for manslaughter, must also consider whether the D might have had a defence, such as self-defence, if charged with the original assault.

The most usual type of offence which will constitute the necessary criminality is likely to be an assault. Offences against property might, however, in some circumstances be sufficient. Examples might be a D who steals a V's medication, thinking that this will cause the V merely inconvenience or discomfort, whereas in fact its absence proves fatal;[190] or a D who tampers with the brakes on a V's car (criminal damage), expecting the V to notice the relevant warning lights before driving the car. Whatever the offence, however, the unlawful act must also be 'dangerous', and this comprises the second element of involuntary manslaughter.

The test of dangerousness in this context was set out in *Church*,[191] where the D assaulted the V, and then threw her into a canal, causing her to drown. The D claimed that at the time he threw her into the canal he thought she was already dead. Edmund Davies J, in the Court of Appeal, stated that:

> ... the unlawful act must be such as all sober and reasonable people would inevitably recognise must subject the other person to, at least, the risk of some harm resulting therefrom, albeit not serious harm.[192]

This test was subsequently approved by the House of Lords in *DPP v Newbury and Jones*.[193] The question before the House was:

186 *Op cit*, Smith and Hogan, fn 72, p 382.

187 This was the view taken in the 19th century case of *Senior* [1899] 1 QB 283.

188 *Op cit*, Ashworth, fn 169, p 291.

189 *Scarlett* [1993] 4 All ER 629.

190 Cf *Watson* [1989] 2 All ER 865, where it was accepted that burglary could constitute an 'unlawful act' for involuntary manslaughter, though the conviction was quashed on other grounds.

191 [1965] 2 All ER 72.

192 *Ibid*, p 76.

193 [1976] 2 All ER 365.

> Can a defendant be properly convicted of manslaughter, when his mind is not affected by drink or drugs, if he did not foresee that his act might cause harm to another?

The House of Lords, adopting the test from *Church* outlined above, answered the question in the affirmative. It is therefore an objective test, not depending on whether the D recognised that the act was dangerous, but on whether a reasonable person would have done so. The reasonable person is deemed to be sober. The intoxication of the D by drink or drugs will therefore be ignored at two stages in this type of manslaughter. First, if (as is likely) the offence which constitutes the unlawful act is one of basic intent,[194] then the intoxication will not be taken into account in deciding whether he had the necessary *mens rea*. An example of this is *Lipman*,[195] where the D, having taken hallucinatory drugs, believed he was being attacked by snakes, and stuffed a sheet into the V's mouth, killing her. Secondly, the intoxication of the D will be ignored in deciding whether he should have foreseen the danger of harm resulting from his actions. The D, whether drunk or sober, will not, however, be attributed with knowledge of facts increasing the risk of injury, unless this would have been something of which the reasonable person would have been aware. Thus, the D in *Daweson*[196] was not taken to have notice of the V's weak heart (since this would not have been obvious to the reasonable person). In *Watson*,[197] however, the frailty (and therefore the susceptibility to injury) of the 87 year old V was something which the reasonable person would have appreciated.[198] There does not seem to be any authority on the position where the D has relevant special knowledge which the ordinary reasonable person would not have. It would seem, however, that, if the D is, for example, aware of the V's heart condition, then this should be taken account in assessing the foreseeability of harm resulting from the D's behaviour, even though the reasonable person, not having the D's special knowledge, would not have appreciated the increased risk.

The danger which should have been foreseen does not need to be of death, or even serious injury, but just 'some harm'. Thus, a minor assault, if by chance it results in death, may nevertheless make the D liable for manslaughter. In *Larkin*,[199] the D had threatened a person (not the V) with a razor (which constituted an assault). The V, who was present, fell against the razor with the result that her throat was cut. The D was convicted of manslaughter of the V, and the Court of Appeal commented that:

194 See Chapter 7, p 206.

195 [1969] 3 All ER 410.

196 (1985) 81 Cr App R 150.

197 [1989] 2 All ER 865.

198 Though the conviction for manslaughter was in fact overturned on other grounds, ie, lack of proof of causation.

199 [1943] 1 All ER 217.

> Where the act which a person is engaged in is unlawful, then, if at the same time it is a dangerous act, that is, an act which is likely to injure another person, and quite inadvertently he causes the death of that other person by that act, then he is guilty of manslaughter.[200]

A similar case in which an assault on X leads to the death of the D occurred in *Mitchell*.[201] There was an altercation in a queue in a post office, which resulted in the D assaulting X. X fell against the V, and they both fell to the ground. X incurred minor injuries, but the V suffered a broken femur, and was taken to hospital. A few days later, following an operation to replace her hip, the V died as a result of a pulmonary embolism attributable to the broken femur. The D was convicted of an assault on X, and of the manslaughter of the V. He appealed on the basis that it was necessary for the offence of unlawful act manslaughter that the act should be 'directed at' the victim, in the sense of having had some immediate impact on her (as had happened in *Larkin*). The Court of Appeal rejected this. As long as there was a sufficient causal link between the D's unlawful act and the V's death, then the charge of manslaughter could be sustained. In reaching this conclusion, the court had to deal with the earlier Court of Appeal decision in *Dalby*.[202] In that case, a conviction for manslaughter had been quashed where the D had supplied the V with a controlled drug, and the V had then injected the drug, with fatal consequences. At one point, Waller LJ had commented:[203]

> In the judgment of this court, where the charge of manslaughter is based on an unlawful and dangerous act, it must be an act directed at the victim and likely to cause immediate injury, however slight.

The court in *Mitchell* distinguished *Dalby* on the basis that the issue in that case was whether there was a sufficient link between the unlawful act (the supply of the drug) and the V's death. In other words, despite the quotation cited above, the case turned on causation, and did not lay down a general requirement that the lawful act must be directed at the victim. With respect, this seems a tenuous argument, given the clear statement by Waller LJ. Nevertheless, the same line was taken in the subsequent decision of *Goodfellow*.[204] The D had set fire to a house, intending that the occupants should escape. Unfortunately, three people died, and the D was convicted of manslaughter. At his appeal, it was argued that his unlawful act of arson was not aimed at anyone, let alone the victims, who comprised his wife, his mistress, and one of his children. The court, having cited the passage from Waller LJ's judgment in *Dalby*, quoted above, suggested that 'what he was ...

200 The case is, of course, also an example of the doctrine of 'transferred malice': see Chapter 2, p 23.

201 [1983] 2 All ER 427.

202 [1982] 1 All ER 916.

203 *Ibid*, p 919.

204 (1986) 83 Cr App R 23.

intending to say was that there must be no fresh intervening cause between the act and the death'.[205] As with the approach taken in *Mitchell*, this is by no means the most obvious interpretation of the statements in *Dalby*. Nevertheless, it seems safe to regard *Mitchell* and *Goodfellow* as representing the current law: thus, all that is needed for this type of manslaughter is a deliberate criminal act, which any reasonable sober person would realise was bound to subject some other human being to the risk of some (not necessarily serious) harm, and which causes the death of the V.

Manslaughter by gross negligence, or recklessness

The leading case on this type involuntary manslaughter is the House of Lords decision in *Adomako*.[206] This concerned alleged negligence by an anaesthetist during a hospital operation, which resulted in the death of the V. The D, the anaesthetist, was charged with manslaughter. This category of manslaughter does not depend on the prosecution proving that the D committed a criminal act, but rather on showing that his behaviour fell so far below the standards to be expected of someone in his position that it should be regarded as giving rise to criminal liability. The steps involved in the process of determining liability were set out by Lord Mackay, and the passage is worth quoting at length. The first step is to decide whether the D owed any duty of care to the V:[207]

> In my opinion, the ordinary principles of negligence apply to ascertain whether or not the defendant has been in breach of a duty of care towards the victim who has died. If such breach of duty is established the next question is whether that breach of duty caused the death of the victim. If so, the jury must go on to consider whether that breach of duty should be characterised as gross negligence and therefore as a crime. This will depend on the seriousness of the breach of duty committed by the defendant in all the circumstances in which the defendant was placed when it occurred. The jury will have to consider the extent to which the defendant's conduct departed from the proper standard of care incumbent upon him, involving as it must have done a risk of death to the [victim], was such that it should be judged criminal.

The three main elements are thus: the establishment of a breach of duty; the issue of causation; the degree of negligence. In contrast to the position in relation to an unlawful act of manslaughter, the first step is to be determined by reference to civil law principles. Would there be a breach of duty under the tort of negligence? The second step is a straightforward causation issue, to be dealt with in the normal way.[208] The third step is the crucial one, for it is here

205 (1986) 83 Cr App R, p 27.

206 [1994] 3 All ER 79.

207 *Ibid*, pp 86–87.

208 See Chapter 2, p 10 *et seq*.

that the leap is made from tortious to criminal liability. Unfortunately, it is also here that the test becomes most vague. The House of Lords in *Adomako* returned to the approach taken in two cases, both 50–60 years old: *Bateman* (1925),[209] and *Andrews v DPP* (1937).[210] In *Bateman* (also a medical negligence case), Lord Hewart CJ had said that, in order to convict in this type of manslaughter, the jury must be satisfied that:[211]

> ... the negligence or incompetence of the accused went beyond a matter of mere compensation and showed such disregard for the life and safety of others as to amount to a crime against the State and conduct deserving punishment.

Similarly, in *Andrews*, which concerned death caused by dangerous driving, Lord Atkin said:[212]

> Simple lack of care such as will constitute civil liability is not enough. For purposes of the criminal law, there are degrees of negligence, and a very high degree of negligence is required to be proved before the felony is established.

As has frequently been pointed out by commentators, this approach to defining the level of gross negligence which will amount to manslaughter has a strong element of circularity. To the question 'what behaviour constitutes a criminal offence?', the answer is given 'behaviour which is so bad that it ought to be criminal'. Lord Mackay in *Adomako* noted this point, but was prepared to accept it.[213] The test of criminality was necessarily a question of degree, and attempts to specify it more closely would only lead to 'a spurious precision':

> The essence of the matter, which is supremely a jury question, is whether, having regard to the risk of death involved, the conduct of the defendant was so bad in all the circumstances as to amount in their judgment to a criminal act or omission.[214]

In reaching this conclusion, he rejected the use of *Caldwell* 'recklessness',[215] as modified by *Lawrence*, as appropriate to this head of manslaughter. This definition had been adopted by the House of Lords in *Seymour*,[216] which was concerned with motor manslaughter, and been applied more generally by the Privy Council in *Kong Chenk Kwan*.[217] The decision in *Seymour* was, however, linked to the offence of 'reckless driving', which had been the context for the *Lawrence* direction. This offence was replaced by 'dangerous driving' by the Road Traffic Act 1991. With the disappearance of the underlying statutory

209 (1925) 19 Cr App R 8.
210 [1937] 2 All ER 552.
211 (1925) 19 Cr App R 8, p 13.
212 [1937] 2 All ER 552, p 556.
213 [1994] 2 All ER 79, p 87.
214 *Ibid*, p 87.
215 See Chapter 2, p 34.
216 [1983] 2 All ER 1058.
217 (1985) 82 Cr App R 18.

provisions, there was no need to retain this special meaning of 'recklessness' in relation to manslaughter. On the other hand, Lord Mackay was content for a judge to use the word 'reckless' in directing a jury, provided that it was used 'in the ordinary connotation of that word'.[218] He went on to say that he thought the word had been used properly in this sense in *Stone and Dobinson*,[219] and *R v West London Coroner ex p Gray*.[220] The reference to *Stone and Dobinson* in this context is perhaps surprising. As we have seen, Lord Mackay refers in the last of the quotations from his speech set out above to the 'risk of death' involved. In *Stone and Dobinson*, however, the facts of which have been given in Chapter 2,[221] the relevant risk was described in the following terms:[222]

> What the Crown has to prove is a breach of...duty in such circumstances that the jury feel convinced that the defendant's conduct can properly be described as reckless. That is to say a reckless disregard of danger to the health and welfare of the infirm person.

The 'recklessness' here is not as regards the likelihood of death, but simply 'health and welfare', which seems a much lower level of risk. Given, however, that the facts of *Stone and Dobinson* suggest that, objectively speaking, there was a risk of death involved in the failure to seek assistance for the V, it may be that the reference to a lower level of harm may be regarded as *obiter*, even though just after the passage quoted above, there is a reference to indifference 'to an obvious risk of injury to health'.[223] At that point, however, the court was merely indicating that 'mere inadvertence' is insufficient for 'recklessness': there must be indifference to an obvious risk, or a determination to run a risk which has been foreseen. In that context, the precise nature of the risk, or the outcome of ignoring it, may not have been expressed with legislative precision. Should, therefore, the risk which gives rise to gross manslaughter be limited to death, as apparently suggested by Lord Mackay in the passage from *Adomako* quoted above? That, perhaps, does not go far enough. Take the example of the D who throws a heavy item out of upstairs window into a crowded street. If he does this intending to cause serious injury to someone passing below he is guilty of murder. If, however, he simply acts carelessly but kills, should it be necessary for the prosecution to prove that there was an obvious risk of death in order to obtain a conviction

218 [1994] 2 All ER 79, p 87, *per* Lord Mackay, referring to Lord Atkin's speech in *Andrews v DPP* [1937] 2 All ER 552, p 556.

219 [1977] 2 All ER 341.

220 [1987] 2 All ER 129.

221 See Chapter 2, p 18.

222 [1977] 2 All ER 341, p 347.

223 It should be noted that Lord Taylor in the Court of Appeal judgment in relation to *Adomako* (reported under *Prentice* [1993] 4 All ER 935, p 943) also refers to 'indifference to an obvious risk of injury to health' as indicating 'gross negligence' for the purposes of manslaughter.

for manslaughter? Surely it should be sufficient to show a risk parallel to the consequences required to be intended for murder, that is, death or really serious harm, and that the D has been grossly negligent in relation to such a risk.

The justification for accepting that even a lower level of risk should be sufficient, if death is the actual consequence, could, of course, be based on the 'rights of the victim' perspective. If acts of the D which are negligent as regards the V's well being have resulted in the V's death, then it is arguable that this ultimate infringement of the V's rights should be recognised by categorising the D's behaviour as a homicide offence, ie manslaughter. It is unlikely, however, that the current line of decisions in this area can be regarded as going quite this far. At face value, *Adomako* limits the relevant risk to one of death. Despite the approving reference to *Stone and Dobinson*, it seems unlikely, therefore, that a risk of anything less than serious injury would have been regarded by the House of Lords as sufficient for this type of manslaughter. Unfortunately, despite the considerable simplification of the law achieved by the House of Lords in this area, the offence of manslaughter by gross negligence continues to contain areas of uncertainty. The safest direction for a judge to give would seem to be to abjure the word 'reckless' and simply ask the jury to consider whether there was an obvious risk of death (or perhaps serious injury) from the D's behaviour, and whether the prosecution have proved beyond reasonable doubt that the D was grossly negligent in relation to the that risk, meaning that he was so negligent that he ought to be criminally liable for it. It was a failure to direct the jury not only that there needed to be an obvious risk, but on the need for gross negligence on the part of the D in relation to it that led to the quashing of the two convictions which were heard by the Court of Appeal together with *Adomako*.[224] One of these was, like *Adomako*, a situation of medical negligence. The other was a case of the negligent electrical wiring of a central heating system, which led to radiators, and other parts of the system being 'live'. The Court of Appeal clearly regarded this as a situation where manslaughter by gross negligence could arise,[225] but quashed the conviction because this had not been properly dealt with in the summing up.

DRIVING OFFENCES

It has long been recognised that juries are reluctant to convict of manslaughter drivers who have been involved in road accidents causing death, other than in the most blatant cases. Special homicide offences have therefore been created

224 *Prentice* [1993] 4 All ER 935.

225 *Ibid*, p 958: '... the case against this appellant may have been strong ...'

to deal with the situations where bad driving has led to death. English law currently has two such offences, both of which are to be found in the Road Traffic Act 1988 (as amended by the Road Traffic Act 1991). The two offences are 'causing death by dangerous driving', and 'causing death by careless driving when under the influence of drink or drugs'. They are dealt with here, in outline, for the sake of completeness.

Causing death by dangerous driving

The offence is set out in s 1 of the 1988 Act:

> A person who causes the death of another person by driving a mechanically propelled vehicle dangerously on a road or other public place is guilty of an offence.

It carries a sentence of up to 10 years imprisonment (whereas manslaughter, of course, can result in life imprisonment). The essence of the offence is 'dangerous driving' which causes death. Dangerous driving is defined by s 2A. A person drives dangerously for these purposes if (s 2A(1):

> (a) the way he drives falls far below what would be expected of a competent and careful driver; and
>
> (b) it would be obvious to a competent and careful driver that driving in that way would be dangerous.

As will be seen, the standard here is one of negligence, and there is no need to show intention or recklessness on the part of the D as regards the dangerousness of his driving. 'Dangerousness' can include risk of serious damage to property, as well as injury to persons.[226] The manner of driving (for example, excessive speed) is the most obvious way in which dangerousness may arise, but s 2A(2) makes it clear that driving a vehicle which is in a state a competent and careful driver would realise made driving dangerous is sufficient. The defect(s), if not actually known to the D,[227] must be obvious 'at first glance'.[228] Relevant 'defects' can include the way in which the vehicle is loaded.[229]

The second requirement is that the dangerous driving caused the death. This is not a particularly onerous burden on the prosecution. There is no need for the D's dangerous driving to be a major cause, or even a substantial cause, as long as it was a cause. The Court of Appeal has recently, in *Kimsey*,[230]

226 Road Traffic Act 1988, s 2A(3).

227 *Ibid*, s 2A(3).

228 *Strong* [1995] Crim LR 428.

229 Road Traffic Act 1988, s 2A(4).

230 [1996] Crim LR 35.

confirmed its decision in *Hennigan*[231] on an earlier version of this offence, to the effect that as long as the contribution by the D's behaviour was more than *de minimis*, the causation element would be satisfied. In *Hennigan*, the court was happy to accept that a D whose contribution to a fatal accident was only one-fifth, could nevertheless be held liable for causing the death. In *Kimsey*, the court indicated its approval of a direction which told the jury that there had to be more than a 'slight or trifling link', as a means of avoiding a reference to 'de minimis'. In practice, therefore, whenever a D has driven dangerously, and is involved in a fatal accident, a charge of causing death by dangerous driving is likely to be sustainable.

Causing death by careless driving

Causing death by careless driving while under the influence of drink or drugs was added to the 1988 Act by the Road Traffic Act 1991, and now appears as s 3A.

There are three main elements of the offence:

(i) driving without due care and attention, or without reasonable consideration for other persons using the road;

(ii) causing the death of a V;

(iii) being unfit to drive[232] through drink or drugs, or being over the prescribed limit for alcohol, or failing to provide a specimen when so required.

The causation element will be dealt with in the same way as for dangerous driving, and so does not require further discussion. The standard of driving implied by (i) is closely akin to the standard required by the civil law of negligence.[233] Anyone who is negligent according to the civil law standard is likely also to be driving without due care and attention. The mere fact that a person is unfit to drive through drink or drugs, however, does not in itself mean that he or she is driving carelessly. There must be some problem with the manner of driving before the offence is committed. All three elements must be present together. Causing death by careless driving is not in itself a specific offence; nor is causing death while driving under the influence of drink or drugs. There must be both carelessness and the influence of drink or drugs. Of course, a D who is sober, but drives carelessly, and kills, can nevertheless be guilty of an offence under this section if he refuses to provide a specimen.

The maximum penalty for this offence is the same as for dangerous driving, that is, 10 years imprisonment.

231 (1971) 55 Cr App R 262.

232 Meaning that D's 'ability to drive properly is impaired': s 3A(2).

233 See, eg, *Scott v Warren* [1974] RTR 104.

CHAPTER 5

NON-FATAL OFFENCES

Non-fatal offences generally involve an interference, or a threat of interference, with the V's bodily integrity, and this provides the basis for making them criminal. In some circumstances, however, particularly in relation to assaults, no such interference is required. The basis of criminalisation is then the infringement of the V's right to 'privacy', in the sense discussed in Chapter 1. As we have seen, the European Court of Human Rights has confirmed that Vs have a right to expect the legal system to provide a criminal process to support their rights in this area. In English law, this is done through a range of offences, from common assault, to attempted murder. All offences are now statutory,[1] though the definition of some elements of some offences are still to be found in the common law, with the main piece of legislation being the Offences Against the Person Act 1861.

'Assault' and 'battery' lie at the heart of non-fatal offences. The approach taken in this chapter is therefore to start with these two offences, and then to move in increasing degrees of seriousness through the other offences, concluding with a discussion of attempted murder.

ASSAULT

Assault is a problematic offence, in that the word 'assault' is used in both a narrow and a broad sense. In the broad sense, which is probably the one more commonly used, it refers to the two offences of 'assault' and 'battery'. This includes the situation where there is physical contact with the V. In the narrow sense, it refers to the situation where there is no physical contact, but where the D's behaviour induces in the V a fear of unlawful violence. The potential for ambiguity is thus great. In attempting to avoid some of the problems arising from the dual use of this word, in this chapter, where 'assault' is used in the narrow sense, it will be in italics – *assault*. Where it is in roman letters, the broad sense will be intended.

---

1 It was confirmed in *DPP v Taylor; DPP v Little* [1992] 1 All ER 299, that common assault and battery have been statutory offences ever since the enactment of the Offences Against the Person Act 1861 (though the accuracy of this analysis was doubted by McCullough LJ in *Cross v DPP* (1995), unreported). Both offences should now be charged as contrary to the Criminal Justice Act 1988, s 39. They are summary offences, punishable with a fine not exceeding level 5 on the standard scale, or imprisonment for up to six months, or both.

The *actus reus* of assault

The definition of the '*actus reus* of assault' seems to be accepted to be as set out in Archbold,[2] that is 'an act – and not a mere omission to act – by which a person ... causes another to apprehend immediate and unlawful violence'. There is no requirement that the response of the V is reasonable, but the general discussion of causation in Chapter 2 may be relevant here.[3] In practice, the liability of the D where the V's response is arguably unreasonable will be dealt with by the mens rea requirements of the offence, discussed below.

This apparently straightforward definition of the *actus reus* in fact needs careful analysis in the light of the cases. In particular, the recent House of Lords decision in *Ireland*[4] seems to have extended the scope of the concept significantly. The court held that to make a phone call and then remain silent was capable of amounting to an assault, provided the relevant *mens rea* could be proved. In the light of this decision, three elements of the definition of *assault*, that is 'act', 'immediate', and 'apprehension of unlawful violence' need to be looked at in detail.

Act

The requirement of an act was at one time thought to mean that words alone could not constitute an *assault*.[5] The threat 'I'm going to beat your head in' would not on this basis be an *assault* unless accompanied with, for example, a raised fist.[6] Indeed, words might have the opposite effect of making clear that an apparently threatening action is not going to lead to violence. Thus, in the classic civil law case on *assault*, *Tuberville v Savage*,[7] the D, in response to an insult, put his hand on his sword. Such a gesture might clearly have been taken to be an act threatening immediate unlawful violence, but it was accompanied by the words: 'If it were not assize time I would not take such language.' This qualification was taken to indicate that the D was not making a threat of immediate attack on the V, and that therefore there was no assault.

---

2 Para 19/166. See, also, *Ireland* [1996] 3 WLR 650, p 653, where Swinton Thomas LJ states that the Archbold definition was approved by the House of Lords in *Parmenter* [1992] 1 AC 699, p 740. It does not in fact seem that there was specific approval for the Archbold definition here, since it appears that it was simply accepted 'as common ground' that the mental element of assault was intention or recklessness as to the causing of an apprehension of immediate and unlawful violence.

3 Chapter 2, p 11.

4 [1997] 4 All ER 225.

5 *Meade and Belt* (1823) 1 Lew CC 184: '... no words or singing are equivalent to an assault.'

6 But cf the *obiter* statement of Lord Goddard in *Wilson* [1955] 1 All ER 744 to the effect that calling out 'Get out the knives!' could in itself amount to an assault.

7 (1669) 1 Mod Rep 3.

The need for an act must now be reconsidered, however, in the light of the House of Lords' decision in *Ireland*.[8] The facts of this case were that the D had made a large number of phone calls to three women – on one occasion, 14 to one of them within an hour. When the phone was answered, the D remained silent, sometimes for several minutes. The women suffered psychological harm as a result of these phone calls, and the D was charged with assault occasioning actual bodily harm, under s 47 of the 1861 Act. On appeal against his conviction, the D argued that there was no assault, in part because silence could not constitute the 'act' necessary for the *actus reus*. In the Court of Appeal, it was suggested that 'The act consists in the making of the telephone call, and it does not matter whether words or silence ensue'.[9] It is difficult to accept, however, that the making of the call itself is sufficient for the *actus reus* of *assault* – the subsequent behaviour is also important. The dialling of the V's number is in itself a neutral act, and simply a way of making contact with the V. Analogous behaviour would be getting into one's car to drive to the V's house, or walking up the path to the V's front door and ringing the bell. With respect to the Court of Appeal, it *does* matter what then follows. If, when the V answers the phone, the D engages in friendly, non-threatening conversation, there is surely no offence. It is only when the D's behaviour is seen as threatening by the V that the *actus reus* of an *assault* occurs. Similarly, walking up to the V's house is neutral, but staring through the windows at the V may constitute an *assault* – as was held in *Smith v Chief Superintendent, Woking Police Station*.[10]

This point, while not addressed directly, seems implicit in the House of Lords speeches in *Ireland*, since they treat the 'act' as being the telephone call *together with* the ensuing silence, thus accepting that what happens after the call is answered is relevant to the issue of whether the *actus reus* of assault has occurred. One situation, however, in which the call itself might constitute an act sufficient for an assault is where, as in *Ireland*, the D makes *repeated* calls. After several of them have been made to a particular V, she will, no doubt, dread the ringing of the telephone. That event in itself, even before the phone had been answered, could in those circumstances engender fear sufficient to form the *actus reus* of assault. In such circumstances, it could be argued that the D would be liable even if he rang off before the V had picked up the receiver. In that case, it clearly would be the case that the making of the telephone call constitutes the act necessary for the *actus reus*. On the other hand, on the first occasion that the D rings a particular V, the making of the call would not produce any apprehension on the part of the V. In that case, it

8 [1997] 4 All ER 225.

9 [1996] 3 WLR 650, p 655.

10 (1983) 76 Cr App Rep 234 – considerable reliance was placed on this case by the Court of Appeal in Ireland.

could only possibly be the *content* of the call, be it words or silence, which could produce the necessary effect.

In coming to the conclusion that a silent telephone call can constitute an assault, the House of Lords accepted that words alone should be capable of constituting an assault, despite the old authorities,[11] that this was not the case. This has long been accepted in Australia, at least as far as the civil law of assault is concerned, by virtue of the decision of the Supreme Court of New South Wales in *Barton v Armstrong*.[12] The case concerned threats uttered to the V over the telephone. As Taylor J put it:[13]

> Threats which put a reasonable person in fear of physical violence have always been abhorrent to the law as an interference with personal freedom and integrity, and the right of a person to be free of insult. If the threat produces the fear or apprehension of physical violence then I am of opinion that the law is breached ...

Lord Steyn, in *Ireland*, with whom the rest of the House concurred, put it this way:[14]

> The proposition that a gesture may amount to an assault , but that words can never suffice, is unrealistic and indefensible. A thing said is also a thing done. There is no reason why something said should be incapable of causing an apprehension of immediate personal violence, for example, a man accosting a woman in a dark alley saying 'come with me or I will stab you'. I would, therefore, reject the proposition that an assault can never be committed by words.

If it is the case, then, that assault can be committed by words, or even silence, would it not be acceptable simply to say that any *behaviour* by the D (whatever form it takes) can constitute the *actus reus* of this offence, provided that it produces the relevant reaction of fear or apprehension in the V? It is submitted that, subject to one limitation, this is indeed the position the law is in post-*Ireland*. Thus it may well be that (subject to the issues of 'immediacy' discussed below) sending a threatening letter can now be categorised as an *assault*. This was the view of the Court of Appeal in *Constanza*, a case similar to *Ireland*, but not referred to by the House of Lords.[15] The one limitation which must surely still apply, is that the behaviour cannot be satisfied by an *omission*. If we were to accept that an omission which causes fear and apprehension in the V constitutes the *actus reus* of an *assault*, this would encompass such situations as the parent who omits to collect a child from school. The child,

11 In particular, *Meade's and Belt's* case (1823) 1 Lew CC 184.

12 [1969] 2 NSWR 451; decided on other grounds by the Privy Council: [1975] 2 All ER 465.

13 [1969] 2 NSWR 451, p 455.

14 [1997] 4 All ER 225, p 236. Lord Hope, apparently trying to make the same point, seems to require a combination of words and gestures – which is arguably what was required under the law prior to Ireland anyway: p 240.

15 [1997] 2 Cr App R 492.

waiting at the school gates may well fear for her personal safety as a result of this omission, but she has surely not been *assaulted* by her parent's behaviour. The discussion in Chapter 2 of situations, generally involving a duty to act on the part of the D,[16] where omissions can constitute an *actus reus*, does not, it is suggested, have any relevance to *assaults*, because of the need for behaviour which induces fear of violence. In relation to the silent telephone call, the *actus reus* is not simply the 'omission' to speak, but the combination of the making of the call, together with remaining silent once it is answered. An omission can, of course, constitute the *actus reus* of a *battery* in appropriate circumstances, so that when assault is used in the broad sense, an omission may be enough to sustain a charge.

Immediate unlawful violence

The apprehension induced by the D's behaviour is required to be of *immediate* unlawful violence. Thus, the D who tells his wife as he is about to leave on a week's business trip that is she is unfaithful in his absence he will beat her on his return does not by that statement commit an *assault*. The conditionality of the threat is probably not an obstacle to liability. The 19th century civil law case of *Read v Coker*[17] confirms that a threat in the form 'If you do not do X, I will hit you' may constitute an *assault*.[18] And, in *Ireland*,[19] as we have seen, Lord Steyn suggested that an assault might be committed by saying 'come with me or I will stab you'. The delay of at least a week, however, prevents the threat being of immediate violence.

'Immediate' does not, however, mean 'instantaneous'. The test to be used is probably the same as that stated by the Divisional Court, when interpreting the phrase 'immediate unlawful violence' in the different context of s 4 of the Public Order Act 1986:[20]

> It seems to us that the word 'immediate' does not mean 'instantaneous', that a relatively short time interval may elapse between the act which is threatening, abusive or insulting and the unlawful violence. 'Immediate' connotes proximity in time and proximity in causation, that it is likely that violence will result in a relatively short period of time and without any other intervening occurrence.

Clearly, the D who sees the V on the other side of the street, waves his fist, and shouts 'I'm going to get you!' thereby commits an *assault*, even though it may

16 See Chapter 2, pp 16–22.

17 (1853) 13 CB 850.

18 See, also, *Ansell v Thomas* [1974] Crim LR 31. The decision to the contrary, in *Blake v Barnard* (1840) 9 C&P 626, should probably not be followed, for the reasons set out by *Williams* [1957] Crim LR 220.

19 [1997] 4 All ER 225, p 236.

20 *Horseferry Road Magistrates ex p Siadatan* [1991] 1 All ER 324, p 329.

take a few minutes for D to cross the traffic, and catch up with the V. Similarly, in *Smith v Chief Superintendent, Woking Police Station*,[21] where the D was held to have *assaulted* the V by looking at her through the windows of her house, it was accepted that the threat that he might do something of a violent nature was sufficiently immediate for the purposes of the offence.[22] How does this requirement of immediacy apply to assaults over the telephone? It is submitted that the general principle of proximity should apply. Clearly, if the threat is uttered over an internal phone to a person in an adjoining office, this is no different to a threat shouted from one room to another, which was implicitly treated as an assault by the Court of Appeal in *Lewis*.[23] The same would be likely to apply where the D is in a phone box in the street outside the V's home. In *Ireland*,[24] Lord Steyn uses the example of a telephone caller 'who says to a woman in a menacing way 'I will be at your door in a minute or two''. What, however, if the D is in a different town, or even a different country, and the V is aware of this? It would be difficult to argue in such a case that the threat induced a fear of *immediate* unlawful violence, unless this was to be inflicted by an accomplice of the D. Thus, in the New Zealand case of *Baron v Armstrong*,[25] in discussing a tortious assault over the telephone, Taylor J commented:[26]

> If, when threats ... are conveyed over the telephone, the recipient has been led to believe that he is being followed, kept under surveillance by persons hired to do him physical harm to the extent of killing him, then why is this not something to put him in fear or apprehension of immediate violence?

This seems entirely consistent with the proximity test. However, a little later in the judgment, Taylor J seems to move from 'an apprehension of immediate violence' to 'an immediate apprehension of violence' as the basis of *assault*, and states that:[27]

> If the threat produces the fear or apprehension of physical violence then I am of the opinion that the law is breached, although the victim does not know when that physical violence may be effected.

To the extent that this suggests that a fear of violence occurring in the remote future is sufficient, then it goes further than other authorities, and seems inconsistent with the generally accepted principle of proximity. This approach seems to have some influence over the Court of Appeal decision in *Ireland*,[28]

21 (1983) 76 Cr App Rep 234.

22 *Ibid*, p 237. Cf *Constanza* [1997] 2 Cr App R 492 – threat by letter.

23 [1970] Crim LR 647. The case concerned an offence under the OAPA, s 20: it would not now be necessary to prove an assault in such a case – see below, p 119.

24 [1997] 4 All ER 225, p 236.

25 [1969] 2 NSWR 451; decided on other grounds by the Privy Council: [1976] AC 104.

26 [1969] 2 NSWR 451, p 455.

27 *Ibid*.

28 [1996] 3 WLR 650, p 652.

leading to a confusion between the immediacy of the contact between the D and the V, and the V's 'immediate' fear, on the one hand, and the fear of the V as to whether violence will 'immediately' follow on the other. In the House of Lords, however, the speeches refer consistently to the need for the V to have a fear that she will suffer violence 'immediately' after the D's actions. This re-establishes without any doubt the orthodox position on this issue, that is that the immediacy refers to the speed with which violence will follow the threat.

The third requirement for the *actus reus* of *assault* is that what should be feared or apprehended by the V is 'unlawful violence' against the V's person.[29] The use of the word 'violence' should not be taken to imply that a high level of injury is involved. Any non-consensual interference with the V's bodily integrity will be sufficient, and reference should be made to the discussion of battery below for the scope of 'violence' in this context. Some confusion has, however, been caused by the decision of the Court of Appeal in *Chan-Fook*[30] that 'psychiatric injury' (though not simply extreme fear or panic) can constitute 'actual bodily harm' for the purposes of s 47 of the OAPA.[31] Although the House of Lords in *Burstow*[32] confirmed *Chan-Fook*, there were passages in the Court of Appeal's judgment in *Ireland*[33] which suggested that they were equating this type of injury with the 'immediate unlawful violence', fear of which is necessary for an assault. This was firmly rejected by the House of Lords in the same case, however. Such psychiatric injury does not constitute a 'battery',[34] nor is it sufficient to constitute the violence needed as part of the definition of an *assault*.[35] What is required is that the V should personal, that is, physical, violence being used against her: in other words, the D's actions cause 'the victim to apprehend an imminent application of force upon her'.[36]

Mens rea

The *mens rea* of *assault* is much more easily dealt with. Since *Venna*,[37] it has been accepted that the prosecution must prove that the D either intended to bring about the *actus reus*, or was reckless as to doing so. That is, the D must

29 If what is feared is violence against a third party, or against property, this will not be an assault, but may involve an offence under the Public Order Act 1986, s 4.

30 [1994] 2 All ER 552.

31 See below, p 114.

32 [1997] 4 All ER 225 – this case was decided together with *Ireland*.

33 [1997] 1 All ER 112, p 118.

34 [1997] 4 All ER 225, p 236, *per* Lord Steyn.

35 *Ibid*, p 240, *per* Lord Hope.

36 *Ibid*, p 236, *per* Lord Steyn.

37 [1975] 3 All ER 788. This, like Ireland, was a case dealing with the OAPA, s 47, but the discussion of the *mens rea* of assault may be taken to be of more general application.

either intend to cause the V to apprehend immediate unlawful violence, or be reckless as to whether that is the consequence of his behaviour. The type of recklessness required is now generally accepted to be *Cunningham* recklessness, rather than *Caldwell* recklessness.[38] The only recent case which supported a test based on *Caldwell* recklessness was the Divisional Court decision in *DPP v K*.[39] This was overruled, however, by the Court of Appeal in *Spratt*.[40] That the test is subjective has also been the view taken other Court of Appeal decisions,[41] and is implicit in the speech of Lord Ackner in the House of Lords in *Savage and Parmenter*.[42] It is, perhaps, unfortunate that he did not address the issue directly. But, in dealing with the mental element required for s 47 of the OAPA,[43] he took it as settled that the mental element of *assault* is derived from *Venna*, which used *Cunningham* as the relevant authority on recklessness. Moreover, in discussing a situation where the D 'neither intends nor adverts to the possibility of' physical contact, he concludes that there would be no offence under s 47 'because there would have been no assault'.[44] Although the point is only made obliquely, it is thus clear that Lord Ackner is using a subjective test of recklessness for *assault*.

What is required, therefore, is that the D realised that his behaviour might cause the V to fear immediate unlawful violence. If no such risk is appreciated by the D, then there will be no liability. To take the facts of *Ireland*, discussed at length above, the V who has been the subject of a series of threatening silent phone calls, may be caused fear simply by the phone ringing. The person who is calling her, however, does not commit an assault, unless he is aware of the effect his action will have on the V.

BATTERY

Whereas the essence of *assault* is the creation of fear or apprehension in the mind of the V, the essence of battery is physical contact (direct or indirect) between the D and the V. As noted above, the word 'assault' is often used to connote both *assault* and battery. This section is, however, concerned solely with battery.

38 For the distinction, see Chapter 2, pp 33–36.

39 [1990] 1 All ER 331. The case is discussed in Chapter 2, p 21.

40 [1991] 2 All ER 210.

41 Eg, *Nash* [1991] Crim LR 768.

42 [1991] 2 All ER 225. This case is discussed further below, in connection with s 20 of the OAPA. See, also, Stone, R, 'Reckless assaults after *Savage and Parmenter*' (1992) 12 OJLS 578, p 582.

43 Assault occasioning actual bodily harm, discussed below, p 114.

44 [1991] 4 All ER 698, p 711.

Actus reus

The definition of the *actus reus* of battery is the application of unlawful force by the D to the V. The D who hits the V with his fist, or a stick, commits battery. No harm to the V is required, however. A mere touching is sufficient to constitute battery. Nor does the V need to be aware of what is about to happen. The D who approaches the V from behind and pats her bottom clearly commits the offence.[45] If he merely touches her shoulder in order to gain her attention, however, there is probably no battery.[46] As was explained by the Divisional Court in *Collins v Wilcock*:[47]

> ... it was held by the Court of Common Pleas in 1807[48] that a touch by a constable's staff on the shoulder of a man who had climbed on a gentleman's railing to gain a better view of a mad ox, the touch being only to engage a the man's attention, did not amount to a battery ... But a distinction is drawn between a touch to draw a man's attention, which is generally acceptable, and a physical restraint, which is not ... Furthermore, persistent touching to gain attention in the face of obvious disregard may transcend the norms of acceptable behaviour, and so be outside the exception.

This exception is probably based on the implied consent of the V, as is the acceptance that the inevitable jostling that occurs in a crowded street, shop, or train, is not an offence. The issue of consent is problematic, however, since it is unclear whether the absence of consent should be regarded as part of the *actus reus*, or whether its presence should constitute an defence to an otherwise valid charge. The current view of the House of Lords, as expressed by the speeches of the majority in *Brown*,[49] is that consent is to be treated as a defence. Detailed discussion of this issue will, therefore, be left until Chapter 7.[50] The point to note here is simply that, although the slightest touch may constitute battery, this does not mean that every contact which forms one of the normal incidents of everyday life will amount to an offence.

It appears that the V's clothes are for these purposes an extension of her person.[51] Thus to grab a sleeve, rather than an arm, may constitute battery. This follows from the *obiter* statement in *Thomas*[52] that 'there could be no dispute that if you touch a person's clothes whilst he is wearing them, that is equivalent to touching him'. In that case, the D was alleged to have touched the bottom hem of the V's skirt, and rubbed it. It was accepted that this could be a battery, though it was not an indecent assault.

45 The D's behaviour may well also constitute an indecent assault: see Chapter 6, p 159.

46 *Collins v Wilcock* [1984] 3 All ER 374, p 378.

47 *Ibid*.

48 Ie, in *Wiffin v Kincard* (1807) 2 Bos & PNR 471.

49 [1993] 2 All ER 75.

50 Chapter 7, p 178.

51 *Day* (1845) 1 Cox CC 207.

52 (1985) 81 Cr App Rep 331, p 334.

As indicated above, a battery can take place by the indirect application of force to the V. A D who fires a stone from a catapult at the V will commit battery if he hits his target. Similarly, if a D pushes V1, who falls against V2, he will commit battery against them both.[53] The question of whether a 'trap' can constitute a battery is less certain. If, for example, the D balances a bucket of water on top of a door, which falls on the V when she opens the door, does this amount to a battery? The case of *DPP v K*[54] would suggest that it does. In that case, the D had poured acid into a hand-drier, which, when operated squirted the acid over the V. It was held that this could amount to an assault for the purposes of s 47 of the OAPA. Since it clearly could not have amounted to an *assault* in the narrow sense, it must have been taken to be a battery. On the other hand, Lord Ackner in *Savage and Parmenter*,[55] noting that Lord Roskill in *Wilson*[56] had held that there could be an infliction of grievous bodily harm under s 20 of the OAPA *without* the need for an assault,[57] used the examples of the infliction of grievous bodily harm by causing panic,[58] or 'interfering with the braking mechanism of a car, so as to cause the driver to be involved in an accident and thus suffer injuries'.[59] If neither of these involves an assault, in the broad sense, then this means that neither involves a battery. The question must be one of the degree of remoteness of the D's acts from the force applied to the V. In relation to the acid in the hand-drier, or the bucket over the door, the force is more direct: the V is injured by the acid, or the bucket. In the case of a D causing panic in a theatre, the resulting 'force' applied to the V will come from the crush of people against each other, or against the exit doors. Similarly, where the D has tampered with the brakes of the V's car, the force will come not from the brakes themselves, but because the car hits some obstacle. It is consistent with this distinction that setting a dog on a person has been said to amount to battery.[60] More dubious is the suggestion that setting a dog on a horse, or striking a horse, and thereby causing the rider to fall, is a battery against the rider.[61] Proximity is probably being stretched to its limits here. A further, though somewhat unlikely, example sometimes given of a 'trap' amounting to a battery is that of the D digging a pit for the V to fall into. In *Martin*,[62] Stephen and Wills JJ thought that this would constitute an assault, and therefore a battery. Since, however,

53 Cf *Mitchell* [1983] 2 All ER 427, discussed in Chapter 4, p 95.

54 [1990] 1 All ER 331.

55 [1991] 4 All ER 698.

56 [1983] 3 All ER 448.

57 *Ibid*, pp 453–54.

58 As, eg, in *Martin* (1881) 8 QBD 54.

59 [1991] 4 All ER 698, p 710.

60 See Smith, JC and Hogan, B, *Criminal Law Cases and Materials*, 6th edn, 1996, London: Butterworths, p 417.

61 *Dodwell v Burford* (1669) 1 Mod 24 – an ancient authority which might, nevertheless, have contemporary relevance in the context of protests about hunting.

the facts of *Martin* itself (causing panic in a theatre, resulting in injury to people attempting to escape) would probably not now be regarded as constituting battery, it may be that the 'pit' example should also be regarded as open to question, and as quite likely being too remote.

The discussion of omissions, in Chapter 2,[63] and in particular the case of *Fagan*,[64] is also relevant to defining the limits of battery. There is authority that for the D simply to stand still and thus obstruct the V, so that the V runs into the D, is not a battery.[65] As Smith and Hogan point out,[66] however, there seems little justification for this limitation, assuming that the D can be proved to have had the relevant *mens rea* when taking the decision not to move out of the V's way.[67] If it were otherwise, the distinction between liability or not would depend simply on whether the V's course led to the D without the D's having to move. If the D steps into the V's path, there is no doubt that this constitutes battery. There seems no reason in principle why liability should depend on the route which the V happened to take. Looked at from the point of view of the interference with the V's rights, the result is the same in both cases, and assuming that the relevant mental responsibility attaches to the D, there seems no reason of policy why the D should not be liable for battery in both cases.

Mens rea

As with assault, the mental element for battery is based on intention, or *Cunningham* recklessness.[68] The consequence that has to be intended or foreseen is the application of force to the body of the V. 'Force' has here, of course, the same meaning as in relation to the *actus reus*, and therefore encompasses all types of touching. The D who throws a snowball in the direction of the V, and is aware that it might hit the V, will technically (and subject to the issue of consent) commit battery if the snowball hits any part of the V. Even if it only strikes the V on the boot, and disintegrates on impact, without causing the V any discomfort, the offence is still committed.

62 (1881) 8 QBD 54.

---

63 Chapter 2, p 16.

64 [1968] 3 All ER 442.

65 *Innes v Wylie* (1844) 1 Car & Kir 257.

66 *Op cit*, Smith and Hogan, fn 60, p 416.

67 This will, of course, be much easier to prove if the D has taken some action to put himself in the V's path.

68 See above, p 109, for the reasons why it is *Cunningham* rather than *Caldwell* recklessness that is relevant.

ASSAULT OCCASIONING ACTUAL BODILY HARM

Section 47 of the OAPA 1861 states that:

> Whosoever shall be convicted on indictment of any assault occasioning actual bodily harm shall be liable ... to imprisonment for not more than five years.

Despite the language of the section, the offence is triable either way.

Actus reus

There are two elements to the *actus reus* of this offence, and both must be proved. First, there must be an assault by the D on the V. Secondly, that assault must have caused actual bodily harm to the V.

In relation to the first element, what is meant is either *assault* or battery (either one being sufficient), as defined in the previous two sections of this chapter. The offence may be committed therefore by a D who either puts the V in fear of immediate unlawful violence, or applies any unlawful force, however, trivial, to the person of the V. If the charge is based on an *assault*, of course, then there will be no need for there to have been any physical contact between the D and the V. Where the D threatens the V, causing her to step backwards, trip over, and bruise her hand, the *actus reus* of the s 47 offence is made out.

As regards the second element, 'actual bodily harm' has never been given a precise definition. It is essentially an issue of fact. The harm can be at quite a low level. Approval was given by some members of the House of Lords in *Brown*[69] to the view of the Court of Appeal in *Donovan*[70] the hurt or injury caused need not be permanent, but must be more than merely transient or trifling. The same line was taken by the Court of Appeal in *Chan-Fook*:[71]

> The word 'harm' is an synonym for injury. The word 'actual' indicates that the injury (although there is no need for it to be permanent) should not be so trivial as to be wholly insignificant.

Thus, to slap a person on the back, through their clothes, is clearly a battery, but is unlikely to involve actual bodily harm. To slap a person in the face, however, may well cause bruising, and thus be within the scope of s 47.[72]

---

69 [1993] 2 All ER 75.

70 [1934] 2 KB 498.

71 [1994] 2 All ER 552, p 557.

72 See, eg, *Taylor v Granville* [1978] Crim LR 482. Note, however, that the Crown Prosecution Service Charging Standards (1996) suggests that minor bruising should normally be charged as common assault under the Criminal Justice Act 1988, s 39.

The main issue before the Court of Appeal in *Chan-Fook* was whether actual bodily harm was limited to *physical* injury, or could encompass affects on the V's mind. The court held that:

> The body of the victim includes all parts of his body, including his organs, his nervous system and his brain. Bodily injury therefore my include injury to any of those parts of his body responsible for his mental and other faculties ...

Accordingly, the phrase 'actual bodily harm' is capable of including psychiatric injury. But, it does not include mere emotions such as fear or distress or panic nor does it include, as such, states of mind that are not in themselves evidence of some identifiable clinical condition.[73]

The House of Lords in *Ireland*[74] approved the decision in *Chan Fook* as being 'based on principled and cogent reasoning', and confirmed that 'bodily harm in ss 18, 20 and 47 [of the OAPA] must be interpreted to include recognisable psychiatric illness'. The emphasis on 'psychiatric illness' means that it is likely, therefore, that if the prosecution is relying on this type of mental injury, it will need to produce medical evidence of the V's condition. Such was the case in *Ireland*[75] where there was psychiatric evidence relating to the effect of the D's silent phone calls on his victims.

The final issue in relation to the *actus reus* is the need to prove that the assault 'occasioned' or 'caused' the actual bodily harm. In most cases, this will not be difficult. There may be problems, however, where the injury suffered by the V is in part attributable to actions taken by the V in response to the assault. The approach to causation in this context is demonstrated by the decision in *Roberts*,[76] which has been discussed in Chapter 2.[77] The case concerned a girl who, having been assaulted by the D, jumped out of his moving car. The test of causation stated by the Court of Appeal was whether the reaction of the V was:

> ... the natural result of what the alleged assailant said and did, in the sense that it was something that could reasonably have been foreseen as the consequence of what he was saying or doing?[78]

This approach was approved by the House of Lords in *Savage and Parmenter*.[79]

---

73 [1994] 2 All ER 552, pp 558–59.

74 [1997] 4 All ER 225. This case has been discussed at length above, p 105, in connection with the definition of an assault.

75 *Ibid*.

76 (1971) 56 Cr App R 95.

77 Chapter 2, p 11.

78 (1972) 56 Cr App R 95, p 102

79 [1991] 4 All ER 698, p 712. For further discussion of causation issues, see Chapter 2, pp 10–16.

Mens rea

The *mens rea* for the s 47 offence is the same as for *assault* or battery. The prosecution must prove that the D intentionally put the V in fear or apprehension of unlawful violence, or intentionally used unlawful force on the V, or was subjectively reckless as to either of these consequences to his behaviour. There is no need to prove any state of mind on the part of the D as regards the causing of actual bodily harm. This was the central issue in *Parmenter*.[80] The D's baby son was injured as a result of the D's rough handling. He was charged under s 20 of the OAPA,[81] with maliciously inflicting grievous bodily harm. He admitted causing the injuries, but claimed they were unintentional, as he did not realise the danger, having no previous experience of dealing with young babies. The judge gave a direction that indicated to the jury that they could convict under s 20 if they felt the D *should* have foreseen the risk of injury to the baby (that is, an objective test). The Court of Appeal held that this was a misdirection in relation to s 20, as the test was the subjective one of whether the D himself realised the risks of some injury to the V. Turning to s 47, the court followed its earlier decision in *Spratt*,[82] which suggested that foresight of the risk of harm following from an assault was a necessary ingredient of the offence. A different view, however, had been taken by the Court of Appeal in *Savage*,[83] which had held that no element of intention or recklessness was required as the actual bodily harm. It was enough that an assault was as a matter of fact followed by such harm. The House of Lords, which considered the appeals in *Savage and Parmenter* together, therefore had to decide between conflicting views of the Court of Appeal on this issue. The House of Lords felt that the approach taken in *Spratt* and *Parmenter* overlooked the effect of the decision in *Roberts*.[84] The Court of Appeal in that case had held that there was no need for the prosecution to prove that the D foresaw that the V might jump from his car as a result of his assault in order for the D to be convicted under s 47. Of course, a totally unforeseeable reaction might break the chain of causation between the assault and the harm (so that the assault no longer 'occasioned' the harm), but otherwise, once an assault was proved from which actual bodily harm resulted then the offence was made out. Thus, the approach taken by the Court of Appeal in *Savage* was to be preferred to that in *Spratt* or *Parmenter*. The prosecution is not obliged to prove that the D intended to cause the V some harm, or was reckless as to whether such harm would be caused, in order to obtain a conviction under s 47.

---

80 [1991] 2 All ER 224, CA; [1991] 4 All ER 698, HL.

81 For which, see below, p 124.

82 [1991] 2 All ER 210. The facts of this case are given below, p 117

83 [1991] 2 All ER 220.

84 (1972) 56 Cr App Rep 95. The facts of this case are given in Chapter 2, p 11.

How would this approach apply in a case such as *Spratt*?[85] In that case, the D had fired an air pistol from his flat. Two pellets struck a girl aged seven playing outside. The D claimed that he had not realised that there were people in the vicinity at the time he fired the airgun, and was adamant that he would not have fired if he had known that there were children in the area. The D pleaded guilty to the s 47 charge following a ruling by the judge that *Caldwell* recklessness was the relevant test. As we have seen, this was reversed by the Court of Appeal, but the House of Lords in *Savage and Parmenter* in its turn overruled the Court of Appeal's view that recklessness as regards actual bodily harm was necessary. Thus, if the D, having the *mens rea* for assault, fired the gun, and someone was injured in a way that was reasonably foreseeable (though not foreseen by the D), then he would be guilty of assault occasioning actual bodily harm. It is by no means clear, however, that the D did have the *mens rea* for assault. As we have seen this covers the *mens rea* for *assault* ('intention to cause the victim to apprehend immediate unlawful violence or recklessness whether such apprehension be caused'), or battery (intention or recklessness as to some application of unlawful force to the victim). The D, however, said that he was unaware that there was anybody in the area into which he fired. He cannot, therefore, have acted intentionally or recklessly as regards causing apprehension; nor can he be said to have intended or been reckless as to the application of unlawful force. As Lord Ackner put it in *Savage and Parmenter*:[86]

> Where the defendant neither intends nor adverts to the possibility that there will be any physical contact at all, then the offence under s 47 would not be made out. That is because there would have been no assault ...

This confirms the point that liability under s 47 depends on the D having the *mens rea* of *assault* or battery. If he has one or the other, and actual bodily harm results from his actions, then it is irrelevant whether he or not he intended or foresaw this consequence. If he has neither, then no offence under s 47 is committed.

The issues which arise from this approach, concerning the fact that the level of offence for which the D may be convicted may depend on the chance outcome of whether the V sustains injuries, and if so their seriousness, are discussed below, in connection with liability under s 20 of the OAPA.[87]

85 [1991] 2 All ER 210.

86 [1991] 4 All ER 698, p 707.

87 See below, p 124.

OTHER AGGRAVATED ASSAULTS

The offence under s 47 is sometimes referred to as an 'aggravated assault', in that it is based on proving an assault which has some feature making it more serious, in this case that it results in actual bodily harm to the V. There are two other offences of this type which should be noted here, namely 'assault with intent to resist arrest', and 'assault on a constable in the execution of his duty'.

Assault with intent to resist arrest

This offence is contained in s 38 of the OAPA 1861:

> Whosoever ... shall assault any person with intent to resist or prevent the lawful apprehension or detainer of himself or any other person for any offence, shall be guilty of a misdemeanour, and being convicted thereof shall be liable, at the discretion of the court, to be imprisoned for any term not exceeding two years ...

The offence is triable either way.

The prosecution needs to prove an assault on the part of the D, and the *actus reus* and *mens rea* for this will be as set out above for *assault* and battery. In addition, the prosecution must prove the further intention as regards resisting arrest, etc. The offence is most likely to be committed by someone trying to escape from the police, or to stop the police arresting a third party, though in theory it could apply to an arrest by any citizen. Questions of mistake of fact may well arise, but these are left for discussion in Chapter 7.[88]

Assaulting a police officer

Section 89(1) of the Police Act 1996 (re-enacting s 51(1) of the Police Act 1964), provides that:

> Any person who assaults a constable in the execution of his duty, or a person assisting a constable in the execution of his duty, shall be guilty of an offence, and liable on summary conviction to a fine not exceeding level 5 on the standard scale or to imprisonment for a term not exceeding six months or to both.

Once again, the *actus reus* and *mens rea* for this offence are those of *assault* or battery. The aggravating element here, that the V of the assault is a constable acting in the execution of his duty, has no *mens rea* element attached to it. Much case law on this section concerns the question of whether the constable was acting in the execution of his duty at the relevant time. If, for example, the

88 See Chapter 7, p 174.

constable has been told to leave private premises, and has no lawful reason to remain, the V who uses force in ejecting the constable will not commit the offence under s 91.[89] The issue is, however, whether the constable is acting in the execution of his duty, not whether the D thinks that he is. There is generally no need for the prosecution to prove intention or recklessness as regards this element of the offence. On the other hand, in certain circumstances the D may be able to raise a mistake of fact as a 'defence'.[90] The mistaken belief that the person exercising a power is not a police officer may mean that force used by the D is not unlawful. The mistake means, therefore, that there is no assault. In effect, if evidence is given to suggest that this was the D's view of the facts, the prosecution will have to prove that he did in fact know that he was dealing with a police officer. This issue (that is, the significance of mistakes made by the D) is discussed further in Chapter 7.[91]

MALICIOUSLY WOUNDING OR INFLICTING GRIEVOUS BODILY HARM

The next most serious offence in the OAPA 1861 after s 47 (assault occasioning bodily harm) is contained in s 20, which states:

> Whosoever shall unlawfully and maliciously wound or inflict any grievous bodily harm upon any other person, either with or without any weapon or instrument, shall be guilty of a misdemeanour, and being convicted thereof shall be liable ... to imprisonment ... for not more than five years.

The offence is triable either way. It will be noted that the maximum penalty is the same as for an offence under s 47. This is an anomaly, since there is no doubt that s 20 is concerned with a more serious offence, generally involving a more extensive infringement with the V's rights. We shall also see, however, that in some circumstances a D who has inflicted grievous bodily harm on the V can only be convicted under s 47, because he does not have the *mens rea* for the s 20 offence. In such a case the infringement of the V's rights is the same, and it might be argued that sentencing powers available to the judge should be equivalent. The argument is a weak one, however, and gives only a spurious justification to what must in the end be accepted as an unsatisfactory aspect of the law of non-fatal offences.[92]

---

89 See, eg, *Davis v Lisle* [1936] 2 All ER 213. For further discussion of police powers, see, eg, Stone, *Textbook on Civil Liberties*, 2nd edn, 1997, Blackstone, London: Chapters 2–4.

90 See, eg, *Williams (Gladstone)* [1987] 3 All ER 411; *Beckford v R* [1987] 3 All ER 425; *Blackburn v Bowering* [1994] 3 All ER 380.

91 Chapter 7, p 174.

92 See, also, Stone, R, 'Reckless assaults after *Savage and Parmenter*' (1992) 12 OJLS 578, pp 584–85.

Actus reus

The *actus reus* of s 20 may be committed in two main ways: first by 'wounding' the V; secondly, by 'inflicting grievous bodily harm' on the V. It is important to note the separateness of these two ways of committing the offence. It is not necessary for a wound to cause grievous bodily harm in order for the offence to be committed; likewise grievous bodily harm may be inflicted without the D's skin being broken. The precise definition of 'wound' and 'inflict grievous bodily harm' will therefore be considered in turn.

The definition of a 'wound' is mainly to be found in 19th century cases, but the general approach was confirmed by the Divisional Court in *JCC v Eisenhower*.[93] Thus, what is required is that there should be a break in the continuity of the whole skin (not the mere cuticle or upper skin).[94] A blow which causes simply internal bleeding will not constitute a wound. Thus, in *JCC v Eisenhower*, the V had been hit by an air gun pellet near his eye, but his skin had not been broken. There was evidence, however, that the blow had caused the rupture of one or more internal blood vessels. This was held not to constitute a wound for the purposes of s 20.[95] The application of this test is in most cases likely to be straightforward. Some difficulties may arise in relation to the distinction between 'internal' and 'external' bleeding. Thus, it has been held that a break in the lining of the urethra,[96] or the skin inside the mouth,[97] does constitute a wound. The same would presumably also be true of a similar breach to the lining of the nose, ear passages, vagina or rectum. There is no authority, however, supporting the view which might well follow from this, that a blow to the nose which causes it to bleed amounts to a 'wounding'.

The second way in which the *actus reus* of the offence under s 20 may be caused is by the 'infliction' of grievous bodily harm. 'Grievous bodily harm' has been stated by the House of Lords in *DPP v Smith*[98] to be synonymous with 'really serious harm'. The lack of a definition means that it will in the end be a decision for the jury as to whether the V's injuries fall into this category. There is no need for the injury to be life-threatening, so that a broken leg, or a severed finger, could come into this category, as well as serious internal injuries. Note that a wound, if serious enough, may also amount to grievous bodily harm. As we have seen, it was held in *Chan-Fook*[99] and *Ireland*[100] that

93 [1983] 3 All ER 230.

94 *Wood* (1830) 1 Mood 278; *Moriarty v Brooks* (1834) 6 C&P 684; *M'Loughlin* (1838) 8 C&P 635; *Beckett* (1836) 1 M&Rob 526.

95 Serious internal bleeding may, of course, be evidence that the V has suffered grievous bodily harm.

96 *Waltham* (1849) 3 Cox 442.

97 *Shadbolt* (1835) 5 C&P 504.

98 [1960] 3 All ER 161.

99 [1994] 2 All ER 552.

100 [1997] 4 All ER 225.

actual bodily harm could include psychiatric injury. In *Burstow*,[101] the House of Lords accepted that severe psychiatric illness, such as 'severe endogenous depression', could amount to grievous bodily harm.

It is not necessary in relation to either a wounding, or the infliction of grievous bodily harm, that the prosecution should prove that there was an assault by the D. The 19th century case of *Clarence*,[102] where the D infected his wife with gonorrhoea, held that the use of the word 'inflict' in s 20 meant that an assault was required, so that the D could not be convicted of this offence. This view was rejected by the House of Lords in *Wilson*,[103] which, following the Australian case of *Salisbury*,[104] held that 'inflict' does not necessarily mean 'assault', though there was some suggestion that it might require at least the indirect application of force to the V's body. The *Wilson* approach was confirmed by the House of Lords in *Savage and Parmenter*.[105] One of the questions considered by the House of Lords was:

> Is a verdict of guilty of assault occasioning actual bodily harm a permissible alternative verdict on a count of alleging unlawful wounding contrary to s 20 of the 1861 Act?

Lord Ackner considered the speech of Lord Roskill in *Wilson* at some length, and then commented:[106]

> Having reviewed the relevant authorities, Lord Roskill was content to accept that there can be infliction of grievous bodily harm contrary to s 20 without an assault being committed. For example, grievous bodily harm could be inflicted by causing panic. Another example provided to your Lordships in the course of the argument in the current appeals was interfering with the braking mechanism of a car, so as to cause the driver to be involved in an accident and thus suffer injuries.

In other words, 'inflicting' is effectively the same as 'causing',[107] and 'wounding' means 'cause a wound', not 'wound by means of an assault'. Nevertheless, Lord Ackner regarded situations in which the distinction would be significant as likely to be rare:

> The allegation of inflicting grievous bodily harm or for that matter wounding ... inevitably imports or includes an allegation of assault, unless there are some quite extraordinary facts.

---

101 Reported with *Ireland* [1997] 4 All ER 225.

102 (1888) 22 QBD 23.

103 [1983] 3 All ER 448.

104 [1976] VR 452

105 [1991] 4 All ER 698.

106 *Ibid*, p 710.

107 See *Mandair* [1994] 2 All ER 715, where the House of Lords approved a verdict of 'causing grievous bodily harm, contrary to s 20'.

One such rare occasion apparently occurred, however, in *Burstow*.[108] The D had 'stalked' the V, with whom he had had a brief social relationship, over a period of some years, harassing her with telephone calls, letters and photographs, and frequent visits to her home. Although there had been no application of physical violence directly, or indirectly, to the V, the Court of Appeal confirmed that the D could be charged with inflicting grievous bodily harm under s 20, because of the psychiatric injury which the V suffered as a result of his behaviour. It is, however, arguable on the basis of *Ireland* that there were in this case one or more *assaults* on the V. She was almost certainly put in fear of unlawful violence by the D's behaviour. Provided that the test of 'immediacy' was satisfied,[109] the elements of an *assault* would seem to be present. Nevertheless, the House of Lords, in confirming the Court of Appeal's decision in *Burstow*, re-affirmed that the offence under s 20 'can be committed where no physical violence is applied directly or indirectly to the body of the victim'.[110] Lord Steyn once again reviewed the earlier authorities. The only case which caused him any difficulty was *Clarence*. He concluded, however, that this decision 'no longer assists', since at the time it was decided the possibility of causing or inflicting *psychiatric* injury was not under consideration.[111] The criminal law has moved on since then, and the developing understanding of the link between the body and psychiatric injury meant that it is no longer necessary to insist that infliction required an assault.

To summarise, the position as regards the *actus reus* of s 20 is that it is enough that the D's behaviour caused a wound or serious bodily harm, and no direct or indirect application of physical violence to the V is necessary. On the other hand, if the harm suffered by the V does not reach the necessary level of seriousness, it will generally be permissible to convict of the lesser offence of s 47, assault occasioning actual bodily harm, since it will be rare that the facts leading to a charge under s 20 do not also involve an assault or battery.

Mens rea

The *mens rea* for the offence under s 20 is stated to be 'maliciousness'. This has been held to mean intention or *Cunningham* recklessness. The leading authority on the mental element required for s 20 is the House of Lords decision in *Savage and Parmenter*.[112] One of the issues before the House of Lords concerned the *extent* of the intention or foresight required to be proved

108 Reported with *Ireland* [1997] 4 All ER 225.

109 See above, p 107.

110 [1997] 4 All ER 225, p 231.

111 *Ibid*, p 235.

112 [1991] 4 All ER 6980.

by the prosecution. Did the prosecution have to prove that the D intended, or foresaw the risk of, a wound or grievous bodily harm, or was it enough that the D intended or foresaw the risk of some harm? Lord Ackner confirmed the view expressed by the Court of Appeal in *Mowatt*,[113] that the latter state of mind was sufficient. He quoted with approval the following passage from Diplock LJ:[114]

> It is quite unnecessary that the accused should have foreseen that his unlawful act might cause physical harm of the gravity described in the section, ie, a wound or serious physical injury. It is enough that he should have foreseen that some physical harm to some person, albeit of a minor character, might result.

This particular phraseology, although perfectly clear in its context, has caused some confusion when quoted in isolation, because of its use of the construction 'should have foreseen'. Some judges and commentators have read this as meaning 'ought to have foreseen'. Indeed, at least one commentator has referred to Lord Ackner's adoption of this passage in *Savage and Parmenter* as a 'slip',[115] since it appears to state an objective test of foresight. In fact, however, Diplock LJ is using the subjunctive, as the context makes clear, and the test is whether the D *did* foresee the particular consequence, not whether he ought to have foreseen it. Diplock LJ is using the phrase as it might be used in the following situation:

> To be buried in sacred ground, it is not necessary that the deceased should have been a member of the Church of England; it is enough that he should have been a member of some Christian faith.[116]

The test is, therefore, whether the D intended, or foresaw, that his actions might cause some harm to the V. It is this requirement of intention or foresight as to some harm that provides the main distinction between s 20 and s 47. As we have seen, it is not necessary for liability under s 47 that the D intends or foresees any harm resulting from his actions; it is enough that actual bodily harm results from his assault.

In considering the relationship between ss 47 and 20, Lord Ackner, in *Savage and Parmenter*,[117] quoted with approval the comment by Professor Smith that the 1861 Act 'is a rag-bag of offences brought together from a wide variety of sources with no attempt, as the draftsman frankly acknowledged, to introduce consistency as to substance or form'.[118] It is thus pointless to seek for complete rationality between liability and penalty in relation to the various

113 [1967] 3 All ER 47.

114 *Ibid*, p 50.

115 *Op cit*, Smith and Hogan, fn 60, p 97.

116 NB: this is not intended to be an accurate statement of canon law, merely an example of the use of a grammatical construction.

117 [1991] 4 All ER 698, p 721.

118 Smith, JC, 'Commentary on the Court of Appeal's decision in *Parmenter*' [1991] Crim LR 43.

offences. The fact that s 47 and s 20 carry the same maximum penalty does not prevent s 20 being regarded as more serious, and requiring a greater degree of intention or foresight on the part of the D as to the consequences of his actions.

What then is the consequence of the differing requirements in relation to ss 47 and 20? How do they apply in different factual situations? Consider the following:

(a) the D assaults the V, but does not intend or foresee any bodily harm. However serious the V's injuries, the D can only be convicted of the s 47 offence;[119]

(b) the D assaults the V, foreseeing the risk of slight harm. The D's liability will depend on the extent of the V's injuries. If they are slight, the D will be liable under s 47. If they are serious, or include a wound, the D will be liable under s 20;

(c) the D, without committing an assault, causes harm to the V. The D cannot be liable under s 47 (because there is no assault). If the harm is serious, or includes a wound, and the D can be shown to have intended or foreseen the risk of some harm, he will be liable under s 20.

As will be seen from these examples, the D's liability depends not only on his intentions and foresight, but also on consequences which may be unforeseen and fortuitous. Can this be justified? It is difficult to do so considering liability purely from the point of view of the D. It is arguable that a sensible relationship between the two offences under s 20 and s 47 should depend on a distinction based on the D's moral responsibility, which in turn should be based on the consequences which the D foresaw as likely to result from his actions.[120] The more serious the consequences foreseen, the more serious the offence. On the other hand, if an approach is used which gives weight to the extent of infringement of the V's rights as an element in the D's liability, as has been suggested in Chapter 1,[121] then the current state of the law becomes more acceptable. The fact that the D1's behaviour has caused more serious injuries to the V1, than the D2's has to the V2, is a justification for convicting the D1 of a more serious offence, even if the *mens rea* of the D1 and the D2 is identical. The same justification may be used in relation to the fact that a D who intends to cause grievous bodily harm, and does so, is guilty of an offence under s 18 of the OAPA, whereas a D who intends to cause grievous bodily harm and kills, is liable for murder.

119 Of course, if the V's injuries do not amount even to actual bodily harm, the D will only be liable for assault or battery.

120 See *op cit*, Stone, fn 92, p 584.

121 See Chapter 1, p 2.

WOUNDING OR CAUSING GRIEVOUS BODILY HARM WITH INTENT

Section 18 of the 1861 Act states that:

> Whosoever shall unlawfully and maliciously by any means whatsoever wound or cause any grievous bodily harm to any person ... with intent ... to do some grievous bodily harm to any person, or with intent to resist or prevent the lawful apprehension or detainer of any person, shall be guilty of an offence, and being convicted thereof shall be liable ... to imprisonment for life ...

Offences under s 18 are indictable.

As will be seen, s 18 contains four offences or, perhaps more accurately, two methods of committing two offences,[122] namely:

(a) wounding with intent to do grievous bodily harm;

(b) wounding with intent to resist arrest;

(c) causing grievous bodily harm with intent to do so;

(d) causing grievous bodily harm with intent to resist arrest.

The *actus reus* and *mens rea* of these offences will now be considered, with the lettering above being used to indicate the different ways of incurring liability.

Actus reus

'Wounding' and 'grievous bodily harm' have the same meaning as under s 20. 'Resisting the lawful apprehension or detainer of any person', in offences (b) and (d) should be approached in the same way as the offence under s 38 of the OAPA, considered above.[123]

It will be noted that this section refers to 'causing' rather than 'inflicting' grievous bodily harm. This distinction from the wording used in s 20 is, however, no longer of any significance, given that, as we have seen, it has been held that an assault is not necessary for the s 20 offence. The breadth of the s 18 offence is nevertheless emphasised by the words 'by any means whatsoever'. Provided there is a sufficient causal link between the D's behaviour and the harm suffered by the V, then the *actus reus* will be committed. The general issues of causation, and liability for omissions, discussed in Chapter 2,[124] will of course be relevant here.

---

122 *Naismith* [1961] 2 All ER 735 – holding that a count is not bad for duplicity if it specifies the alternatives of 'intent to do grievous bodily harm' and 'intent to resist lawful apprehension'.

123 See above, p 118.

124 Chapter 2, p 10 *et seq*.

Mens rea

There are two elements to the *mens rea* of s 18 offences. First, the *actus reus* must be committed 'maliciously'. Secondly, it must be committed with intent to produce one of two consequences.

The word 'maliciously' is to be interpreted in the same way here as in relation to s 20. That is, it means the D must intend, or be subjectively reckless, as to the causing of the wound, or some harm (not necessarily serious harm), to the V. Of course, if the offence is charged is in the form of (c), above, then the word 'maliciously' and the *mens rea* implied by it, is redundant. It is absorbed into the requirement that the D intended grievous bodily harm when causing the *actus reus*. If the charge is on any of the other three bases, however, then the prosecution will have to prove both that the D acted 'maliciously' as regards the *actus reus*, and also had the relevant 'ulterior' intent.

The two intentions – to cause grievous bodily harm, or to resist lawful apprehension – are referred to as 'ulterior', because they go beyond what is required in terms of the actus reus. The D may cause V a wound which is relatively minor, and which would certainly not in itself amount to grievous bodily harm; if, however, the prosecution can prove that the D acted with the intention of causing the V serious injury, then the offence under section 18 is made out. The proof of intention will be approached in the same way as in relation to murder.[125] In other words, the prosecution will have to prove either that the D desired the consequence, or that he saw it as virtually certain. If the latter state of mind is proved, then the jury may (not must) find that the D intended the consequence.

The offences under s 18 will therefore apply in the following ways:

(a) the D, who is trying to kill the V, hits her over the head. If the V suffers serious injury (for example, a cracked skull), D is liable for the offence of causing grievous bodily harm with intent to cause grievous bodily harm.[126] If the V is less seriously injured, the D will be liable for the s 47 offence;

(b) D1, who is trying to enable D2 to escape from the police, shoots at police officer, causing her a minor flesh wound. D1 is liable under s 18 for wounding with intent to prevent lawful apprehension (of D2) (or, possibly, with intent to cause grievous bodily harm);

(c) the D, who wishes to frighten the V, sets her house on fire. Unknown to the D, the V is in the house at the time, and suffers serious injuries. The D is almost certainly not liable under s 18 (no intent to cause grievous bodily

---

125 See Chapter 2, p 24 *et seq*. Authority for the proposition in the text is provided by *Purcell* (1986) 83 Cr App Rep 45; *Bryson* [1985] Crim LR 669.

126 The D may also be liable for attempted murder – see below, p 127.

harm).[127] He may be liable under s 20, if he can be said to have been subjectively reckless as to the causing of some injury (not necessarily to the V). If he states that he foresaw no risk of injury, and the prosecution fails to prove otherwise, he will not be liable for any offence against the person, but may be liable for an offence under s 1 of the Criminal Damage Act 1971.[128]

ATTEMPTED MURDER

The offence of attempted murder covers three possible situations. One is where the D, intending to kill the V totally fails in the attempt, because, for example, he is arrested before he can complete his plan, or he shoots but misses his target. The second is where the V has died, and there is some evidence that the D intended her death, but it is impossible to establish that the D's actions were the cause of death. This is most likely to arise in 'mercy-killing' cases.[129] The third situation is where the D causes the V to suffer some harm, possibly very serious harm, but does not kill her. It is this situation (which is probably the most common one in which this offence is charged), which provides the justification for dealing with this offence in this chapter. In other words, attempted murder is a charge which may be available where the V has been on the receiving end of an assault[130] which has resulted in injury, but not death.

Actus reus

The approach here is the same as for all other attempts – that is, the D must have acted in a way which was 'more than merely preparatory' towards committing the offence.[131] This requirement will provide no difficulty where the D has violently assaulted the V, nor where an attempt to kill has been carried out, but has for some other reason proved unsuccessful. It is only where the D has abandoned the enterprise, or has been arrested prior to completing the attempt, that the issue will need consideration. If it does, then the approach will be as discussed in Chapter 3.[132]

---

127 Cf *Nedrick* [1986] 3 All ER 1. Discussed in Chapter 2, p 29.

128 Recklessly endangering life by intentionally causing criminal damage – the recklessness here is objective.

129 See, eg, *Arthur* (1981) 12 BMLR 1.

130 Or, indeed, other action by the D, short of an assault.

131 For detailed discussion of this issue, see Chapter 3, pp 48–52.

132 *Ibid*.

An example of the use of an attempted murder in the context of a non-fatal violent assault is to be found in *Walker and Hayles*.[133] The Ds visited the V who was the ex-boyfriend of a sister of one of the Ds. The V was asked to hand over the key to the woman's flat. A fight followed, in the course of which the V suffered a head wound. The fight culminated in the V being thrown from a third floor balcony. The V somehow survived. There was evidence that in the course of the fight one of the Ds had threatened the V with a knife, and that just before V was thrown one of the Ds had said: 'You deserve to die. I am going to kill you. We don't like you.' The V was found lying on the ground, bleeding and in pain. The report does not, however, indicate that his injuries were life-threatening. If the V had suffered relatively minor injuries, the only substantive offence with which the Ds could be charged would be s 47. This charge might well be thought not to reflect appropriately the seriousness of the Ds behaviour. Even if a charge under s 18 were possible, which in the case of *Walker and Hayles* was possible because of the head wound,[134] it might be thought that the Ds aim of bringing about the Vs death should be reflected in the charge, to distinguish it from the case where serious injury is intended, but no more.[135] The Ds were charged with attempted murder. There is no doubt that if the Ds were trying to kill the V when they threw him over the balcony, they had committed the *actus reus* of the offence. The basis of the Ds appeal against conviction, was on the issue of *mens rea*, which is discussed below.

Mens rea

The *mens rea* of all attempts is the intention to bring about the *actus reus* of the substantive offence. The *actus reus* of murder is the acceleration of the death of the V. That is what must be intended for the offence of attempted murder. In *Whybrow*,[136] the D was alleged to have tried to kill his wife, with whom he was 'on bad terms', by electrocuting her while she was taking a bath. He had apparently wired the metal soap dish to the mains. His wife received an electric shock, but did not suffer serious injury. The D was convicted of attempted murder. His appeal was successful because the judge had directed the jury on the basis of the *mens rea* required for murder – that is, an intent to kill *or cause grievous bodily harm*. For attempted murder only, an intention to kill will suffice. Lord Goddard explained the point as follows:[137]

> It may be said that the law ... is somewhat illogical in saying that, if one attacks a person intending to do grievous bodily harm and death results, that is

133 (1990) 90 Cr App Rep 226.

134 Ie, the Ds were also charged with wounding with intent to cause GBH.

135 Though of course, if serious injury is intended, and death results (even if not intended), the D will be guilty of murder: Chapter 4, p 63.

136 (1951) 35 Cr App Rep 141.

137 *Ibid*, p 147.

> murder, but that if one attacks a person and only intends to do grievous bodily harm, and death does not result, it is not attempted murder, but wounding[138] with intent to do grievous bodily harm. It is not really illogical because in that particular case, the intent is the essence of the crime, while, where the death of another is caused, the necessity is to prove malice aforethought, which is supplied in law by proving intent to do grievous bodily harm.

A further issue relating to the intention necessary for attempted murder was considered in *Walker and Hayles*. It might be thought that the issue was relatively straightforward on the facts of this case, since if it was accepted that the statement quoted above was made by the Ds, then they would seem to clearly have had the desire, and therefore the intention, to kill the V. The jury, however, having been given a direction along the lines that they could convict if they thought that the Ds were 'trying to kill' the V, sought further clarification. The judge at that point decided to give a direction dealing with the possibility of inferring intention from foresight.[139] He told the jury that they could infer intention if the death of the V was a highly probable consequence of the Ds actions, and the Ds 'knew quite well that in doing [what they did] there was a high probability' of such a consequence.[140] It was argued on appeal that this direction was too favourable to the prosecution, particularly since *Nedrick*[141] indicated that it was only where a consequence was 'virtually certain' (rather than 'highly probable'), and foreseen as such, that intention could be inferred. The Court of Appeal rejected this argument. Taking into account the views of the House of Lords in *Hancock and Shankland*,[142] as well as those of the Court of Appeal in *Nedrick*, it was not wrong (though probably undesirable) to refer to a 'very high degree of probability' rather than a 'virtual certainty' as providing the basis for an inference of intention. This view must now be considered in the light of *Woollin*, discussed in Chapter 2,[143] where the House of Lords, in discussing the *mens rea* of murder rejected the judge's use of 'substantial risk' as the test, preferring *Nedrick*'s 'virtual certainty'. It is this phrase which should it is submitted also be used in directing a jury on attempted murder. Similarly, the judge should refer to the juries entitlement to 'find', rather than to 'infer' intention.

The decision in *Walker and Hayles*, nevertheless, makes it clear that as far as intention in attempts is concerned, the same test should be applied as in relation to 'intention' in other areas of the criminal law. It is not necessary to prove that the D *desired* a consequence in order to convict of an attempt in

138 Or causing grievous bodily harm.

139 See Chapter 2, pp 25–32.

140 (1990) 90 Cr App Rep 226, p 229.

141 [1986] 3 All ER 1; see Chapter 2, p 29.

142 [1986] 1 All ER 641; see Chapter 2, p 28.

143 See Chapter 2, p 31.

relation to it, though that often will be the situation. Thus the D who belabours his V around the head with an axe, and claims that he only intended to cause her grievous bodily harm, may nevertheless be guilty of attempted murder if the jury feel that he must have realised that death was a virtually certain consequence, and that it is thus proper to find that he intended her death. The problem for the prosecution in this situation is, however, arguing that something which has not in fact occurred (that is, the death of the victim) was nevertheless a virtually certain consequence of the D's actions. For this reason, the broader approach to intention may in fact be more likely to be used in situations where the attempt from an incomplete or frustrated enterprise on the part of the D, rather than an attack which has been completed, but which has not proved fatal.

Other offences under the OAPA 1861

In addition to the offences discussed above, there are a number of other non-fatal offences under the Offences Against the Person Act 1861 which require consideration. They are dealt with basically in the order in which they appear within the Act, though there is also some grouping according to topic.

Threats to kill: s 16

This section makes it an offence, triable either way, to make, without lawful excuse, a threat to kill the person to whom the threat is addressed (V) or a third party.[144] The *mens rea* required is that the D intends that the V should fear that the threat would be carried out. It is not strictly part of the *actus reus* that the V believes the threat, as long as the D intends that she should. This distinguishes the offence from *assault*, where fear or apprehension on the part of the V is required. There is nothing to suggest that the threat needs to be accompanied by an action: words are sufficient. Moreover, it would seem that the threat does not need to be made in person, but can be transmitted through any medium – for example, a letter, phone call, fax, or e-mail.

A lawful excuse would arise where, for example, the threat is made in self-defence. A woman who fears she is about to be raped might, for example, threaten to kill her prospective attacker, but would not by so doing commit the offence under s 16.

The offence carries a maximum penalty on indictment of 10 years imprisonment. It is, therefore, potentially more serious than an offence under s 47 or s 20 of the OAPA, despite the fact that the V may suffer no harm at all (particularly if the threat is not believed).

144 A 'third party' does not include an unborn foetus: *Tait* [1990] 1 QB 290.

Attempted choking: s 21

The *actus reus* of this indictable offence can be committed in two ways: first by actually attempting to choke, suffocate or strangle the V; secondly by attempting to render the V 'insensible, unconscious or incapable of resistance'. In the second case, the attempt must be carried out by means calculated to choke, suffocate or strangle the V. The difference presumably relates to the D's intention. In the first case, the D is trying to choke, suffocate and strangle; in the second, these consequences may be the incidental result of the D's intention of rendering the V unconscious or incapable of resistance. There is no need, however, in the second case for the prosecution to prove an intention to choke, suffocate or strangle the V.[145]

It is presumed that 'attempt' will be interpreted in the same way as the general law of attempts, and will therefore mean doing something 'more than merely preparatory' towards the achievement of the D's objective.[146]

A further *mens rea* element is that the attempt must be carried out with the intention of enabling the D or another to commit an indictable offence, or of assisting another to commit such an offence. It would apply to a D who grabbed a guard round the throat in order to prevent him giving the alarm in relation to a burglary being carried out by the D's accomplice; or to a D who puts his arm across the throat of the V whom he is planning to rape in order to stop her calling for help.

The offence is punishable with a maximum of life imprisonment, and is therefore as serious as attempted murder (which may well be an alternative charge on facts falling within the scope of s 21).

Use of chloroform or other stupefying drugs: s 22

This offence, like that under s 21, deals with means used against a V to enable an indictable offence to be committed. It covers the unlawful application or administration to the V, or the causing of the V to take, 'chloroform, laudanum, or other stupefying or overpowering drug, matter, or thing'. The actus reus may also be committed by an attempt to cause such a substance to be administered to, or taken by, the V. The latter form of the *actus reus* would cover, for example, the spiking of drink, food, or medication which was discovered before being consumed by the V. The definition of the substances which may be used to effect the *actus reus* is wide, and could certainly cover alcohol. Plying the V with alcoholic drinks in order to make her sufficiently inebriated that she does not realise that the D is committing an offence (for example, the theft of money or keys from the V's bag) would certainly fall within the section.

145 It is assumed here that 'calculated' means 'objectively likely', rather than 'intended'.
146 See Chapter 3, pp 48–52.

As with s 21, the prosecution must also prove that the D had the ulterior intention of enabling himself or another to commit an indictable offence, or of assisting another to commit such an offence.

The maximum penalty is life imprisonment, despite the fact that the harm to the V may be slight, or non-existent (in relation to the 'attempt' mode of committing the offence).

Administering poison, or other noxious substance: ss 23, 24

Sections 23 and 24 both deal with the administration of poison, or other noxious substances, to the V. They are distinguished by the level of seriousness of the offence, with s 23 carrying a maximum of 10 years imprisonment, but s 24 only five years.

The *actus reus* of both offences requires the prosecution to prove that the D 'unlawfully and maliciously' administered to, or caused to be administered to or taken by the V, 'any poison, or other destructive or noxious thing'. The meaning of 'administer' was considered in *Gillard*,[147] where it was held by the Court of Appeal that it was wide enough to cover:

> ... conduct which not being the application of direct physical force to the victim nevertheless brings the noxious thing into direct physical contact with his body.

Thus, in that case, spraying CS gas into the face of the victim could amount to 'administering' a noxious substance.

In relation to s 23, the prosecution must also prove either that the V's life was thereby endangered, or that she suffered grievous bodily harm. Whether a substance is 'noxious' is a question of fact for the jury, and they may have to take into account the quantities administered. Although the fact that something which is in common use (such as medicine for insomnia) is *potentially* harmful if given in sufficiently large quantities will not make it noxious,[148] if the D has in fact administered it in such quantities to have that effect this will entitle the jury to find that it was in the circumstances noxious.[149]

The *mens rea* of both offences involves proof that the D acted 'maliciously'. In *Cunningham*,[150] it was held that this means that it must be proved that the D either intended the relevant consequences of his actions, or was aware of the risk of those consequences occurring.

147 (1988) 87 Cr App Rep 189.

148 *Cato* [1976] 1 All ER 260; though in *Cato* itself the substance was heroin, which the court viewed as a noxious substance whatever the quantities involved.

149 *Marcus* [1981] 2 All ER 833. Cf *Weatherall* [1968] Crim LR 115 where the trial judge ruled that two-thirds of a sleeping tablet in a cup of tea did not constitute a noxious substance.

150 [1957] 2 All ER 412. The case is discussed further in Chapter 2, with reference to the concept of recklessness which is derived from it: see pp 33–34.

In relation to s 23, the wording could be read as requiring the proof of 'maliciousness' as regards all elements of the *actus reus* – that is, both the administration, etc, of the substance, and the consequences suffered by the D. It was held in *Cato*,[151] however, that it is only in relation to the first part that intention or recklessness need be proved. Thus, the D who deliberately administers a poisonous substance to the V cannot escape liability by claiming that he did not realise that it would endanger the V's life, or cause her serious bodily harm, if that is in fact its effect.

By contrast, in s 24 it is explicit that in addition to the maliciousness as regards the administration of the substance, an ulterior intention must be proved. This is that the D intended to 'injure, aggrieve or annoy' the V. An intention to injure must involve an intention to cause some physical harm. Thus the intention of keeping the V awake is not in itself an intention injure.[152] Nor will an intention to make the V sleepy while the D searches her handbag apparently fall within the scope of any of the intentions required for s 24.[153]

Offences involving explosives or other noxious substances: ss 28–30

Section 28 contains an offence relating to the causation of injury by explosives. Sections 29 and 30 deal with the situation where the D has an intention to cause serious bodily harm with explosives or other noxious substances, but does not necessarily succeed in this aim. All three offences are indictable: ss 28 and 29 are punishable with a maximum of life imprisonment; s 30 with a maximum of 14 years.

The *actus reus* of the offence under s 28 is the burning, maiming, disfiguring, disabling or doing of any grievous bodily harm to the V, by means of an unlawful explosion of gunpowder, or other explosive substance. The requirement of unlawfulness presumably means that the licensed use of explosives for mining, quarrying, etc, would not come within the section. The *mens rea* of the offence is that the D acted maliciously. In other words, he must have intended, or foreseen the risk of, some injury to the V. By analogy with s 20,[154] it is assumed that the D does not have to foresee serious injury.

For s 29, the *actus reus* may be committed in a number of ways:

(i) causing gunpowder, or other explosive substance, to explode;

(ii) sending or delivering to the V any explosive or other dangerous or noxious thing;

(iii) causing the V to take or receive any explosive or other dangerous or noxious thing;

151 [1976] 1 All ER 260.

152 *Hill* (1986) 83 Cr App Rep 386, HL.

153 *Weatherall* [1968] Crim LR 115 (trial judge's ruling).

154 See above, p 122.

(iv) putting or laying at any place any corrosive fluid, or destructive or explosive substance;

(v) casting or throwing at or upon, or applying to, the V any corrosive fluid, or destructive or explosive substance.

The action must in each case be 'unlawful'. No harm to any V need result from these actions in order for the offence to be made out. The D can be liable whether or not the V suffers any injury.

The *mens rea* is that the D must commit the *actus reus* 'maliciously', that is with intention or foresight. In addition, the prosecution must prove that the D had the ulterior intent to 'burn, maim, disfigure, or disable any person, or to do some grievous bodily harm to any person'.

The *actus reus* of s 30 is committed by a D who places or throws any gunpowder or other explosive substance in, into, upon, against, or near any building, ship or vessel. As with ss 28 and 29, the action must be unlawful. There is no need for any explosion to take place, or for anyone to be injured in order for the D to be liable.

The *mens rea*, as with s 29, is that the D must commit the *actus reus* 'maliciously'. In addition the prosecution must prove that the D had the ulterior intent to do some bodily injury to any person.

Setting of spring-guns, man-traps and other engines: s 31

The common law allows the occupier of premises to use reasonable force to expel or repel trespassers, the level of force being determined by the circumstances. A landowner is not, however, generally allowed to set up lethal booby-traps. This general principle of the civil law is reinforced by the specific offence under s 31 of the OAPA, which criminalises the setting of spring guns, man traps, etc. in certain situations.

The *actus reus* is committed by setting or placing, or causing to be set or placed, 'any spring-gun, man-trap, or other engine calculated to destroy human life or inflict grievous bodily harm'. The wide scope of this is then narrowed by the proviso that it does not apply to customary action taken with the intention of destroying vermin. Nor does it apply to such devices which are intended for the protection of a dwelling house, between the hours of sunset and sunrise. Subject to these provisos, the *actus reus* may also be committed by an occupier coming into possession of land containing such devices, who 'knowingly and wilfully' allows them to remain in place. The meaning of 'engine' in this section was considered in *Munks*.[155] The Court of Appeal held that it meant a 'mechanical contrivance'. An arrangement of wires which was designed to give an intruder an electric shock if on touching

155 [1964] 1 QB 304.

one of them, was not, therefore, an 'engine', and did not fall within the scope of the section.

There is no specific *mens rea* element attached to this offence. The D who falls within the previous paragraph will be guilty if the device 'may destroy or inflict grievous bodily harm upon a trespasser or other person coming in contract' with it. If, however, the device would not have this effect (for example, because the trigger mechanism in the man-trap is defective) then the D may still be guilty if the prosecution prove that it was his intention 'to destroy or inflict grievous bodily harm' upon trespasser or other person. If the D has knowingly and wilfully allowed the devices to remain on land which he has taken over, this intention will be presumed.

The penalty for this indictable offence is a maximum of five years imprisonment.

Endangering railway passengers: ss 32–34

The three offences contained in ss 32, 33 and 34 are all concerned with actions which may endanger the safety of people travelling on a railway. Sections 32 and 33 are concerned with what may generally be termed vandalism – s 32 in relation to the railway line, and s 33 in relation to trains travelling on it. They are both indictable offences, punishable with a maximum of life imprisonment.

Section 34 is a much broader offence concerning acts or omissions which may affect safety. It is triable either way, and punishable with a maximum of two years imprisonment.

The *actus* reus of the s 32 offence may be committed in several ways:

(i) putting or throwing upon or across the railway, any wood stone or other matter or thing;

(ii) displacing any rail, sleeper or other matter or thing belonging to the railway;

(iii) turning, moving, or diverting any points or other machinery belonging to the railway;

(iv) making or showing, hiding or removing, any signal or light upon or near to a railway;

(v) doing or causing to be done any other matter or thing.

In each case, the actions must be done 'unlawfully'. The generality of (v), however, even if interpreted *eiusdem generis* with (i) to (iv), indicates that the main ingredient in this offence is the *mens rea* element. This is that the acts are done 'maliciously',[156] and with the intention of endangering 'the safety of any person travelling or being upon' the railway.

156 To be interpreted in the usual way as covering intention and subjective recklessness.

The *actus reus* of the s 33 offence is committed by unlawfully throwing, or causing to fall or strike, at, against, into or upon any engine, tender, carriage or truck used on a railway, any wood, stone, or other matter or thing. The *mens rea* is that the action is done 'maliciously',[157] and with the intention of injuring, or endangering the safety of any person in or on the engine, etc, or any part of a train of which it forms part.

The s 34 offence is committed by any unlawful act or by any wilful omission or neglect which endangers or causes to be endangered the safety of any person conveyed or being in or upon a railway. A person aiding or assisting such an act or omission also commits an offence under the section. No separate *mens rea* element is stated, other than that which may be implied from the requirement that any omission or neglect (but not any unlawful act), should be wilful. The House of Lords' approach in *Sheppard*,[158] though dealing with a different statutory provision,[159] would suggest that wilfully here should be interpreted as meaning 'deliberately, or with a reckless disregard for safety'. A genuine failure to appreciate the danger would not be 'wilful'.

Furious driving: s 35

This offence was passed to deal with horsedrawn carriages, but is expressed in wide enough terms also to cover bicycles,[160] and motor vehicles. However, the offences under the Road Traffic Act 1988 will generally be used in relation to the drivers of motor vehicles, unless they are being driven on private land.

The *actus reus* of the offence may be committed by a D in charge of a carriage or vehicle who does, or causes to be done, some bodily harm to a V, by:

(a) wanton or furious driving or racing;

(b) other wilful misconduct; or

(c) wilful neglect.

It is thus an offence which combines both behaviour ((a)–(c) above), and consequences (bodily harm).

No *mens rea* is specified for this offence, though 'wanton' may imply recklessness. 'Wilful' means only that the behaviour which constitutes the misconduct is intentional.[161] The standard of whether it falls below acceptable standards is objective. There seems no reason, however, why 'wilful neglect'

157 Ie, covering intention and subjective recklessness.

158 [1980] 3 All ER 899.

159 Children and Young Persons Act 1933, s 1(1).

160 *Parker* (1895) 59 JP 793.

161 *Cooke* [1971] Crim LR 44.

should not be interpreted in the same way as in other areas, as described in relation to the offence under s 34, above.

Procuring abortion: ss 58, 59

The termination of pregnancy is legal if it falls within the provisions of the Abortion Act 1967. The details of this legislation are beyond the scope of this book, but it only legalises terminations which are carried out by a registered medical practitioner, on the fulfilment of certain other conditions. Terminations which are not protected by the 1967 will be liable to be offences under s 58 or 59 of the OAPA 1861.

Section 58 deals with two situations. The first is where a pregnant woman acts to bring about her own miscarriage. The prosecution must prove that she administered to herself some 'poison or other noxious thing',[162] or used some instrument or other means, with the intention of procuring her own miscarriage. The second is where a D takes similar action in relation to a woman (whether pregnant or not), with the intention of procuring a miscarriage. The offence is inchoate, in that it is not necessary for a miscarriage to follow in either case. Indeed, such a result would be impossible where the D acts in relation to a woman who is not pregnant.

The first situation is unusual, in that it involves criminalising actions taken by a woman in relation to her own body. As we have seen, it is not in any other situation an offence to damage or mutilate your own body. Nor is it generally accepted that the unborn child has any rights independent of its mother.[163] Indeed, the House of Lords has held that a mother has the right to refuse medical procedures which, if not carried out, would put the survival of her unborn child at risk.[164] The rights analysis which is one of the themes of this book has difficulty coping with this offence. It is one of those areas, like the criminalisation of assaults consented to by the V, where there must be a public policy operating which overrides the rights of the individual. The policy must relate to the protection of the foetus, despite the fact that this is not regarded as having independent rights.

The *actus reus* of the offence under s 58 is the action taken to terminate the pregnancy; the *mens rea* is the intention that the pregnancy should be terminated. Recklessness is not sufficient. A pregnant woman, having been warned that taking, for example, heroin, will increase the risk of a

162 It is not enough that the D believed the substance to be poisonous or noxious: *Isaacs* (1862) LJMC 567; *Hollis* (1873) 12 Cox 463. Whether a substance is 'noxious' may depend on the quantity in which it is administered (or, under s 59, supplied): *Cramp* (1880) 5 QBD 307. It does not need to be an abortifacient (*Marlow* (1965) 49 Cr App Rep 49), provided that it is harmful to the human system, *Hennah* (1877) 13 Cox 547.

163 Eg, *Attorney General's Reference (No 3 of 1994)* [1997] 3 WLR 421; *St George's Healthcare* [1998] 3 All ER 673.

164 *St George's Healthcare National Health Service Trust v S* [1998] 3 All ER 673.

termination, does not commit an offence simply by continuing to do so. The prosecution would have to prove that she realised that the termination was a virtually certain consequence of her actions, so that intention might be found.[165]

The offence under s 58 is indictable, and punishable with a maximum of life imprisonment.

Section 59 is essentially an 'aiding and abetting' offence. It makes it an offence to procure or supply the means of bringing about a termination. The *actus reus* is the procurement or supply of 'any poison or other noxious thing, or any instrument or thing whatsoever.' The mens rea is knowledge that what is procured or supplied is intended to be used for the unlawful, and intentional, purpose of procuring the miscarriage of 'any woman, whether or not she be with child.'

The offence under s 59 is indictable, punishable with a maximum of five years imprisonment.

165 See Chapter 2, pp 28–32, for discussion of the process by which the fact that the D foresaw a consequence as virtually certain may permit a decision that the D intended the consequence.

CHAPTER 6

SEXUAL OFFENCES

Sexual offences involve interference with the V's privacy, infringing the most intimate areas of an individual's personality. They often also involve interference with the V's bodily integrity. This combination of infringements of the V's rights makes this type of offence potentially very serious. Thus a touching which would in itself amount only to the most minor battery, may, if deemed to be sexual, become an offence punishable with 10 years imprisonment.[1]

The issue of consent is also of major importance in this area. For example, the act of sexual intercourse between consenting couples can be the expression of the deepest and most intimate love, and a source of great mutual pleasure. The same act performed without consent constitutes one of the most serious assaults that may be committed by one person on another. For this reason, although the main general discussion of consent appears in Chapter 7, the topic will also be referred to at various points in this chapter, particularly in connection with the offence of rape.

The order of treatment in this chapter is to deal first with the most serious offence, rape, then with indecent assaults, and then with a range of other sexually related offences mainly contained in the Sexual Offences Act 1956 (SOA).

RAPE

The offence of rape is defined mainly by statute, though some elements have been the subject of case law interpretation. The relevant provision is s 1 of the SOA, as amended by the Criminal Justice and Public Order Act 1994. The section states:

> (1) It is an offence for a man to rape a woman or another man.
>
> (2) A man commits rape if:
>
> (a) he has sexual intercourse with a person (whether vaginal or anal) who at the time of the intercourse does not consent to it; and
>
> (b) at the time he knows that the person does not consent to the intercourse or is reckless as to whether that person consents to it.

1 Ie, as an indecent assault, under s 14 or 15 of the Sexual Offences Act 1956: see below, p 157.

A number of initial points should be noted concerning this definition, before the details of the *actus reus* and *mens rea* are considered. First, the offence can only be committed by a man, though the V may be either a man or a woman. Secondly, and related to the first point, the only type of sexual congress that falls within the definition is the insertion of the D's penis into the V's vagina or anus. The D who compels the V to perform *fellatio* does not commit rape. Nor does he do so by inserting either an object, or some part of his body other than his penis, into the V's vagina or anus. Such actions will amount to indecent assaults, but not rape. Thirdly, since the House of Lords decision in *R*,[2] rape may be committed by a husband against his wife.[3] Finally, there is no longer any presumption that boys under the age of 14 are incapable of sexual intercourse, and therefore rape.[4]

Actus reus

The *actus reus* of rape requires the combination of a certain physical act by the D, together with a particular state of mind on the part of the V.

As we have noted above, the physical act required is the insertion of the D's penis into the V's vagina or anus. A further indication of the nature of the act required is given by s 44 of the SOA, which states that:

> Where ... it is necessary to prove sexual intercourse ... it shall not be necessary to prove completion of the intercourse by emission of seed, but the intercourse shall be deemed to be complete upon proof of penetration only.

Although this provides that the D does not need to achieve orgasm or ejaculation, it does not specify what degree of penetration will suffice. The issue was dealt with in several 18th and 19th century cases. In *Russen*,[5] there was evidence that the V's hymen was intact, which was taken to be a mark of virginity. There was other evidence, however, which suggested that there had been some penetration of the V's vagina. A panel of 12 judges agreed with the direction of the trial judge, Ashurst J, that any penetration, however small, was sufficient for the *actus reus* of rape.[6] A more explicit statement along the same lines was given by Parke B in *Lines*.[7] Directing a jury on the offence of carnally knowing and abusing a female under the age of 10, he said:

> I shall leave it to the jury to say, whether, at any time, any part of the virile member of the prisoner was within the labia of the pudendum of the

2 [1991] 4 All ER 481.

3 This extension of the offence is probably the reason why the current statutory definition no longer refers to 'unlawful' sexual intercourse.

4 Sexual Offences Act 1993, s 1.

5 (1777) 1 East PC 438; also noted at 9 Car & P 753.

6 The ruling was accepted as an accurate statement of the law relating to rape in (1841) 9 Car & P 752.

7 (1844) 1 Car & K 393.

> prosecutrix; for if it was (no matter how little), that will be sufficient to constitute a penetration, and the jury ought to convict the prisoner of the complete offence.

It is clear, therefore, that any degree of penetration is sufficient. Although the cases cited deal only with vaginal intercourse, there is no reason to doubt that the same approach should be taken in relation to anal intercourse.

It should be noted that s 44 states that the intercourse shall be 'complete', not 'completed', upon penetration. Commenting on a similar provision in s 127 of the New Zealand Crimes Act 1961, Lord Scarman said that:[8]

> 'Complete' is used in the statutory definition in the sense of having come into existence, but not in the sense of being at an end. Sexual intercourse is a continuing act which only ends with withdrawal.

Thus, if the V consents to the initial penetration, but then changes her mind, the D will commit the *actus reus* of rape simply by leaving his penis inside her.[9] The offence is not so much the omission to withdraw, as the continuation of the penetration. Once the D is aware that the V is not consenting, he should withdraw immediately.

The second part of the *actus reus* of rape is the lack of consent on the part of the V. Very often, this will not be in doubt, since the D will have used force to engage in the intercourse. Difficulty may arise, however, where the V has been tricked into allow the D to have intercourse, or has submitted through fear of what the D might otherwise do to her, or a third party. The two types of situation need to considered separately. The first involves a mistake by the V as to some aspect of her dealings with the D; the second does not involve any such mistake, but the question of whether the D's submission is properly regarded as consent. A third category of case which also needs consideration is where the V is unconscious a the time of the intercourse.

Mistake

As regards the general issue of mistakes, whether induced by the D's fraud or not, the Court of Appeal in *Linekar*[10] suggested that in effect they were two situations that needed consideration, these being where there was doubt about the V's *consensus quoad hanc personam* (that is, mistake as to identity), or about her *consensus quoad hoc* (that is, mistake as to the act of intercourse). Provided that the V consented to an act of intercourse with the particular D, the fact that this consent was obtained by a misrepresentation would not make the D guilty of rape. In *Linekar*, the V was a prostitute. The D had told

8 *Kaitamaki* [1984] 2 All ER 435, PC, p 437.

9 *Ibid*. Though the facts of the case concerned not a change of mind on the part of the V, but a realisation on the part of the D, after the initial penetration, that the V did not consent.

10 [1995] 3 All ER 69.

her that he would pay her £25 for intercourse. He did not, in fact, have such a sum on him, and so his promise was clearly fraudulent. After intercourse had taken place, the D made off without paying. The V then complained that she had been raped. The judge gave a direction indicating that if the D never intended to pay, and the V's consent had therefore been obtained by fraud, the D could be guilty of rape. D was convicted on this basis.[11] The Court of Appeal disagreed. The V consented to an act of intercourse, and there was no mistake as to the D's identity. The fact that V's consent may have been obtained by false pretences on the part of the D did not vitiate it. The Court adopted *dicta* taken from the Australian case, *Papadimitropoulos v R*,[12] where it was stated:[13]

> Rape is carnal knowledge of a woman without her consent: carnal knowledge is the physical act of penetration; it is the consent to that which is in question; such a consent demands a perception as to what is about to take place, as to the identity of the man and the character of what he is doing. But, once the consent is comprehending and actual, the inducing causes cannot destroy the reality and leave the man guilty of rape.

Thus, the D who induces the V's consent by stating that he loves her, or that he intends to marry her, or that he is a millionnaire, will not commit rape, even if his statement is untrue, and made with the sole purpose of obtaining intercourse with her.

There are, therefore, only two types of mistake that will vitiate consent: mistake as to the D's identity, and mistake as to the nature of the act. Looking first at mistaken identity, one aspect of this is dealt with specifically by a statutory provision. Section 1(3) of the SOA states that:

> A man also commits rape if he induces a married woman to have sexual intercourse with him by impersonating her husband.

The specific recognition of this one type of impersonation should not, however, necessarily be taken to mean that other, similar, tricks will not involve rape. In *Elbekkay*,[14] the D had been staying with the V and her boyfriend. One night, when they had both been drinking, The D entered the V's bedroom and climbed on to the bed. The V, assuming that it was her boyfriend allowed the D to kiss her, and commence intercourse. As soon as she realised the mistake it seems that she terminated the intercourse, punched the D, and also cut him with a knife. At the trial, the D argued that the V had consented to the intercourse. The trial judge ruled that if V had only allowed the intercourse because she thought that the D was her boyfriend, then she

---

11 This was made clear by a statement from the foreman of the jury.

12 (1957) 98 CLR 249.

13 *Ibid*, p 261.

14 [1995] Crim LR 163.

could not be said to be consenting. The Court of Appeal agreed, considering that:

> To find that it is rape to impersonate a husband, but not if the person was merely, say, a long term, live-in lover, or in even more modern idiom, the 'partner' of the woman, would be extraordinary.[15]

There is no good reason why this principle should not apply, even though the statutory rule was re-enacted in the Criminal Justice and Public Order Act 1994 revision of s 1 of the SOA, in terms, as we have seen, that refer only to husbands. Despite this piece of 'remarkable incompetence'[16] on the part of the legislature, and despite the fact that certain weight was placed in *Elbekkay* on the fact that the rule relating to husbands was not (at the time of the case) of recent origin, it cannot seriously be doubted that the courts will follow that decision, and apply the 'impersonation' rule beyond the area of husbands and wives. If that is so, there is no reason why the principle should not also apply to a male V, who mistakenly thinks that the D is his lover. If, however, the scope of mistaken identity as vitiating consent beyond the specific statutory provision, does this mean that any mistake as to the identity of the D will have this effect? The statements in *Linekar* on this issue are equivocal. At one point, the court suggests that 'it is immaterial whether the perpetrator is impersonating a husband, a cohabitee or a lover'.[17] This might be taken as suggesting a limited scope for mistaken identity. On the other hand, at other points the court refers to the issue in general terms,[18] and cites with approval passages from other judgments which do not limit the scope of this type of mistake. Thus, the court agrees with a passage from Stephen J in *Clarence*,[19] where he states:

> The only sorts of fraud which so far destroy the effect of a woman's consent as to convert a connection consented to in fact into a rape are frauds as to the nature of the act itself, or as to the identity of the person who does the act.

It also, as we have seen, cites with approval *Papadimitropoulos*,[20] and in particular a passage which includes the following:

> Consent demands a perception as to what is about to take place, *as to the identity of the man* and the character of what he is doing (emphasis added).

What then, is the position of the D who persuades the V that he is a particular famous film star, and thereby induces her to have sex with him? If the broader statements relating to mistaken identity are accepted then he is guilty of rape.

15 [1995] Crim LR 163, p 164.

16 Smith, JC and Hogan, B, *Criminal Law Cases and Materials*, 6th edn, 1996, London: Butterworths, p 469.

17 [1991] 3 All ER 69, p 73.

18 Eg, *ibid*, p 74j, referring to the 'husband' cases simply as of a more general principle of 'no *consensus quoad hanc personam*'.

19 [1886–90] All ER Rep 133, p 144.

20 (1957) 98 CLR 249.

The V is mistaken as to the person with whom she is having intercourse, and this vitiates her consent.[21] It would surely be different, however, if the D had falsely told the D that he was a millionaire, or even if he had simply claimed to be a 'film star' without assuming the identity of a real person. In these cases, the V's mistake, although based on the D's fraud, would not be sufficient to vitiate her consent. She would still be intending to have sex with the D, rather than with another specific individual whom the D was pretending to be. To borrow from terminology sometimes used in the law of contract, her mistake would have been as to the D's *attributes*, rather than his *identity*.[22] It would be a mistake of the same kind as that made by the V in *Linekar*, who thought that the D was a man in possession of £25 which he was going to give her after they had intercourse.

The above approach would follow from a broad concept of mistake vitiating consent. As has been noted, however, *Linekar* also contains statements suggesting that mistakes as to identity which would be regarded as vitiating consent should be limited to the situation where the V thinks that the D is her husband, cohabitee or lover. Is there any justification for this narrower view? It might be argued that the common factor of the categories mentioned – husband, cohabitee or lover – is that they will presumably all have had sexual intercourse with the V on a previous occasion.[23] The decision to have intercourse with another person is probably most significant on the first occasion. On subsequent occasions when the possibility arises, both parties are likely, in the absence of indications to the contrary, to assume the consent of the other. This will certainly be the case where the parties are in a relationship which has lasted some time, and has regularly involved intercourse. It would be possible, therefore, to justify distinguishing the impersonation of 'husband, cohabitee or lover' from other mistakes as to identity, in that in these cases the V's consent is likely to be less of a conscious decision, and more in the nature of an assumption arising out of the relationship. On the other hand, in referring to the three categories mentioned the court in *Linekar* cites with approval para 2.25 of the *15th Report of the Criminal Law Revision Committee on Sexual Offences*,[24] which states that there is:

> ... no reason to distinguish between consent obtained by impersonating a husband and consent obtained by impersonating another man, so that latter case should also constitute rape.

---

21 The prosecution would, of course, have to prove the causal link between the deception and the giving of consent.

22 Though, as the courts dealing with this distinction in the contract area have shown, it is not easy to apply: see, eg, Stone, R, *Principles of Contract Law*, 3rd edn, 1997, London: Cavendish Publishing, p 194. Indeed, Lord Denning suggested in [1972] 2 All ER 229 that it was 'a distinction without a difference'.

23 There could, of course, be exceptions, eg the virgin bride who is visited by the fraudulent D on her wedding night.

24 (1983) Cmnd 9213, London: HMSO.

This, therefore, gives support to the broad rather than the narrow approach to mistaken identity.

To sum up on this issue, there are at least three arguable propositions as to the current English law as to which mistakes of identity will vitiate consent to sexual intercourse:

(a) the narrowest is that the law is stated simply by s 1(3) of the SOA, so that the only relevant mistake is where the D impersonates the V's husband;

(b) the second possibility is that suggested by *Elbekkay*, and to some extent by *Linekar*, to the effect that impersonation of a cohabitee, lover, boyfriend, or other regular sexual partner, will be sufficient to vitiate consent;

(c) the broadest proposition is that based on the *dicta* in *Clarence*, and *Papadimitropoulos*, and supported by the CLRC, to the effect that any mistake as to the identity of the person with whom the V has intercourse will vitiate consent.

There is no clear authority as to which of these currently represents English law. It seems likely, however, that the courts will be prepared to move at least as far as proposition (b). Whether they will go as far as proposition (c) must remain doubtful, despite the support for this in academic commentaries,[25] and the CLRC. Prosecutors will no doubt proceed with caution, and given that relevant factual situations are not likely to occur with great frequency, the law seems destined to remain in its current uncertain state on this issue.

Turning now to the other type of mistake which may vitiate consent, that is, mistake as to the nature of the act – the position is much clearer. If the V does not understand that the act is one of sexual intercourse, but thinks that it has some other purpose, there will be no *consensus quoad hoc*.[26] The fact that V has not, therefore, consented to sexual intercourse will potentially render the D liable for rape (subject to proof of *mens rea*). There are two reported cases in which a mistake of this kind was considered: *Flattery*[27] and *Williams*.[28] In *Flattery*, the 19 year old V had been taken by her mother to the D, who ran a 'medical' stall at an open market. The V suffered from fits. The D told her mother that he needed to 'break nature's string' in order to cure the V. The mother, not understanding what the D meant, gave him permission to attempt to do this. D took V to a nearby inn, and there had intercourse with her, to which the V made 'but feeble resistance, believing that she was being treated medically, and that what was taking place was a surgical operation'.[29]

25 Eg Ashworth, A, *Principles of Criminal Law*, 2nd edn, 1995, Oxford: Clarendon, p 343.

26 See, eg, May CJ in (1884) 15 Cox CC 579, p 587.

27 (1877) 2 QBD 410.

28 [1923] 1 KB 340.

29 (1877) 2 QBD 410, p 413. The issue was raised as to whether a girl of 19 could be said to be unaware of the nature of sexual intercourse. Kelly CB pointed out, however, that there was no rule of law presuming such awareness. Moreover, 'she might suppose that penetration was being effected with the hand or with an instrument'.

It was held that the fact that the V misunderstood the nature of what was happening meant that she did not consent to sexual intercourse, and the D's conviction for rape was upheld. The case was not one of consent induced by fraud, but of lack of consent. The decision in *Flattery* was followed and approved in *Williams*.[30] The D in this case was a choirmaster. He told one of his 16 year old pupils that she was not singing as she should. He made her lie down, and carried out a spurious examination, involving the placing of a barometer on her body. He then engaged in sexual intercourse with the V, explaining that he was 'going to make an air passage' to improve her breathing. The D was convicted of rape, and the Court of Criminal Appeal, in upholding this conviction, approved the direction which Branson J had given to the jury. This stated that where the V:

> ... is persuaded that what is being done to her is not the ordinary act of sexual intercourse but is some medical or surgical operation in order to give her relief from some disability from which she is suffering, then that is rape although the actual thing that was done was done with her consent, because she never consented to the act of sexual intercourse. She was persuaded to consent to what he did because she thought it was not sexual intercourse and because she thought it was a surgical operation.[31]

The position as regards this type of mistake, involving lack of *consensus quoad hoc*, thus seems to be as follows. If the V does not realise that the D is placing his penis in her vagina or anus (if, for example, she thinks he is using his finger or an instrument), then she clearly does not consent to the act of intercourse. Where she does realise what the D is doing, however, she may still not consent to intercourse, if she thinks that the D's actions are part of a medical procedure, or carried out for some other non-sexual purpose. The focus is thus on the V's perception of the D's motive for putting his penis inside her. Only if she realises that his motive is sexual pleasure, and nevertheless allows him to continue, can she be said to consent to intercourse. This means in addition that a V who through youth or mental infirmity does not understand the nature of the act will also not be held to consent. Certain 19th century authorities which suggested that 'animal instinct' was sufficient to amount to consent,[32] should no longer be regarded as good law.[33]

Improper pressure

We now turn to the situation where the V, knowing the D's identity, and fully understanding the nature of the act, does not resist intercourse, but nevertheless is regarded as not having consented to it. The leading modern

30 [1923] 1 KB 340.

31 *Ibid*, p 347.

32 *Fletcher* (1859) *Bell* CC 63; followed in *Fletcher* (1866) LR 1 CCR 39; *Barratt* (1873) LR 2 CCR 81.

33 See *Dee* (1884) 15 Cox CC 579.

authority on this issue is *Olugboja*,[34] in which the Court of Appeal referred with approval to the distinction between 'submission' and 'consent', quoting the comment by Coleridge J in *Day*[35] to the effect that 'every consent involves a submission, but it by no means follows that a mere submission involves consent'.[36] As other commentators have pointed out, however,[37] the distinction is one that is very difficult to apply in practice. Agreement to sexual intercourse may involve a state of mind ranging from enthusiasm, through indifference and reluctant acquiescence, to terrified acceptance. To identify the precise point on this scale at which 'consent' changes into 'submission' is a philosophical conundrum which is probably inappropriate for juries to determine. A more pragmatic approach is to recognise that in all these situations the V 'consents' to intercourse, but that, in certain situations, the consent will be regarded as invalidated by illegitimate pressure placed on the V. The task then becomes that of deciding what pressure is illegitimate. Clearly direct threats of violence against the V or a third party will come into this category. The V who consents to intercourse having been told that otherwise she will be killed, or her child will be harmed, has undoubtedly been raped. Beyond this, the circumstances may imply a threat. In *Olugboja*, the 16 year old V was initially raped by X, an associate of the D. She had been tricked into going to X's bungalow by an offer of a lift home. After the initial rape, she was left in a room with the D who told her 'he was going to fuck her'. She told him that she had already had sex with X, and asked why the D could not leave her alone. The D then told her to take her trousers off, which she did, because she said she was frightened. The D pushed her on to a settee and had intercourse with her. She did not resist, struggle, or cry out. The D was charged with rape. The judge directed the jury that as regards the issue of the V's consent the question was the reason why the V allowed the D to have intercourse:

> Was it circumstances in which she was consenting, or was it circumstances in which there was constraint operating on her mind, fear or constraint, so that in doing that, she was doing it without her consent?

The jury convicted, and the Court of Appeal held that there had been no misdirection. It would have been better not to have used the word 'constraint', but since it was linked to 'fear' its use was 'unexceptional'. The decision indicates, therefore, that 'fear', however caused, may vitiate consent. In particular, there is no need for the fear to be induced by an explicit threat from the D. Beyond this, however, the judgment is unhelpful in indicating the parameters of the offence, leaving it to the jury to decide whether in all the circumstances the V did or did not consent. It seems to be implicit in the

34 [1981] 3 All ER 443.

35 (1841) 9 C&P 722.

36 [1981] 3 All ER 443, p 448.

37 Eg, *op cit*, Smith and Hogan, fn 16, p 471.

comments on the judge's direction referred to above, however, that 'fear' of what will otherwise happen is the main factor which will vitiate consent. This seems, however, to encompass not only fear of violence, but also other consequences. Is consent vitiated if the V agrees to intercourse to avoid being reported for a criminal offence, to avoid being dismissed from her job, or to avoid her husband being told of her previous career as a prostitute? The Court of Appeal in *Olugboja* appeared to accept the possibility that all of these cases might involve lack of consent, and therefore could potentially be categorised as rape. In such a situation, the judge would need to direct the jury very carefully:[38]

> They should be directed to concentrate on the state of mind of the victim immediately before the act of sexual intercourse, having regard to all the relevant circumstances, and in particular the events leading up to the act, and her reaction to them showing their impact on her mind.

Referring then to the distinction between 'consent' and 'submission' referred to above, the court suggests that the place where the line is to be drawn is for the jury to decide 'applying their combined good sense, experience and knowledge of human nature and modern behaviour to the facts of the case'.

The conclusion thus seems to be that it is only 'fear' that will vitiate consent, but there is no rule of law limiting the type of consequences which must be feared by the V. Whether any particular fear has vitiated consent is an issue that must be determined by the jury on the facts of each case.

This does not seem a very satisfactory result, since it leaves the law in a very unpredictable state. On the other hand, it does place considerable weight on the reaction of the particular V to the pressure placed on her.[39] This may be said to reflect the desirability of giving proper recognition to the protection of V's rights in the definition of criminal offences.[40] From this perspective, it might well be argued that the dominant approach to the *actus reus* of rape should be based on the point of view of the V. Did she feel that she was violated by the intercourse? Such a feeling is clearly incompatible with freely given 'consent'. The approach taken in *Olugboja* might then be seen as a practical approach to determining the answer to this question.

Unconscious victim

This approach, based on the V's view of whether she has been violated, might also be used in relation to the final category of situations where the issue of consent may arise in relation to rape – that is, where the V is unconscious, through sleep, drugs or alcohol, at the time when the intercourse takes place.

38 [1981] 3 All ER 443, p 449.

39 As pointed out by Gardner, S, 'Appreciating *Olugboja*' (1996) 16 Legal Studies 275.

40 Which is one of the themes of this book – see Chapter 1, p 2.

It is generally said that, since an unconscious person cannot consent, intercourse with such a V will always constitute the *actus reus* of rape.[41] While in most cases this will be true, it is not impossible to envisage the situation, particularly where the couple have been having intercourse regularly over a period of time, in which a V would not feel violated by intercourse in such circumstances. While not strictly speaking consenting at the time, she would not on regaining consciousness (which might be while the intercourse was continuing), feel distress at what had happened. Since it would presumably not be rape if the V had beforehand given express permission for intercourse to take place while she was unconscious, it would seem that it should be possible to imply such permission from previous conduct, particularly if it arises out of a long term relationship. It will, however, be rare for the courts to be faced with a case involving such circumstances. In the more common situation where the D has been prosecuted for simply having taken advantage of the V's unconsciousness to engage in intercourse, there is no doubt that it is correct to categorise this as 'intercourse without consent', therefore, constituting the *actus reus* of rape.

Mens rea

Section 1(2) of the SOA states:

> A man commits rape if:
>
> (a) he has sexual intercourse with a person (whether vaginal or anal) who at the time of the intercourse does not consent to it; and
>
> (b) at the time he knows that the person does not consent to the intercourse or is reckless as to whether that person consents to it.

The *mens rea* of rape is thus set out in s 1(2)(b), and is based on the D's knowledge or recklessness as regards the V's lack of consent. 'Knowledge' in this context must be interpreted as at least including, if not in effect meaning, 'belief', since it is impossible that the D can know for certain what the V's state of mind is at a particular time, even if she has just said either 'yes' or 'no' to intercourse. This is not, of course, to suggest support for the view that women often say 'no' when they mean 'yes'. It is simply that consent is a state of mind, and while this may be evidenced by words or behaviour, one person can never be 100% certain of the state of mind of another.

As regards 'recklessness', there was some uncertainty following the House of Lords decision in *Caldwell*[42] as regards the use of the same word in the Criminal Damage Act 1971,[43] as to whether the same approach should apply

41 See, eg, *Mayers* (1872) 12 Cox 311; *Young* (1878) 14 Cox 114.

42 [1982] AC 341.

43 See the discussion in Chapter 2, pp 34–36.

to rape. In other words, would it be enough to satisfy the *mens rea* of rape for there to be a risk that the V was not consenting which would have been obvious to a reasonable person, but which the D failed to recognise? Some decisions of the Court of Appeal appeared to give support to such an approach,[44] but the decision in *Satnam*[45] seems to have settled that *Cunningham*[46] recklessness is what is required.[47] In other words, it is only if the D himself foresaw the risk that the V was not consenting that he will be regarded as being 'reckless' in relation to her consent. This is taken to include the situation where the D was 'indifferent' to the issue of the V's consent. In deciding whether the D was reckless as to whether the V wanted to have intercourse, if the jury:

> ... came to the conclusion that he could not care less whether she wanted to or not, but pressed on regardless, then he would have been reckless and could not have believed that she wanted to, and they would find him guilty of reckless rape.[48]

In reaching this conclusion, the Court of Appeal was influenced by the fact that the definition of the *mens rea* of rape contained in the Sexual Offences (Amendment) Act 1976,[49] followed the recommendations of the Heilbron Committee.[50] These re-affirmed the law on the mental element of rape as stated by the House of Lords in *DPP v Morgan*,[51] which of course pre-dated *Caldwell*. Moreover:[52]

> The word 'reckless' in relation to rape involves a different concept to its use in relation to malicious damage or, indeed, in relation to offences against the person. In the latter cases, the foreseeability, or possible foreseeability, is as to the consequences of the criminal act. In the case of rape, the foreseeability is as to the state of mind of the victim.

It was justifiable, therefore, to use a subjective test of recklessness, focusing on the foresight of the D rather than a reasonable person, but including the D who 'could not care less'. Later cases have, however, held that a direction which tells the jury that they may find the D was reckless as to whether the V was consenting 'where, if any thought had been given to the matter, it would have been obvious there was a risk she was not' is permissible, provided it is

44 In particular, *Pigg* (1982) 74 Cr App R 352, though the wording used in this case, and in *Thomas* (1983) 77 Cr App R 63 and *Bashir* (1983) 77 Cr App R 59, was ambiguous, in that it did not make it clear to whom the risk had to be obvious – the D or a reasonable observer.

45 (1984) 78 Cr App R 149.

46 [1957] 2 QB 396.

47 See Chapter Two, pp 33–34.

48 *Satnam* (1983) 78 Cr App R 149, p 155.

49 And now incorporated into the SOA 1956, s 1.

50 Ie, *The Report of the Advisory Group on the Law of Rape* (1975) Cmnd 6352, London: HMSO.

51 [1976] AC 182.

52 *Satnam* (1983) 78 Cr App R 149, p 154.

made clear that it means 'obvious to the defendant, as opposed to obvious to a reasonable man'.[53]

The consequence of this is that the D who genuinely, albeit unreasonably, believes that the V is consenting to intercourse, is not guilty of rape. This is confirmed by s 1(2) of the SOA, which also derives from the recommendations of the Heilbron Committee. It states:

> It is hereby declared that if at a trial for a rape offence the jury has to consider whether a man believed that a woman or man was consenting to sexual intercourse, the presence or absence of reasonable grounds for such a belief is a matter to which the jury is to have regard, in conjunction with any other relevant matters, in considering whether he so believed.

The reasonableness of the D's belief is thus just one factor in the consideration of the question of whether he did in fact have such a belief. If the jury is convinced on all the evidence that, despite the unreasonableness of his so doing, the D held the belief that the V was consenting, it must acquit.[54] This approach derives from the House of Lords decision in *DPP v Morgan*.[55] In this case, M had invited the Ds (with whom he worked) to his house, and had encouraged them to have intercourse with the V, his wife. The Ds alleged that M had told them that they should ignore signs of resistance from the V, since this was mere pretence from which she stimulated her own sexual excitement. The Ds had intercourse with the V, who did resist, and was held down during the intercourse. At the trial, the judge directed the jury that they could convict the Ds of rape if they thought that the Ds belief in the V's consent was not based on reasonable grounds. This was ruled by the House of Lords to be a misdirection. The essence of the argument appears in the following passage from Lord Hailsham's speech:[56]

> Once one has accepted, what seems to me abundantly clear, that the prohibited act in rape is non-consensual sexual intercourse, and that the guilty state of mind is an intention to commit it, it seems to me to follow as a matter of inexorable logic that there is no room either for a 'defence' of honest belief or mistake, or of a defence of honest and reasonable belief and mistake. Either the prosecution proves that the accused had the requisite intent, or it does not. In the former case it succeeds, and in the latter it fails. Since honest belief clearly negatives intent, the reasonableness or otherwise of that belief can only be evidence for or against the view that the belief and therefore the intent was actually held ...

Although Lord Hailsham speaks here only of 'intention', it is clear that he includes within this recklessness of the kind outlined above, since he later

53 See *Pearson* (1985) 80 Cr App R 335, p 343. Also, *Taylor* (1984) 80 Cr App R 327.

54 The burden of proof is, of course, on the prosecution to prove beyond reasonable doubt that the D had the relevant *mens rea*.

55 [1976] AC 182.

56 *Ibid*, p 214.

refers to the mental element of rape as being intention to have intercourse without consent 'or the equivalent intention of having intercourse willy-nilly not caring whether the victim consents or not'. In either case, however, the 'inexorable logic' applies, and the D who genuinely believes in the V's consent does not have the required state of mind. The reasonableness or otherwise of the D's belief is not irrelevant, however, since it will be one of the factors which the jury will consider in deciding whether the D did have such a belief. This is illustrated by the decision in *Morgan* itself where, despite the fact that there had been a misdirection, the House of Lords upheld the convictions, on the basis that there had been no miscarriage of justice.[57] In other words, they did not think that there was any possibility that a jury, even if properly directed, would have believed the Ds story and acquitted them.

The decision in *Morgan* was controversial, with some commentators suggesting that it was too favourable to the Ds (despite the outcome in *Morgan* itself). The government responded by setting up the Heilbron Committee. The report of this Committee, however, as we have seen, confirmed the approach taken in *Morgan*, but led to the statutory enactment of the rule that a jury is to have regard to the reasonableness of the D's alleged belief in the V's consent in deciding whether it was actually held.[58] The principles as stated by the House of Lords in *Morgan* thus remain good law as regards the mental element in the offence of rape, and other offences where knowledge or recklessness as regards the V's lack of consent must be proved by the prosecution. Subsequent decisions of the Court of Appeal have held, however, that there is no need for the judge to direct the jury on the issue of 'belief in consent' where the real issue in the case is whether the V actually consented or not.[59] For example, if the V gives evidence that she was protesting at the time of the intercourse, and the D claims that she was not, a jury which believes the V will convict, whereas one that believes the D will acquit. The question of 'honest belief' in consent is not, on the facts, relevant.

ATTEMPTED RAPE

The offence of attempted rape is, of course, governed by the general law on attempts, as set out in the Criminal Attempts Act 1981, and discussed in Chapter 3.[60] This requires that the D has carried out acts which are 'more than merely preparatory', with the intention of committing the complete offence. The particular application of these principles to the offence here is perhaps

57 Applying the proviso to the Criminal Appeal Act 1968, s 2(1).

58 Now contained in SOA 1956, s 1(2), quoted above.

59 See, eg, *Taylor* (1984) 80 Cr App R 327; *Pearson* (1985) 80 Cr App R 335.

60 Chapter 3, p 48.

somewhat surprising, and so is considered in a little more detail here. The *actus reus* and *mens rea* will be discussed in turn.

Actus reus

As we have seen in Chapter 3, the interpretation of the phrase 'more than merely preparatory' has been problematic. The case law is not consistent as to how close to completion of the substantive offence the D must be in order to fulfil this criterion. The test has been stated as whether the D 'has embarked on the crime proper'.[61] In *Attorney General's Reference (No 1 of 1992)*,[62] the facts were that the D had been walking the V home. Both had been drinking. The D at one stage pushed the V to the ground, lay on top of her, put his hand over her mouth and threatened to kill her if she did not stop screaming. The V lost consciousness, whereupon the D dragged her up some steps into a shed. The V regained consciousness and was crying and trying to scream. The D lowered his trousers, and there was evidence that he had touched the V's genitals. The D, however, subsequently claimed that he was unable to maintain an erection because of his intoxicated state. He had therefore been unable to attempt to penetrate the V's vagina. On this basis, the trial judge directed that the jury should acquit the D of attempted rape, on the basis that there was no *actus reus*. The Attorney General referred the following question to the Court of Appeal: '... whether, on a charge of attempted rape, it is incumbent on the prosecution, as a matter of law, to prove that the defendant physically attempted to penetrate the woman's vagina with his penis.'

The Court of Appeal held that this was not necessary. Facts such as those of the present case were sufficient for it to be left to the jury to decide whether the D had done acts which were more than merely preparatory towards the commission of the offence, and had embarked on committing the offence itself.[63] Impotence, therefore, from whatever cause, is no barrier to a charge of attempted rape, provided that the relevant intention can be proved. The decision suggests that, in the case of rape, actions which are some way from the commission of the full offence can nevertheless be sufficient for the *actus reus* of an attempt. It is not clear, however, at what stage in the D's enterprise the law will step in. It is presumably more likely to do so where the D has already assaulted the V, as opposed to the situation where, for example, the D has climbed into bed with the sleeping V intending to have intercourse without waking her, but then changes his mind, or is simply unable to perform.

---

61 Chapter 3, p 50.

62 [1993] 2 All ER 190.

63 *Ibid*, p 194.

A further issue relating to the *actus reus*, concerning whether the prosecution needs to prove that the V would not have consented, is discussed below, in connection with related *mens rea* issues.

Mens rea

The *mens rea* for attempted rape is the intention to have intercourse with the V, knowing that the V will not consent, or being reckless (as defined above) in relation to that consent. The governing authority is the Court of Appeal's decision in *Khan*.[64] The court here rejected the argument put forward by some commentators[65] to the effect that s 1(1) of the Criminal Attempts Act 1981[66] requires the prosecution to prove intention as to every element of the full offence. It held that this was not necessary in relation to the D's state of mind about the circumstances which contributed to the offence, as opposed to the actions taken to commit it. Thus, as regards attempted rape, the offence could be analysed as follows:[67]

> (a) the intention of the offender is to have sexual intercourse with a woman;
>
> (b) the offence is committed if, but only if, the circumstances are that:
>
> (i) the woman does not consent; and
>
> (ii) the defendant knows that she is not consenting or is reckless as to whether she consents.

This confirms that recklessness (in the sense of 'couldn't care less') in relation to the V's consent is sufficient. It should surely not be necessary, however, to require the prosecution to prove element (b)(i). The Criminal Attempts Act 1981 makes it clear that a D may be found guilty of attempt even if commission of the full offence would have been impossible (for example, attempting to murder someone who is already dead).[68] There seems no reason, therefore, why there should not be liability for attempted rape even if the prospective V would in fact have consented to the intercourse.

PROCUREMENT OF A WOMAN TO HAVE SEXUAL INTERCOURSE

Sections 2 and 3 of the SOA 1956 contain offences of procurement of a woman to have sexual intercourse by 'threats or intimidation' (s 2(1)), or 'false

64 [1990] 2 All ER 783.

65 Eg, Professor Griew in his annotations to the Criminal Attempts Act 1981.

66 For which see Chapter 3, p 48.

67 [1990] 2 All ER 783, p 787.

68 See Chapter 3, p 51.

pretences or false representations' (s 3(1)). The intercourse can take place anywhere in the world. There is no offence, however, unless intercourse occurs. This was the view taken in *Johnson*[69] which was concerned with the similar offence under s 23 of the SOA.[70] The court, however, made it clear that the same approach should apply to ss 2 and 3. In that case, intercourse had not occurred, and a conviction of attempt was substituted.

The offence can be committed by the D procuring the V for intercourse either with X, or with himself. In either case, there is the problem of what type of threats, intimidation or fraud will constitute the offence. The problem is similar to that of the issue of lack of consent in rape.[71] There must be some types of low-level threat which will not constitute the offence (for example, 'If you don't have sex with me I will never speak to you again'). But, what of the employer who tells his employee 'Be nice to client X, or you will not get promoted'? It has been suggested above that this type of threat will not lead to a finding that intercourse which subsequently occurs is non-consensual.[72] Can it, nevertheless, constitute the offence under s 2? There is no clear answer, and there is little case law to provide guidance. It has been suggested that the test should be whether the threat is one which a woman of the age and characteristics of the V could not reasonably be expected to resist.[73] It is difficult to think of any other practical approach to the issue, even though it leaves the scope of the offence shrouded in considerable uncertainty.

A similar difficulty exists in relation to the type of false statements which will be sufficient to commit the offence. Here, the degree of overlap with the offence of rape is smaller, in that, as we have seen, it is only a limited range of mistakes which will be taken to vitiate consent.[74] Nevertheless, it cannot be that every false statement will amount to 'procurement', unless every seducer who whispers 'I love you' without meaning it is to be regarded as a criminal. The only authority on the issue appears to be *Williams*,[75] which was decided on a previous version of this offence contained in s 3(2) of the Criminal Law Amendment Act 1885. Here, it was held that the offence was committed by a false promise of marriage. It was recognised by Hewart CJ that the section goes 'far beyond the case of rape'. Indeed, it seems that the limits of the offence cannot be fixed by law, but must be left to be determined by the common sense of prosecutors and courts.

69 [1964] 2 QB 404.

70 Procuring a woman under 21.

71 See above, p 146.

72 X would therefore not be guilty of rape, even if he knew of the D's threat.

73 *Op cit*, Smith and Hogan, fn 16, p 475.

74 See above, pp 144–46.

75 (1898) 62 JP 310.

In relation to both the offences, it is those cases which fall just short of amounting to rape, or conspiracy to rape (where the D is procuring for X), which will provide the most obvious situation in which to charge them.

ADMINISTERING DRUGS FOR THE PURPOSES OF SEXUAL INTERCOURSE

Section 4(1) of the SOA 1956 states that:

> It is an offence for a person to apply or administer, or cause to be taken by, a woman any drug matter or thing with intent to stupefy her so as thereby to enable any man to have unlawful sexual intercourse with her.

The use of the word 'unlawful' here means that the offence is not committed where the intended outcome is intercourse between husband and wife. This was confirmed by *Chapman*,[76] though the case was specifically concerned with s 19 of the SOA.[77] Where a husband administers drugs to his wife with a view this facilitating X to have intercourse, however, he will commit an offence under this section. In this case, unlike the offences under ss 2 and 3 of the SOA, there is no need for intercourse to take place. The *actus reus* is the administration of the drugs. Indeed, if intercourse does follow, it will be likely to amount to rape, for which the D who has administered the drug may be liable as principal (if he has intercourse with the V) or accessory (if X does).

INTERCOURSE WITH GIRLS UNDER 13 OR 16

Sections 5 and 6 make it an offence for a man to have unlawful sexual intercourse with a girl under 13, or 16, respectively. In relation to s 5, the prosecution does not have to prove that the D knew the true age of the girl, and in relation to s 6 it will not generally be necessary for it to do so. This follows from the decision in *Prince*,[78] where it was held that as regards offences of this kind,[79] a reasonable belief that the girl was older than the specified age provides no defence. The only exception to this is that, under s 6(3), a D who is under 24 does not commit an offence under s 6 if he reasonably believed that the V was over 16, and has not been previously

76 [1959] 1 QB 100.

77 Abduction of an unmarried girl under 18.

78 (1875) LR 2 CCR 154.

79 The case concerned the offence under Offences Against the Person Act 1861, s 55 – taking a girl of under 16 out of the possession of her parents.

charged with 'a like offence'.[80] If the girl is in fact under 13, however, such a D will commit an offence under s 5.

Both sections refer to 'unlawful' sexual intercourse. This presumably means that if the D is, by virtue of the law of another jurisdiction under which he is domiciled, legally married to the V, no offence is committed. In addition, D has a defence under s 6(2) if he reasonably thinks he is married to the V under English law, whereas in fact the marriage is invalid under s 2 of the Marriage Act 1949 or s 1 of the Age of Marriage Act 1929.

INTERCOURSE WITH 'DEFECTIVES'

Sections 7 and 9 of the SOA 1956 contain offences involving intercourse with a woman who is a 'defective'.[81] This term is defined by s 45 of the SOA as meaning:

> ... a person suffering from a state of arrested or incomplete development of mind which includes severe impairment of intelligence and social functioning.

The interpretation of this provision is a matter for the jury, applying the ordinary meaning of the words used.[82]

Section 7 makes it an offence to have unlawful sexual intercourse with such a woman, and s 9 to procure such a woman for such intercourse. In both cases the D will have a defence if he did not know, and had no reason to suspect, that the woman was a defective.

If, of course, the V's impairment is so substantial that she cannot be said to be capable of consenting to intercourse (because, for example, she does not understand the nature of the act), then D will be liable to be charged with rape.[83]

INDECENT ASSAULT

This type of assault is the second most serious type of sexual offence, after rape. It will be applicable to any kind of sexual attack which does not involve vaginal or anal penetration with the D's penis. Fellatio, or the insertion of something other than the D's penis into the V's anus or vagina, will fail to be

80 Ie, an offence under s 6, or an attempt to commit such an offence (s 6(3)).

81 Note, also, the offences under the Mental Health Act 1959, s 128, concerning intercourse with mentally disordered patients by staff at a hospital or nursing home, or a person having guardianship or custody of such a person.

82 *Hall (John Hamilton)* (1988) 86 Cr App R 159 – considering specifically the words 'severe impairment'.

83 See above, p 139 *et seq*.

dealt with as an indecent assault. It can, however, also cover minor touching of a sexual nature, and need not, as we shall see, involve contact between the D and the V at all. The offence deals, therefore, with a wide range of criminal behaviour, without the gradation of offences which exists in relation to non-sexual assaults. It is triable either way, with the maximum penalty on indictment being 10 years imprisonment, and on summary conviction, six months or a fine not exceeding the statutory maximum, or both.[84]

The offence is in fact contained in two sections of the Sexual Offences Act 1956, each being specific as regards the sex of the V. Section 14 deals with indecent assault on a woman, and s 15 with indecent assault on a man. In either case, the offence may be committed by any 'person', so that the D may be either a man or a woman. The wording of the two sections is virtually identical, apart from a specific provision dealing with the effect of an invalid marriage to a girl under the age of 16 (s 14(3)). The following discussion, therefore, deals with the offences under both sections together. Unless otherwise indicated, the sex of the V is irrelevant to the discussion.

Actus reus

The first requirement of the *actus reus* of this offence is that there should be an 'assault', meaning either an *assault* or a battery.[85] The rules applicable to the definition of these concepts in the non-sexual context will be applicable here. For example, it will be enough to constitute the offence if the V is put in fear of immediate unlawful sexual violence, even though the D does not in fact touch the V. The D who advances threateningly towards the V, indicating that he is going to rape her, commits an indecent *assault*, even if before he is able to carry out his threat she escapes, or he changes his mind.[86] It must also be possible in certain circumstances, following the decision in *Ireland*,[87] for an indecent *assault* to take place over the telephone. Certain types of sexual harassment, if they produce the appropriate apprehension in the V, will therefore also have the potential to be categorised as an indecent *assault*. On the other hand, an invitation by the D for the V to touch his penis will not involve an *assault*, and therefore cannot be an indecent *assault*.[88]

More commonly, however, the indecent assault will involve a battery. The rules relating to non-sexual battery will apply, so that the slightest touching

84 Sexual Offences Act 1956, s 37 and Sched 2.

85 See Chapter 5, p 103, for the distinction between assault and battery.

86 See, eg, *Rolfe* (1952) 36 Cr App Rep 4.

87 [1997] 4 All ER 225: see Chapter 5, p 105.

88 *Fairclough v Whipp* (1951) 35 Cr App R 138. If the V is another male, however, this may constitute the offence of 'procuring gross indecency' under SOA, s 13; or, if a male or female under 14, the offence of 'inciting an act of gross indecency' under the Indecency with Children Act 1960.

will have the potential to constitute the offence.[89] Two particular issues need consideration, however. First, there is the question of the consent of the V; secondly, there is the issue of what turns a battery into an *indecent* assault.

On the issue of consent, generally speaking, if there is genuine consent on the part of the V, there will be no assault, and therefore no indecent assault.[90] The question of the genuineness of the consent should be treated in the same way as consent in rape. The V's misapprehension as to the identity of the D, or the nature of the act will have the potential to nullify any consent apparently given.[91] There is a distinction here, however, in that there will be some types of serious sexual assault to which the V will be deemed unable to give a valid consent. The position is governed by the House of Lords decision in *Brown*,[92] which is discussed in detail in Chapter 7.[93] The effect is that if the assault results in injuries which are more than merely 'transient or trifling' the consent of the V is irrelevant. Thus, the D who, for their mutual sexual pleasure, whips the V's buttocks until they bleed, will almost certainly commit an indecent assault[94] (though, in *Brown*, such activities were charged as serious non-sexual assaults), despite the fact that the V welcomes the beating.

More difficulty surrounds the issue of what makes an assault 'indecent'. In particular, to what extent is the motive or intention of the D relevant to this issue? In many cases, of course, there is no problem categorising the assault as indecent. If the D touches the V's breasts, or sexual organs, whether through clothing or not, this will constitute the *actus reus* of an indecent assault. But what of the D who puts his hand on the V's thigh, or round the V's shoulders? Is it relevant whether the D acted out of a sexual motive? And what of the D who gains sexual pleasure from cutting the V's hair, or washing her feet? Can such activities ever constitute an indecent assault? The governing authority is the House of Lords decision in *Court*.[95]

The facts of *Court* involved a 26 year old D, who was a shop assistant. The V was a 12 year old girl who had visited the shop several times. On one occasion, the D had asked the V if she had ever been spanked, to which she replied that she had not. On a subsequent visit, the D asked the V if she would let him spank her. She said 'No', but the D pushed her to the back of the shop, and sitting on a chair pulled her face down across his knee. He then smacked

---

89 See Chapter 5, p 111.

90 But note that persons under 16, and 'defectives' (as defined in the SOA 1956, s 45), cannot, as a matter of law, consent to an indecent assault: s 14(2), (4), s 15(2), (3).

91 See, above, pp 141–46.

92 [1993] 2 All ER 75.

93 Chapter 7, p 178 *et seq*.

94 This follows from [1988] 2 All ER 221, discussed below. If only the V was gaining sexual pleasure, the offence would not be an indecent assault, but simply a wounding under the OAPA 1861, s 20.

95 [1988] 2 All ER 221.

her bottom about 12 times over the shorts which she was wearing. At this point, the V's brother came into the shop, and D stopped. The V reported what had happened to her parents, and the D was interviewed by the police. What had occurred was clearly an assault. When the D was questioned by the police about why he had spanked the V he replied: 'I don't know; buttock fetish.' The D was then charged with indecent assault. At the trial the judge allowed the evidence of his statement about his buttock fetish to be given, on the basis that it was relevant to the issue of the D's indecent intention at the time of the assault. The D was convicted, and appealed on the basis that his secret motive in carrying out the assault (that is, to gratify his own sexual feelings) could not turn an ordinary assault into an indecent assault. His argument was that the only mental element which was relevant to the offence of indecent assault was intention or recklessness as to the assault itself. The indecency should arise from the circumstances, not from the intentions or motives of the D.

The House of Lords (Lord Goff dissenting) rejected the D's appeal. The main speech was delivered by Lord Ackner. In the central part of his analysis, he identified three different categories of assault.[96] First, there are those assaults which are incapable of being indecent. In this category, he placed *George*,[97] in which the D removed or attempted to remove the V's shoes. Although the D admitted that this action gave him sexual gratification, the judge ruled that none of the assaults involved circumstances of indecency, and therefore could not possibly amount to indecent assaults. Evidence of the D's motives was thus irrelevant. The second category of case is where the D's actions are *ambiguous*. That is, they are *capable* of amounting to an indecent assault, but do not necessarily do so. In such a case, the intentions and motives of the D may be relevant. The majority of the House of Lords felt that the assault in *Court* fell into this category. The D's actions were capable of being construed as simply chastisement for some misbehaviour by the V, or they might have a sexual motive. Evidence of all the circumstances, including the D's reasons for spanking the V, were therefore relevant. The final category is where the D's assault is inherently indecent. The example given by Lord Ackner where the D removes the V's clothing against her will. In this case, the question of:

> ... whether he did so for his own personal sexual gratification or because, being a misogynist or for some other reason, he wished to embarrass or humiliate his victim seems to me to be irrelevant.[98]

This approach was followed by the Court of Appeal in *C*,[99] where it was held that, in relation to inherently indecent assaults, there was no need to establish

96 [1988] 2 All ER 221, pp 229–30.

97 [1956] Crim LR 52.

98 [1988] 2 All ER 221, p 230.

99 [1992] Crim LR 642.

a specific indecent intention. It is clearly possible, however, even in relation to such an assault to plead that the consequences were accidental. Lord Ackner does not think that the clumsy passenger on a rush hour tube train who rips a woman's clothes in his panic to alight should be guilty of an indecent assault, rather than simply an assault.[100] It will also be possible to plead 'lawful justification', for example, where the D undresses an unconscious V in the course of a medical emergency. Here, of course, the lawful justification will generally prevent there being an assault, let alone an indecent assault.

It will be seen that this analysis makes it difficult to separate the *actus reus* from the *mens rea* of this offence. If the motive of the D is a relevant issue in deciding whether an assault is indecent, this suggests that the two elements are not capable of being distinguished. It is possible, however, to define the *actus reus* as any assault which falls into one of the latter two categories identified by Lord Ackner – that is, assaults capable of being indecent, and assaults inherently indecent. The D will only be guilty of an indecent assault, however, if he has the required state of mind, which, as we shall see below, includes an intention to commit an assault which is indecent.[101]

The remaining difficulty with the House of Lords' analysis in *Court* is the practical one of defining those assaults which fall into the category of those which are *capable* of being indecent, but are not inherently so. Spanking is probably a particularly clear example of this category. Beating the buttocks can be simply a form of punishment. Nevertheless, the buttocks are an erogenous zone, and the use of spanking in a sexual context is well established not only in pornography, but also in popular culture,[102] and even in serious literature.[103] It is difficult to identify other behaviour, however, which has a similar ambiguity. It is at this, rather belated, point that we should consider exactly what the courts mean by 'indecency'. The definitions, such as they are, applied in other contexts (such as outraging public decency,[104] or the Protection of Children Act 1978)[105] are unlikely to be of much assistance here. Lord Ackner's definition in *Court*, which he repeats on several occasions is that an indecent assault is one which is 'so offensive to contemporary standards of modesty and privacy as to be indecent'.[106] The issue is primarily one of fact, to be decided by the jury. The focus is, however,

100 [1998] 2 All ER 221, p 229.

101 Or recklessness as to the indecency.

102 See, eg, the musical *Kiss Me Kate*, or the films of John Wayne, such as *Donovan's Reef*, and *McClintock*, where a woman is spanked by a man in a situation where there is sexual tension between them. Cf, also the Madonna song, 'Hanky Panky', which contains the line 'I don't want you to thank me, you can just spank me'.

103 Eg, Robert Coover, *Spanking the Maid*.

104 See, eg,*Gibson* [1991] 1 All ER 439.

105 See, eg, *Graham-Kerr* [1988] 1 WLR 1098.

106 [1988] 2 All ER 221, pp 229, 231.

on *modesty* and *privacy*. This is echoed by Lord Goff, in his dissenting speech, where he comments that:

> If a man gives a young woman a good spanking on the backside, the jury will ... have to consider whether the assault was such an affront to her modesty as to amount to an indecent assault.[107]

This quotation puts the emphasis on the affront to the modesty of the V; Lord Ackner's formulation seems to leave it as a more objective standard, leaving open the possibility that an assault can be regarded as indecent by the jury, even if the V did not treat it as such. It is submitted, however, that since the offence here is primarily concerned with the level of assault which the V has suffered, rather than maintaining public standards of decency, evidence as to the V's view of the nature of the assault should be relevant. This is not to suggest that there can only be an indecent assault where the V, *at the time*, regards it as being indecent. This would exclude assaults on Vs who were sleeping, or otherwise unconscious. But, in the same way as it has been suggested above that, in relation to rape, the V's feelings of violation are relevant,[108] so, in relation to indecent assault, the V's view as to whether or not the assault had a sexual element should be taken into account. Where the V was not conscious of the assault at the time, her subsequent attitude, on becoming aware of what the D had done, would provide the relevant test. This approach would have the effect of giving appropriate recognition to the infringement of the V's rights. It does not mean, however, that any assault which the V regards as indecent would lead to the D being guilty of that offence. In the first place, the D would still have to have the required state of mind for guilt (see below), and the V's evidence would only be relevant in relation to assaults which were objectively regarded as being capable of being indecent.

This brings us back to the question of what type of assaults, other than spanking, will fall into this intermediate category of assaults which are capable of being indecent, but are not inherently so. In the light of the above paragraph, the test is whether, applying contemporary standards, the assault is capable of being an affront to the V's modesty or privacy. On the basis of this test, it is suggested that the two examples given at the beginning of this discussion (cutting the V's hair, or washing the V's feet), would fall outside the category of possible indecent assaults. Even if the D gets sexual pleasure from the act, it is merely an assault, not an indecent assault.[109] There is insufficient affront to the V's modesty or privacy to move it into the 'ambiguous' category. More difficulty arises with an assault which involves tying up the V. As with spanking, there is a well recognised connection

107 [1988] 2 All ER 221.

108 See above, p 148–149.

109 Ie, it falls into the same category as the shoe fetishism in *George* [1956] Crim LR 52, above, p 160.

between bondage and sexual activity. Does this mean, for example, that a burglar who ties up the V in the course of a burglary, and incidentally gets sexual pleasure from doing so, is guilty of an indecent assault? Applying the approach in *Court*, the answer would seem to be 'Yes', assuming that the relevant mental state on the part of the D can be proved. Surely this is a situation, however, where, although it may fall into the category of 'capable of being indecent', the attitude of the V should also be relevant? If she treated the tying up as simply an incident of the burglary, then the fact that the D is found to be in possession of bondage pornography, and subsequently admits that he enjoyed tying the V up, should not alter the nature of any assault charge. In other words, the test of indecency should involve looking at contemporary standards, the motivation of the D, and the attitude of the V. All three elements should be important. This, it is admitted, goes beyond the decision of the majority in *Court*, but it does not directly conflict with it, and there are clear advantages in adding the attitude of the V into the analysis.

Finally, it should be noted that the reference to contemporary standards means that what is indecent may change over time.[110] This means that it is possible for certain behaviour to come to be recognised as having sexual overtones, and therefore possibly to move into the category of 'capable of being indecent'. This might, perhaps, be the case with the practice of 'toe sucking', which has been given prominence by the interest of the tabloid press in the activities of the Duchess of York. It might be that there has been a change in the contemporary view of what is indecent, so that a D who (going further than the shoe fetishist in *George*)[111] having removed the V's shoe, sucks her toes could be committing an indecent assault. On the other hand, the fact that the standards are to determined by 'right-thinking' persons means that only those standards which have general acceptance within society as a whole will be applied. Thus, the fact that the D and the V are members of a religious group who regard it as indecent for a man and woman to hold hands in public, will not turn the D's clasping of the V's hand in the street against her will into an indecent assault. Nor will the fact that, for example, the V is a strict follower of a version of the Islamic religion which requires her to be fully veiled in public mean that she would be indecently assaulted by a D who pulls aside her veil, revealing her face. The D will have assaulted her, but the assault will not be indecent, because according to the contemporary standards of 'right-thinking' people it is not an affront to modesty or privacy for a woman to expose her face in public. Such an assault thus falls into the category of those which are incapable of being indecent.

Applying all the above to the two examples given at the beginning of this discussion, it is submitted that for the D to place a hand on the V's thigh is an

110 See *Boyea* [1992] Crim LR 574, recognising the need to take account of changing social attitudes.

111 [1956] Crim LR 52.

act capable of being indecent, since in some circumstances it will amount to an affront to the V's modesty and privacy; on the other hand, for the D to put an arm around the V's shoulders will not involve such an affront, and so is not capable of being an indecent assault.

Mens rea

This issue has already received some discussion above. The position is that stated by Lord Ackner at the conclusion of his speech in *Court*, and with which the majority of the House of Lords agreed. He stated that:

> On a charge of indecent assault, the prosecution must prove (1) that the accused intentionally assaulted the victim, (2) that the assault, or the assault and the circumstances accompanying it, are capable of being considered by right-minded persons as indecent, (3) that the accused intended to commit such an assault as is referred to in (2) above.

The mental element of indecent assault, therefore, contains two parts. First, the prosecution must prove the same *mens rea* as is necessary for a common *assault* or battery.[112] This means intention or *Cunningham* recklessness. Secondly, following the decision in *Court*, the prosecution must prove that the D acted intentionally or recklessly as regards committing an assault which was capable of being indecent. In arriving at this conclusion, the majority of the House of Lords in *Court* gave support to the ruling of the trial judge in *Pratt*.[113] The Vs, two 13 year old boys who were fishing at night, were accosted by the D. He threatened them with a gun, and ordered them to undress. As each boy did so, the other was required to shine a torch on him. There was no contact between the D and the Vs. The judge admitted evidence from the D that his intention in causing the boys to expose themselves was to search for cannabis which he allege that they had taken from him the previous day. The prosecution had objected to this evidence, in that all that was required for the offence was that there was an assault (for which intention or recklessness must be proved) in circumstances of indecency. The House of Lords in *Court*, however, held that the judge had been correct in allowing the evidence. The D's story, though implausible, did provide evidence that he had no intention of committing an assault which was indecent, and this, if believed, would entitle him to an acquittal. Conversely, in *Court* itself, the evidence of the D's intention in committing the assault was relevant to establishing that he did have an indecent intention, in circumstances which were ambiguous.

As regards the assault element of the offence, since consent will generally provide a defence, then belief in the V's consent will also lead to an acquittal.

112 For which, see Chapter 5, p 109.

113 [1984] Crim LR 41.

Following the principle established in relation to this issue by *Morgan*,[114] in respect of rape, the belief does not have to be reasonable. This was confirmed by the Court of Appeal decision in *Kimber*.[115] The V was a mental patient, suffering from schizophrenia. The D was found to have interfered with her in a way which, if done without her consent, would clearly have amounted to an indecent assault. D's defence was that he thought that the V was consenting. The judge refused to allow the jury to consider this issue, directing them that such a belief was not a defence. The Court of Appeal, following *Morgan*, ruled that the judge's direction was wrong. If there was a genuine belief in consent, then this meant that the D did not have the *mens rea* for an assault. There has to be a positive belief, however. As with rape, indifference to whether the V is consenting will not provide a defence. Thus, in *Kimber*, the D had stated in evidence: 'I was not really interested in [the V's] feelings at all.'[116] The Court of Appeal held that this indicated that the D did not have a genuine belief that the V was consenting, and it therefore allowed his conviction to stand, despite the judge's misdirection on the issue.

This principle will not, with one exception, protect the D, however, if the V is under 16, or a 'defective'.[117] Such persons are deemed to be unable to give consent to an indecent assault.[118] The one exception is where the V is the 'wife' in a marriage which is invalid because she is under 16. Here, if the D believes her to be his wife, and has reasonable cause for the belief, he will not be guilty of an indecent assault simply because of the statutory presumption of lack of consent.[119]

The provisions deeming defectives, and those under 16, as being unable to give a valid consent, give rise to some difficulty in relation to medical treatment. If an examination or treatment is performed on a person in these categories, and it involves touching the patient in a way which, if performed by a non-medical person would be inherently indecent, what prevents this from being an indecent assault? The issue was considered by the Court of Appeal in *Court*.[120] The view expressed there was that consent may be given by the parent or guardian of a V who falls into one of the protected categories. Even if no such consent has been given, however, there would still be no assault, if the touching was carried out for a 'genuine medical purpose':

114 [1976] AC 182; [1975] 2 All ER 347; above, p 151.

115 [1983] 3 All ER 316.

116 *Ibid*, p 318.

117 Defined in SOA, s 45, as 'a person suffering from a state of arrested or incomplete development of mind which includes severe impairment of intelligence and social functioning'.

118 SOA, s 14(2), (4); s 15(2), (3).

119 *Ibid*, s 14(3).

120 [1987] 1 All ER 120, p 125.

> Neither the girl examined, nor the right-thinking members of society, would regard such an examination as an affront to the modesty of the girl or conduct which contravened normal standards of indecent behaviour.

The majority of the House of Lords did not deal directly with this point, but presumably would come to the same conclusion. Lord Ackner refers to the fact that an 'inherently indecent' assault may have a lawful justification,[121] and this would presumably include necessary medical examinations or treatment. What of the situation where the person carrying out the examination or treatment has a dual motive? That is, the examination or treatment is genuinely required on medical grounds, but the person carrying it out also gains sexual pleasure from doing so. On the Court of Appeal's analysis in *Court*, which Lord Goff agreed with in the House of Lords, the intention of the D as regards the indecency of the assault is irrelevant. Provided the circumstances are objectively 'decent', a secret improper motive will not render them indecent. This means that the doctor or nurse acting with a dual motive would not commit an assault. The majority of the House of Lords in *Court*, however, held, as we have seen, that the intention of the D is relevant evidence. The implication of this is that an improper motive can turn an otherwise lawful medical examination, genuinely required by the V for medical reasons, into an indecent assault. It should be noted, however, that this only applies where the statutory presumption against consent operates. If the patient is competent to give consent, and the examination is needed, then the consent will prevent it from being an assault at all, let alone an indecent one.

BUGGERY: SOA, s 12

Section 12 of the SOA deals with two types of sexual activity. The first is anal intercourse by a man with another man or woman; the second is any type of sexual intercourse between a man or a woman and an animal.

Both versions of the offence are triable only on indictment. The maximum penalty where the offence is committed with a person under 16 or an animal is life imprisonment. If the D is over 20 and the other party under 18, the maximum is five years; in all other cases it is two years.

Anal intercourse

Non-consensual anal intercourse now constitutes, as we have seen, the offence of rape.[122] Consensual anal intercourse will only be an offence where either or

121 [1988] 2 All ER 221, p 230.

122 See above, p 140.

both of the parties are under the age of 18, or the intercourse does not take place in private.[123] The act ceases to be 'private' for these purposes, if both parties are male:

(a) when more that two persons take part or are present; or

(b) in a lavatory to which the public have or are permitted to have access, whether on payment or otherwise.

There is no special definition of 'in private' in relation to heterosexual buggery. It will be a question of fact to be determined in all the circumstances.[124]

Both parties to the buggery commit the offence, if it is consensual.

The extension of the offence of rape to cover non-consensual anal intercourse has reduced the role for this offence. Where, however, a female V is under 18 and there is evidence of both vaginal and anal intercourse, the prosecution may find it easier to get a conviction for buggery, since here the issue of consent (the absence of which can sometimes be difficult to prove beyond reasonable doubt) is irrelevant.

Intercourse with an animal

For a man or a woman to have sexual intercourse with an animal constitutes the offence of buggery. Generally, this will not be an 'offence against the person' since the 'victim', if any, is the animal. The facts of *Bourne*,[125] however, show that there may in some cases be a human victim. Here, the D had compelled his wife to have intercourse with a dog. The D was convicted of aiding and abetting the offence of buggery. It is assumed that his wife, although she had intentionally committed the *actus reus*, would have had a defence of 'duress'.[126]

Assault with intent to commit buggery: SOA, s 16

Section 16 of the SOA simply states that 'it is an offence for a person to assault another person with intent to commit buggery'. The offence is triable on indictment and punishable with a maximum of 10 years imprisonment.

The *actus reus* of this offence is that of *assault* or battery.[127] The *mens rea* requires proof of intention or *Cunningham* recklessness as regards the assault;

123 SOA, s 12(1A).

124 See, eg, *Reakes* [1974] Crim LR 615.

125 (1952) 36 Cr App R 125.

126 See Chapter 7, p 187 *et seq*.

127 See Chapter 5, pp 104 and 111. Cf, also, the discussion of indecent assault, above, p 159.

in addition, there must be the ulterior intention to commit buggery. What is not clear is whether the phrase 'commit buggery' should be interpreted as 'commit the offence of buggery', or 'commit the physical acts involved in buggery', that is, anal intercourse. If the former interpretation is correct, the offence is greatly reduced in scope since many cases of non-consensual anal intercourse have now been re-categorised as 'rape'.[128] It would only apply in effect to assaults on persons under the age of 18. It seems unlikely that this was the intention of parliament, and so it is submitted that the preferable interpretation is to treat 'buggery' in this section as meaning 'anal intercourse' rather than the offence of buggery.[129]

It seems that there is no offence of assault with intent to rape,[130] though many such assaults could amount to an attempted rape.[131]

INDECENCY WITH CHILDREN UNDER 14

Section 1(1) of the Sexual Offences Act 1960 contains two versions of an offence involving indecency with children. The first is committing an act of 'gross indecency' with or towards a child under the age of 14. The second is inciting a child under that age to commit such an act with the D or another. The offence (in either version) is triable either way, punishable on indictment with up to two years imprisonments, and on summary conviction with up to six months, or a fine not exceeding the prescribed sum.

'Gross indecency' is not defined, but cases have identified activities such as masturbating in the presence of a child,[132] or allowing a child to leave her hand on the D's penis.[133] The offence will be appropriate where there is indecency without any assault (as, for example, in *Fairclough v Whipp*),[134] thus precluding a charge of indecent assault.

INDECENT EXPOSURE

Where a man exposes his penis to a woman, there is the possibility of this being charged either as the common law offence of 'outraging public decency'

128 As a result of the Criminal Justice and Public Order Act 1994.

129 This is the view taken in *Archbold*, para 20-172.

130 *Ibid*, para 20-15.

131 For which, see above, p 152.

132 *Francis* (1989) 88 Cr App R 127 – since the act must be directed towards the child, the D must at least be aware that the child is watching.

133 *Speck* (1977) 65 Cr App R 161.

134 [1951] 2 All ER 834 – see above, p 186.

(triable only on indictment), or the statutory offence under s 4 of the Vagrancy Act 1824 (triable only summarily). In practice, the latter is the much more common charge, and that is the one that will be discussed here. It should be noted, however, that the common law offence is potentially much wider in scope, not being limited to exposure of the penis, but including any kind of indecency, whether the D is male or female.[135]

Actus reus

The *actus reus* of the offence is constituted by the D 'openly, lewdly and obscenely' exposing his 'person' (meaning his penis). Unlike the common law offence, that under the Vagrancy Act does not have to be committed in public,[136] nor does there have to be more than one other person present. The requirement of 'lewdness' and 'obscenity' will be more easily satisfied if the penis is erect, but this is not a necessary element in the *actus reus*. Much will depend on the circumstances. What is acceptable on a beach (in particular one where nude bathing is permitted) or at a swimming pool, will be different from a public street, or in a shop. In practice, this issue is likely to be subsumed into consideration of the intention of the D, which is considered next.

Mens rea

The Act requires that that the D acts 'wilfully' (presumably meaning intentionally), and 'with intent to insult any female'. The prosecution must therefore prove either that there was a female present whom the D was intending to insult, or at least that the D though that such a female was present. If the D's actions are directed towards another male then no offence is committed under the 1824 Act, thought it may well still be possible to charge an offence of outraging public decency under the common law. As far as the requirement of 'insulting' is concerned it is likely that the act itself will be found to be intended to be insulting, unless the D can produce some explanation why it should not be found to be so. For example, the D might claim that he mistakenly thought that the woman to whom he was exposing himself was his wife or girlfriend, and that he had not reason to anticipate that she would be insulted by his actions. It is unlikely, however, that in the vast majority of cases any plausible explanation of this kind will be available, and the burden of proof, while remaining on the prosecution, will not be very onerous in relation to this element of the offence.

135 See, eg, *op cit*, Smith and Hogan, fn 37, pp 489–91.

136 *Ford v Falcone* [1971] 2 All ER 1138.

Penalty

The maximum penalty for an offence under s 4 of the 1824 Act is three months' imprisonment, or a fine not exceeding level 3, or both. On a second offence, the D may be committed to the Crown Court for sentence, where the maximum term of imprisonment is 12 months.

CHAPTER 7

DEFENCES

This chapter is concerned with the defences which may be available to a D charged with one of the offences against the person outlined in Chapters 4 and 6. Some special defences to murder, that is provocation and diminished responsibility, were considered in Chapter 4. These have the effect of reducing the offence of murder to manslaughter. The defences discussed in this chapter provide, if successful, a complete answer to the charge, and entitle the D to an acquittal. They are also 'general' in that they will potentially be available in relation to a range of offences against the person. It is for this reason that they are dealt with here in a separate chapter. They are not, however, necessarily available across the board. As we shall see, some defences, such as consent and duress, are not available in relation to the most serious levels of offence. By contrast, intoxication will only operate as an excuse in relation to offences requiring a specific mental element, which generally means the more serious offences.[1]

It is important to remember in considering 'defences' that the burden of proof generally remains on the prosecution. In other words, if the evidence provides at least some basis for the D being able to claim a defence, it is up to the prosecution to prove beyond reasonable doubt that the defence should not be available. Those exceptional cases where the burden is on the D will be specifically noted. In all other cases, it should be assumed that the burden lies on the prosecution.

A further general issue which needs to be noted before the particular defences are discussed is the distinction which is sometimes drawn between defences which 'justify' the D's conduct, and defences which 'excuse' it. The role of this distinction in the modern analysis of criminal law is generally acknowledged to derive from the work of George Fletcher, in particular, Chapter 1 of his book, *Rethinking Criminal Law*.[2] It has subsequently been adopted and developed by other writers.[3] Although the distinction has not been given much attention by the courts, it can be useful in explaining the differences between the ways in which various defences operate. If the D's action is 'justified' by the defence, this means that the action is approved, and no wrong has been committed by the D. If, on the other hand, the action is

1 Eg, it is available in relation to murder, but not manslaughter.

2 Fletcher, G, *Rethinking Criminal Law*, 1978, New York: Little, Brown.

3 See, eg, Slater, J, 'Making sense of self-defence' (1996) 5 Nott LJ 140, pp 146–47, and Clarkson, CMV and Keating, HM, *Criminal Law: Text and Materials*, 4th edn, 1998, London: Sweet & Maxwell, pp 276–87.

'excused', the D's behaviour is acknowledged to involve a wrong against the V, but avoids being categorised as criminal because of the excusatory circumstances. Thus, the woman who, in resisting an attempted rape, uses violence against her attacker, will be regarded as being justified in doing so. Her actions, which would otherwise constitute a serious assault, are regarded with approval – she is entitled to act in this way against an aggressor. On the other hand, the D who is so drunk that he does not realise what he is doing when he uses lethal force against the V, may be excused from liability for murder, but will remain liable for manslaughter. His actions are not justified, but they may be, to a limited extent, excused by the circumstances. Of the defences considered here, self-defence and consent are justificatory; the others (with the possible exception of necessity) are excusatory.

SELF-DEFENCE AND PREVENTION OF CRIME

The extent to which a person can use personal force against another who is engaging in criminal activity is governed by a mixture of common law and statute. The relevant statutory provision is s 3 of the Criminal Law Act 1967, which states:

> (1) A person may use such force as is reasonable in the circumstances in the prevention of crime, or in effecting or assisting in the lawful arrest of offenders or suspected offenders or of persons unlawfully at large.
>
> (2) Sub-s (1) above shall replace the rules of the common law on the question when force used for a purpose mentioned in the sub-section is justified by that purpose.

It might appear that this provision has removed the need for any common law defence of self-defence, in that any situation justifying the use of force against an aggressor will also involve the prevention of crime. This is not strictly true, as it is possible that the aggressor will also have a defence, such as insanity, duress or mistake, which will mean that he or she is not in fact committing any crime. Nevertheless, the principles which are to be applied are the same whether the defence arises under the statute or the common law. There is no need, therefore, in the following discussion to make any rigid distinction between the two.

What type of situation will justify the use of force against another person by a D? The most obvious example is where the D himself is under attack. He is not expected to turn the other cheek, but is entitled to respond with appropriate force. Such force may also be used to intervene in the commission of an offence against a third party – the person concerned does not have to have any familial or other connection with the D. It is perfectly legitimate to intervene to restrain an assault by X on Y, even though the D himself thereby commits an assault on one or other of the parties. More difficult is whether the

D is entitled to use force to protect his, or other people's, property. It seems clear that, in some situations, he is. Indeed, in *Hussey*,[4] the Court of Criminal Appeal went so far as to approve a passage in Archbold to the effect that a person may kill a trespasser who would forcibly dispossess him of his house. This must be of doubtful authority as regards the extent of the force which can be used, but there is no doubt that in appropriate circumstances an assault on person who is damaging or interfering with the D's property will be justified. The D who sees someone attempting to break into his car (or, indeed, that of a third party) is clearly entitled to grab the person, or push them away in a manner which would otherwise constitute a battery. The question is in every case, as s 3 of the 1967 makes clear, whether the use of such force is reasonable in the circumstances.

The test of 'reasonableness' in this context must involve considerations of 'proportionality'. Not only must the use of force be reasonable, but the D must not use more force than is necessary and appropriate. For example, a D who is threatened with fists will not generally be entitled to stab or shoot the aggressor. The courts allow a degree of latitude here, however, and there is no hard and fast rule that the D must only respond at the same level as his assailant. The approach taken is well stated in the following passage from Lord Morris's speech in *Palmer v The Queen*:[5]

> If there has been an attack so that defence is reasonably necessary, it will be recognised that a person defending himself cannot weigh to a nicety the exact measure of his necessary defensive action. If a jury thought that in a moment of unexpected anguish a person attacked had only done what he honestly and instinctively thought was necessary that would be the most potent evidence that only reasonable defensive action had been taken.

The question is therefore whether the D's action was within the reasonable range of responses to the perceived threat. This problem is particularly acute where the D is an armed soldier or police officer. As Lord Lloyd noted in *Clegg*:[6]

> In most cases of a person acting in self-defence ... there is a choice as to the degree of force to be used, even if it is a choice which has to be exercised on the spur of the moment, without time for measured reflection. But in the case of a soldier in Northern Ireland, in the circumstances in which Pte Clegg found himself,[7] there is no scope for graduated force. The only choice lay between firing a high-velocity rifle which, if aimed accurately, was almost certain to kill or injure, and doing nothing at all.

4 (1924) 18 Cr App R 160.

5 [1971] AC 814.

6 [1995] 1 All ER 334, p 344.

7 Ie, attempting to stop a car containing suspected terrorists.

The main areas of difficulty, however, which have arisen in relation to this defence are:

(a) is the test of reasonableness objective, or can the D who has made a mistake about the need for force still take advantage of the defence?;

(b) if the D has any alternative to the use of force, must this alternative be taken?;

(c) can the D engage in a 'pre-emptive' strike against someone whom he believes is about to attack him?

These issues will now be considered in turn.

Mistake

There are two issues which may be involved where the D has made a mistake. First, the D may have misread the situation, and thought that it was one where force was justified, whereas in fact it was not. Secondly, the D may have felt justified in using more force than is objectively reasonable. As we shall see, the courts have adopted a subjective approach to the first type of mistake, but an objective one to the second.

As regards the mistake as to whether any force is justified, the current law derives from the Court of Appeal's approach in *Gladstone Williams*,[8] as approved by the Privy Council in *Beckford*.[9] In *Gladstone Williams*, the D observed the V apparently attacking a third party, X. The D intervened on X's behalf, and assaulted the V. What the D did not know was that the V had observed X mugging a woman, and was trying to arrest him. The judge directed the jury that in order to decide whether the D's assault was justified as action taken in defence of X, they should consider the D held an honest belief based on reasonable grounds that reasonable force was necessary to prevent a crime. The D was convicted, and appealed on the basis that this constituted a misdirection. The Court of Appeal held that the jury should have been directed that, if the D was labouring under a mistake of fact, his behaviour was to be assessed on the basis of his mistaken view, whether or not this was reasonable. Reasonableness was only relevant in this context as part of the decision as to whether or not the D actually held the belief he claimed. Once it was accepted that he did, then he was entitled to be judged on the basis of the circumstances as he believed them to be. If those circumstances, had they been as the D believed, would have justified the use of the force which the D in fact used, then he was entitled to be acquitted. As Lord Griffiths pointed out in *Beckford*[10] this conclusion was a logical

8 (1984) Cr App R 276.

9 [1987] 3 All ER 425.

10 *Ibid*, p 431.

development from the view of mistake of fact set out by the House of Lords in *DPP v Morgan*,[11] in the context of rape.

As regards the need for force, therefore, the test is subjective, based on the circumstances as the D believed them to be. What, however, if, in circumstances that justify some force, the D uses more force than is reasonable? Is the test similarly subjective, or should an objective view of what is permitted be applied here? The wording of s 3 of the 1967 Act suggests that an approach based on objective reasonableness ('such force as is reasonable in the circumstances') is the correct one, and, after some uncertainty,[12] this has now been confirmed by the House of Lords in *Clegg*.[13] In this case, the D was a soldier, serving in Northern Ireland, who shot at a car approaching a roadblock. The evidence was that three shots were fired at the windscreen, and a fourth after the car had passed the D. The final shot killed the V, one of the occupants of the car. The D was charged with murder, but argued that he was acting in defence of himself or his fellow soldiers manning the roadblock. This was accepted as regards the first three shots, but not in relation to the fourth, which was fired once the danger had passed. In relation to that shot, which was the fatal one, the D was convicted of murder. His appeal was rejected by the Northern Ireland Court of Appeal, but that court certified a question for the House of Lords raising the possibility of someone using excessive force in self-defence or prevention of crime, being convicted of manslaughter, rather than murder. This approach had at one time been taken in Australia,[14] but had never been accepted in any part of the United Kingdom. The House of Lords in *Clegg* held that the same approach should apply whether the D was relying on force used in self-defence, the prevention of crime, or the arrest of a suspect. In each case the D was only entitled to use such force as was reasonable in the circumstances as he believed them to be. If he used force which was excessive (the clear implication being that this is to be judged objectively), and the V died, then, assuming that the D can be proved to have intended to cause death or grievous bodily harm, the offence is murder, not manslaughter. On the facts, the only basis on which the D could be said to have been justified in the use of force was to arrest the driver of the car. In respect of this:

> The Court of Appeal were entitled to hold, having reviewed all the evidence, that the use of lethal force to kill or wound the driver of the car in order to arrest him was, in the circumstances, so grossly disproportionate to the mischief to be averted as to deprive him of a defence under s 3, and that any

11 [1975] 2 All ER 347, above, p 151.

12 Arising principally from *Scarlett* [1993] 1 All ER 334; but, cf *Owino* [1995] Crim LR 743.

13 [1995] 1 All ER 334.

14 See, eg, *R v Howe* (1958) 100 CLR 448, and *Viro v R* (1978) 141 CLR 88, which were rejected by the High Court of Australia in *Zecevic v DPP (Victoria)* (1987) 162 CLR 645.

> reasonable tribunal of fact, if properly directed, would inevitably have so found.[15]

The phraseology here again assumes an objective test in relation to the question of whether the force used is excessive. The conclusion that this is the approach favoured by the House of Lords is affirmed by the fact that the possibility of objectively excessive force reducing murder to manslaughter is rejected; if the use of such force cannot have this mitigating effect, there is clearly no justification for it operating as a full defence.

To conclude on this issue, therefore, the test is that the where the D makes no mistake as to the circumstances, he may use only such force as is reasonable in those circumstances; where a mistake is made, the D is entitled to the defence where he has used only such force as would have been reasonable if the circumstances had been as the D believed them to be.

The final point to be noted is that if the D is voluntarily intoxicated at the relevant time, then he will not be able to rely on a mistaken belief that self-defence was necessary. This was established in *O'Connor*,[16] following *obiter* comments to the same effect in *O'Grady*.[17] The charge in *O'Connor* was murder, but there is no reason to suppose that the principle would not be of general application.[18]

Possibility of an alternative to use of force

If the D has the possibility of using some other means of achieving the same objective, can he nevertheless still rely on self-defence or prevention of crime? If, for example, there is an opportunity to escape from an attack, should this be taken? The basic principle that the force used must be reasonable in the circumstances suggests that there should be no absolute obligation to take any possible opportunity to escape or retreat. English law having for a time taken a different view, now follows this line. In *Julien*,[19] it was stated that the D should have made some indication of a wish to withdraw or disengage, before being allowed to rely on self-defence. In the later cases of *McInnes*[20] and *Bird*,[21] however, the view was taken that the fact that there might have been the possibility of escape is simply one factor to be taken into account in assessing the reasonableness of the D's actions. This will presumably also apply any other alternative to force which might have been open to the D. The

15 [1995] 1 All ER 334, pp 344–45.

16 [1991] Crim LR 135.

17 [1987] 3 All ER 420.

18 For further discussion of intoxication as a defence, see below, p 204.

19 (1969) 53 Cr App R 407.

20 (1971) 53 Cr App R 551.

21 [1985] 1 WLR 816.

fact that the D chose force rather than any other possible option will not preclude the use of the defence, provided that the choice is regarded as being reasonable in the circumstances.

Is a pre-emptive strike permissible?

So far, it has been assumed that the D is acting in response to an attack on him, or the actions of a person who appears to be engaged in committing a criminal offence. Is it permissible, however, for the D to 'get his retaliation in first'? If he suspects that he is about to be attacked, or that the V is about to commit an offence, can the D use force against the V immediately, or must be wait until the V has started to act? The answers to these questions follow on to some extent from the discussion above about the possibility of a duty to retreat. In other words, the test is once again whether the D's action is reasonable in the circumstances. The possibility of a defence in such circumstances was recognised by McDermott LJ in the Northern Ireland case of *Devlin v Armstrong*,[22] where he stated:

> The plea of self-defence may afford a defence where the party raising it uses force, not merely to counter an actual attack, but to ward off or prevent an attack which he has honestly and reasonably anticipated. In that case, however, the anticipated attack must be imminent.[23]

The matter was considered further in the *Attorney General's Reference (No 2 of 1983)*.[24] In this case, the D's shop had been attacked in rioting. Fearing further attacks, he made some petrol bombs, though they were never used. He was charged with an offence under s 4 of the Explosive Substances Act 1883, which allows a defence of 'lawful object'. The trial judge ruled that 'self-defence' could in the circumstances constitute a 'lawful object'. This point was referred to the Court of Appeal by the Attorney General. The court concluded that self-defence can cover not only the actions of the D taken directly against aggression, but also 'acts immediately preparatory' to such actions. The defence therefore extended to a D taken preparatory steps towards self-defence, provided that:

> ... his object was to protect himself or his family or his property against imminent apprehended attack and to do so by means which he believed were no more than reasonably necessary to meet the force used by the attackers.

This case was, of course, concerned with the specific defence available under the 1883 Act, but there is no reason to doubt that the principle stated can have

22 [1971] NI 13.

23 At this point, he referred to *Chisam* (1963) 47 Cr App R 130, and the Scottish case of *Owens v HM Advocate* (1946) SC (J) 119.

24 [1984] 1 All ER 988.

more general application to self-defence. The passage quoted above, however, would presumably need to be amended, in the light of the current position in respect of mistakes as to the level of force which may be used,[25] by removing the words 'he believed'. The D may use such force against an imminent apprehended attack as is reasonable in the circumstances.

The major limitation on the 'pre-emptive' strike is that the attack must be, or be believed to be, imminent. This is why this defence has not been of great use to battered women who have taken the opportunity of their aggressors being asleep, or otherwise off guard, to attack them.[26]

CONSENT

The issue of consent has already been given some consideration in the discussion of sexual offences, in particular rape, and indecent assault.[27] Here, we are looking more generally at the scope of consent of the V in providing a defence to offences against the person. If we approach the subject from the point of view of the V, then it seems that consent should be a complete defence. To the extent that the criminal law in this area is directed at protecting the rights of Vs, then it would be anomalous to convict a D who has only done what the V has asked. If the V is happy with the D's actions, how can there be any infringements of the V's rights; and if there is no infringement of the V's rights, why should there be criminal liability attaching to the D's behaviour. As we have seen, however, in Chapter 1,[28] the rights of the V are not the only consideration in relation to the criminalisation of offences against the person; there is also a more general public interest which is deemed to justify some behaviour being categorised as criminal, even where it is carried out with the V's consent. The leading authority on the current state of the law in relation to consent as a defence, is the House of Lords decision in *Brown*.[29] Before looking in detail at this decision, however, we should note certain the effect of certain earlier decisions which provide the background to *Brown*, and identify the issues which have tended to cause problems.

First, there is the issue as to whether lack of consent is part of the definition of an offence, so that if there was consent one of the elements of the offence is missing. This is undoubtedly the position in relation to rape, since the statute specifically refers to 'intercourse without consent' in defining the

25 Above, pp 174–76.

26 Cf the discussion of this area in Chapter 4, pp 77–82.

27 See Chapter 6, pp 141–46.

28 See Chapter 1, pp 2–7.

29 [1993] 2 All ER 75.

actus reus.[30] The matter is unclear in relation to assaults (including indecent assaults), and other offences against the person, but, as we shall see, the majority of the House of Lords in Brown seemed to treat lack of consent as not being part of the definition. This may help to explain the decision which was reached in that case.

Secondly, there is the question of whether there is a limit to the level of violence to which a V can consent, and, if so, what that limit is. There is no dispute that express or implied consent can be given to the kind of physical contact which forms part of the incidents of every day life. For example, brushing against another person in a crowded shop or train, is not an offence (because of implied consent); nor is it one to cut someone's hair at their request (express consent). At the opposite end of the scale, there is no dispute that under current English law the D who deliberately kills the V will be liable for murder, even if the V has pleaded with the D to do so.[31] 'Mercy killing' is no defence (though some argue that it should be). The problem lies with the point between these two extremes at which the law should ignore consent. What level (if any) of violence or injury should override the V's agreement to it? Linked with this is the question of how the law should treat injuries resulting from what are accepted to be legitimate activities, such as sports (football, rugby, boxing), religious ritual (circumcision), or cosmetic enhancement (body piercing, tattooing). Should the issue of consent be treated differently in these areas, or should the general rule apply? The following discussion will centre on these issues.

Prior to *Brown*, there were two main English authorities dealing with this area, neither of them entirely satisfactory. They were *Donovan*,[32] and the *Attorney General's Reference (No 6 of 1980)*.[33] In *Donovan*, the V was a prostitute of 17. After some telephone conversations in which the D made it clear that he wished to beat her for his sexual gratification, they met. The D asked 'Where would you like to have your spanking, in Hyde Park or in my garage?'. The V went with the D to his garage, where he beat her with a cane, leaving seven or eight marks which a medical witness said was indicative of 'a fairly severe beating'. The D was charged with indecent assault and common assault, and was convicted. He appealed on the basis that the V had consented to the beating. His appeal succeeded because the jury had not been directed on the issue of the burden of proof in relation to consent. The Court of Criminal Appeal also held, however, that consent could not generally apply to provide a defence where the D had inflicted bodily injury calculated to interfere with the health or comfort of the V, which was more than merely transient or

30 See Chapter 6, p 139.

31 The only exception is a killing as part of a suicide pact, which will reduce the offence to manslaughter: see Chapter 4, p 89.

32 [1934] 2 KB 498; [1934] All ER Rep 207.

33 [1981] 2 All ER 1057.

trifling. It was up to the jury to decide whether in a particular case the D had inflicted or intended to inflict bodily injury in this sense. *Donovan*, therefore, provided authority, albeit in the form of *obiter dicta*, for the proposition that consent is not relevant once the injury caused on intended amounts to what is in effect 'actual bodily harm' (as under s 47 of the OAPA 1861).[34, 35] The Court did not, however, consider in any detail the exceptions in relation to this general rule, which clearly exist in relation to sporting activities, etc. This issue was taken a little further in the *Attorney General's Reference (No 6 of 1980)*.[36] Here the principal concern was the legality of fighting between two people who had agreed only to use reasonable force. The precise question before the Court of Appeal was:

> Where two persons fight (otherwise than in the course of sport) in a public place can it be a defence for one of these persons to a charge of assault arising out of the fight that the other consented to fight?

The court did not think that the reference to a 'public place' had any relevance to a charge of assault: the same principles should apply to actions which take in public or in private. It also felt that 'it is an essential element of an assault that the act is done contrary to the will and without the consent of the victim', the burden lying on the prosecution to disprove consent. However, in certain circumstances the public interest will intervene to override consent. The question is, what are those circumstances? The court took the view that the answer to that question is:

> ... that it is not in the public interest that people should try to cause each other actual bodily harm for no good reason. Minor struggles are another matter. So, in our judgment, it is immaterial whether the act occurs in private or in public; it is an assault if actual bodily harm is intended and/or caused. This means that most fights will be unlawful regardless of consent.

This decision, therefore, like that in *Donovan*, draws the line at 'actual bodily harm'. The court recognises, however, that in some circumstances there may be a 'good reason' for the actual bodily harm. This may result from the fact that the perpetrator of the harm is acting in the exercise of a legal right, as will be the case with 'lawful chastisement or correction'.[37] Alternatively, it may be that the 'public interest' will provide the 'good reason'. This will be the case in relation to 'properly conducted games and sports ... reasonable surgical interference, dangerous exhibitions, etc'. Public interest may, therefore, pull in

---

34 See Chapter 5, p 114.

35 As pointed out by Lord Mustill, in *Brown* [1993] 2 All ER 75, p 112, this conclusion seemed to require the jury to consider the D's liability for an offence with which he had not been charged (that is, assault occasioning actual bodily harm) and for that reason alone should perhaps be treated with caution.

36 [1981] 2 All ER 1057.

37 Ie, generally, of a child by his or her parent. Note that the legality of such punishment does not in this case depend on the consent of the victim! See the comment to this effect by Lord Mustill in *Brown* [1993] 2 All ER 75, p 110. See, also, below, p 197.

two opposite directions. First, it may operate to take certain assaults outside the range of those to which consent may validly be given; alternatively, other considerations of public interest may bring such assaults back within the scope of valid consent. The problem with this approach, however, is that it leads to uncertainty in the law. How is the D to know before he acts whether a court will view his actions as being protected by considerations of the public interest? The Court of Appeal itself recognised this point, but commented:

> ... it does not seem to us that the particular uncertainty enshrined in the reference has caused practical inconvenience in the administration of justice during the last few hundred years. We would not wish our judgment on the point to be the signal for unnecessary prosecutions.

It was against this background of a defence the scope of which was not very clear that the House of Lords came to deliver its view on the issue in *Brown*.

This case was concerned with assaults which occurred in the context of consensual sado-masochistic activities between a group of homosexual men. These had been going on for a number of years. They only came to the attention of the authorities because the group had made videotapes of some of their sessions, and these fell into the hands of the police during the course of other investigations. The men were charged with offences under s 47 (assault occasioning actual bodily harm), and s 20 (unlawful wounding) of the OAPA 1861. They were convicted, but appealed on the basis that all the 'assaults' and 'woundings' had taken place with the consent of the alleged victims. The Court of Appeal upheld the convictions, but gave leave to appeal to the House of Lords, certifying the following point of law of general public importance:

> Where A wounds or assaults B occasioning him actual bodily harm in the course of a sadomasochistic encounter, does the prosecution have to prove lack of consent on the part of B before they can establish A's guilt under s 20 and s 47 of the 1861, Offences Against the Person Act?[38]

There was no doubt that the activities engaged in by the Ds, and which formed the basis of the charges against them, involved actual bodily harm. The Vs were subjected to genital torture, and violence to the buttocks, anus, penis, testicles and nipples. There were also instances of wounding, such as the insertion of a fishhook through the V's penis, or the nailing of the V's scrotum to a board. It was accepted, however, that no permanent injury was caused, nor did any of the Vs require medical treatment.

The majority of the House of Lords (Lord Templeman, Lord Jauncey and Lord Lowry) dismissed the appeal, answering the certified question in the negative. It is implicit in all three speeches, though only explicitly referred to in that of Lord Jauncey,[39] that lack of consent is not a necessary ingredient of

38 [1993] 2 All ER 75, p 77.
39 *Ibid*, p 92.

an assault, but that consent may in some cases provide a defence.[40] Starting from this position, the majority then took a similar line to that taken by the Court of Appeal in the *Attorney General's Reference (No 6 of 1980)*.[41] In other words, consent will generally provide a defence to common assault. As regards more serious assaults, however, the defence's argument that the line at which the general presumption of a defence of consent should be drawn ought to be between actual bodily harm and wounding on the one hand, and grievous bodily harm on the other was rejected.[42] The majority of the House of Lords took the view that this was not supported by earlier case law, nor by arguments based on public interest. It would also be difficult for juries to apply, in that it would mean treating different versions of the offences under s 20 in different ways, in that consent would be an available defence to a charge of wounding, but not to a charge of inflicting grievous bodily harm.[43] Indeed Lord Templeman makes the somewhat surprising comment that 'The differences between actual bodily harm and serious bodily harm cannot be satisfactorily applied by a jury in order to determine acquittal or conviction.'[44] Since this distinction has to be applied in determining whether the *actus reus* of the D's offence falls within s 47 or s 20, it is difficult to see why it should not also be applied in the context of a defence. Nevertheless, the opinion of the majority is summed up by Lord Lowry's conclusions to his discussion of *Donovan* and the *Attorney General's Reference (No 6 of 1980)*:

> Thus, we are left with the proposition that it is not in the public interest that people should try to cause, or should cause, each other actual bodily harm for no good reason and that it is an assault if actual bodily harm is caused (except for good reason).[45]

The next question, therefore, was whether the fact that the defendants were engaging in private activities, as part of an expression of their sexuality, provided a 'good reason' for allowing consent to provide a defence. The majority were clearly influenced here by their distaste for the homosexual sado-masochism of the defendants, and gave short shrift to arguments based of privacy, and invoking Art 8 of the European Convention on Human Rights.[46] Thus, Lord Templeman: 'I am not prepared to invent a defence of

---

40 Though the burden of proof remains on the prosecution in situations where consent is a possible defence.

41 [1981] 2 All ER 1057.

42 Some of the defendants argued that the line should be simply between s 47 and s 20, thus including all woundings in the category of injury to which consent would not provide a defence.

43 See the comments of Lord Jauncey to this effect: [1993] 2 All ER 75, p 91. Lord Slynn (of the minority), however, appeared to have no difficulty in drawing the line at this point: p 124.

44 [1993] 2 All ER 75, p 82.

45 *Ibid*, p 99.

46 Establishing the right to respect for private life.

consent for sado-masochistic encounters which breed and glorify cruelty and result in offences under ss 47 and 20 of the 1861 Act';[47] Lord Jauncey: 'I have no doubt that it would not be in the public interest that deliberate infliction of actual bodily harm during the course of homosexual sado-masochistic activities should be held to be lawful';[48] Lord Lowry: 'Sado-masochistic homosexual activity cannot be regarded as conducive to the enhancement or enjoyment of family life or conducive to the welfare of society.'[49]

By contrast, Lord Mustill, in the first sentences of his speech states:

> My Lords, this is a case about the criminal law of violence. In my opinion, it should be about the criminal law of private sexual relations, if about anything at all.[50]

This distinction between focusing on violence, rather than sex as the central issue, together with the treatment of consent as a defence, rather than lack of consent as an element in the definition of the offences, provides the basis for the difference between the conclusions of the majority and the minority in *Brown*. The outcome of the decision is that, in relation to behaviour which causes actual bodily harm, wounding, or serious bodily harm, consent is only a defence in exceptional circumstances. The list of exceptions cannot be regarded as closed, but the majority of the House of Lords in *Brown* did not significantly expand the categories recognised in the *Attorney General's Reference (No 6 of 1980)*. Thus, the exceptions include organised sport (including boxing), surgery, ritual circumcision of males,[51] tattooing, and ear-piercing (and, presumably, the cosmetic piercing of other parts of the body). To this list Lord Mustill added 'rough horseplay' such as may occur 'in the school playground, in the barrack-room and on the factory floor',[52] relying on the decisions in *Bruce*[53] and *Jones (Terence)*.[54] In these cases, the express or implied consent of the victim to actual bodily harm or wounding will provide a defence. The precise level of injury permissible will depend on the particular circumstances. Clearly in relation to surgery consent can be given to actions which otherwise would constitute grievous bodily harm (for example, an amputation). A much lower level of injury will generally apply in respect of the other permitted activities.[55] There is also one other situation where the

---

47 [1993] 2 All ER 75, p 83. It should be noted that the European Court of Human Rights also rejected arguments by the Ds based on Art 8 – *Laskey, Jaggard and Brown v UK* (1997) 24 EHRR 39

48 [1993] 2 All ER 75, p 92.

49 *Ibid*, p 100.

50 *Ibid*, p 101.

51 Female circumcision is illegal under the Prohibition of Female Circumcision Act 1985.

52 [1993] 2 All ER 75, p 110.

53 (1847) 2 Cox CC 262.

54 (1986) 83 Cr App R 375. See, also, *Aitken* [1992] 1 WLR 1006.

55 Though, in *Jones (Terence)* (1986) 83 Cr App R 375, it extended to serious harm (ruptured spleen).

public interest allows the infliction of actual bodily harm, even though the victim may not consent. This is the lawful punishment of children.[56]

It is difficult to determine the linking factor that allows such activities to be consented to, even if in some circumstances they may result in serious harm, while nullifying consent as a defence to lesser harm resulting from sado-masochistic practices. By no means all of those activities on the 'accepted' list can be said to be 'conducive to the enhancement or enjoyment of family life or conducive to the welfare of society', as Lord Lowry put it in refusing to extend the defence in *Brown*.[57] The law is currently in a confused state, and the position has not been helped by the post-*Brown* decision of the Court of Appeal in *Wilson*.[58] In this case, the V wanted her husband to tattoo his initials on her buttocks. Since he was unable to do this, he, with her agreement, tried to achieve a similar result by branding her with a hot knife. The Court of Appeal held that her consent meant that the D was not liable for the offence of assault occasioning actual bodily harm. The court was clearly reluctant to intervene in the private relationship between husband and wife: 'Consensual activity between husband and wife, in the privacy of the matrimonial home, is not, in our judgment, normally a proper matter for criminal investigation, let alone criminal prosecution.'[59] It drew an analogy with tattooing. The injuries suffered here were of much the same level of seriousness, and were inflicted for the purposes of personal adornment, rather than primarily for sexual gratification (as in *Brown*). *Brown* was distinguishable, and the wife's consent prevented her husband being liable for the offence.

What are the consequences for *Brown* and *Wilson* as regards to consent in the context of indecent assault? Lord Mustill in *Brown* commented, in discussing *Donovan*, that indecent assault 'is an offence to which, it is common ground, consent is a defence'.[60] Similarly, Lord Lowry, again discussing *Donovan*, and the fact that he was only charged with common assault and indecent assault, notes that 'there were two counts in the indictment, to which the consent of the victim was a complete defence'.[61] None of the other speeches deal with this issue directly. The suggestion is, however, that consent is a defence to indecent assault, whatever the level of injury suffered by the V. It is difficult to see, however, why this be show if consent is not a defence to a

56 Note that the corporal punishment of children in schools is unlawful, the law having been changed following adverse decisions against the UK under Art 3 of the European Convention on Human Rights: eg, *Campbell and Cousans v United Kingdom* (1982) 4 EHRR 293. The use of severe corporal punishment by parents has been found to be in breach of the Convention by the European Court on Human Rights in *A v United Kingdom* (103/1997/864/1098) (September 1998, unreported).

57 [1993] 2 All ER 75, p 100.

58 [1996] 3 WLR 125.

59 *Ibid*, p 128.

60 [1993] 2 All ER 75, p 112.

61 *Ibid*, p 97.

charge under s 47 of the OAPA. The reasoning cannot be that indecent assault as an essential element requires proof of an assault, to which consent is a defence, since this would apply equally to s 47. There seems no reason, in the light of the approach taken by the majority in *Brown*, why an indecent assault which has resulted in actual bodily harm should not result in a conviction, even if the victim consented. It is certainly an odd situation if consent can provide a defence to indecent assault, which carries a maximum penalty of 10 years imprisonment, but not to the apparently less serious offence under s 47, which carries a maximum penalty of only five years. The decision of the Court of Appeal in the earlier case of *Boyea*,[62] assumed that at a certain level of injury a conviction for indecent assault could be maintained irrespective of the V's consent. The precise level of injury is unclear, however. The court took the view that the 'level of vigour in sexual congress which was generally acceptable' was probably higher in 1992 than it had been in 1934 (that is, the time of the decision in *Donovan*). It then simply drew a distinction between 'minor injury' and the more serious injury which the V in the case in fact suffered as a result of the insertion and twisting of the D's hand in her vagina. It is not clear, however, whether the court was drawing the line at 'actual bodily harm', or somewhere above this. In the light of *Brown*, however, it would seem that if indecent assault is to be treated in the same way as non-sexual offences, the cut-off point for the efficacy of consent should be at the level of actual bodily harm.

A further issue relating to consent is the question of the genuineness of the consent, if, for example, there is a question that it might have been induced by improper pressure. This issues has been discussed at length in Chapter Six, in the context of rape,[63] but the fact that it can arise in other contexts is demonstrated by the Southern Rhodesian case of *McCoy*.[64] The D was the manager of an air-line, and the V was a probationary air-hostess. The D accused the V of failing to wear her safety belt during a landing. He threatened her with dismissal or grounding (the latter penalty having serious financial consequences for her). Further conversation resulted in the D offering the V the alternative of being caned. This she agreed to, and this punishment was then carried out. The D was subsequently convicted of an assault. On appeal, he raised the defence of consent. The court was of the view that, even if the defence of consent were available here (which it felt it was not, given the level of the harm inflicted),[65] the consent of the V had not been obtained freely, but under duress, as a result of the fear of being dismissed or grounded. It was therefore in any case ineffective as a defence to the charge of

62 [1992] Crim LR 574

63 See Chapter 6, pp 146–48.

64 1953 (2) SA 4 (AD).

65 The court was here following *Donovan* [1934] 2 KB 498.

assault. So, in those cases where consent is a possible defence it is only where it is freely given that it will in fact excuse the D's conduct.

A final issue to be considered in this area is the question of consent and medical treatment. Many types of medical examination and treatment involve actions which would constitute the *actus reus* of assault. The basic position is that, provided that the patient consents to this treatment, then no offence will be committed. On the other hand:

> Every human being of adult years and sound mind has a right to determine what shall be done with his own body; and a surgeon who performs an operation without his patient's consent commits and assault ...[66]

Thus, a doctor has no right to perform an operation, or give other medical treatment, which might amount to an assault, against the V's will, even though the doctor may feel that it is in the best interests of the V. This principle was confirmed by the Court of Appeal in *St George's Healthcare National Health Service Trust v S*,[67] where it was held that a woman had the right to refuse to undergo a caesarean section, even though a natural delivery would pose serious risks to both her own health and that of her unborn child. The only exception to this is where circumstances mean that it is not possible to obtain consent. The leading case is the House of Lords decision in *Re F*.[68] This concerned a mentally handicapped adult woman, who had formed a sexual relationship with a male patient in the hospital where they were both resident. The woman's mother, and the medical staff of the hospital, were of the view that it would be in the woman's best interest for her to be sterilised. The woman was incapable of giving an informed consent to this operation. The House of Lords held that in such circumstances it was permissible to act without the patient's consent – though it was good practice for a declaration from the court to be sought before action was taken. Lord Goff, with whom the majority agreed, saw this as an example of a more general principle, also operating in other areas of the law,[69] to fall within which:

> ... not only (1) must there be a necessity to act when it is not practicable to communicate with the assisted person, but also (2) the action taken must be such as a reasonable person would in all the circumstances take, acting in the best interests of the assisted person.[70]

This principle legitimises medical assistance given to those who are unconscious, eg as a result of an accident, as well as those who are incapable of giving consent for other reasons. The treatment which will be permissible

66 Cardozo J in *Schloendorff v Society of New York Hospital* (1914) 105 NE 92, p 93; quoted by Lord Goff in *Re F* [1990] 2 AC 1, p 73. See, also, *S v McC* [1972] AC 24, p 43.

67 [1998] 3 All ER 673.

68 [1990] 2 AC 1.

69 Eg, 'agency by necessity', for which see, eg, Stone, R, *Law of Agency*, 1996, London: Cavendish Publishing, p 35.

70 [1990] 2 AC 1, p 75.

must be assessed by the test set down in *Bolam v Friern Hospital Management Committee*,[71] which means that the person providing the assistance must act in accordance with a responsible and competent body of relevant professional opinion.

The problematic nature of the defence of consent, as indicated by the above discussions, has led to extensive consideration by the Law Commission, and its suggestions for reform are outlined in Chapter 8.[72]

DURESS

The D may try to argue that he was forced to commit an assault, etc, by a third party. This raises the issue of 'duress', which if successfully pleaded will result in complete acquittal. The defence is 'excusatory' rather than 'justificatory'; the D admits that his act was, as regard the V, unlawful, but seeks to be excused on the basis that he was not, in effect, acting as a free agent in committing it. At times, the courts refer to the situation as one in which the D's will is overborne. This is not, however, a very helpful way of considering the matter. The D knows what he is doing, and chooses to commit the offence against the V. It is not, therefore, accurate to say that he had 'no alternative'. It is simply that he is to be regarded as having been faced with an alternative (such as his own death or serious injury) which it was reasonable for him to reject, even though the consequence was for him to cause harm to the V.

Where duress is raised, the burden of proof remains on the prosecution, which must disprove that the D was under such pressure that it is appropriate to excuse his otherwise criminal act.

The essence of the defence of duress is that the pressure emanates from the threats of a third party. The related defence of 'duress of circumstances' is considered under the heading of 'Necessity', below. The principal issues which need to be considered are:

(a) the nature of the threats which will give rise to the defence;

(b) the effect that the threats must have on the D;

(c) the issue of the 'immediacy' of the threat;

(d) the offences in relation to which the defence is available.

The leading authorities on the modern English law of duress are the decisions of the Court of Appeal in *Graham*,[73] and of the House of Lords in *Howe*.[74] *Graham* contains the more general discussion of the nature of the defence, but

71 [1957] 1 WLR 582.

72 See Chapter 8, p 229.

73 [1982] 1 All ER 801.

74 [1987] 1 All ER 771.

its rulings were approved by the House in *Howe*. The focus in *Howe* itself was issue (d), above, the scope of the defence. In *Graham*, the correct approach to the defence was said to be based on two questions:[75]

> (1) was the [D], or may he have been, impelled to act as he did because, as a result of what he reasonably believed [X] had said or done, he had good cause to fear that if he did not so act [X] would kill him or (if this is to be added) cause him serious injury? (2) if so, have the prosecution made the jury sure that a sober person of reasonable firmness, sharing the characteristics of the [D], would not have responded to whatever he reasonably believed [X] said or did by [committing the offence]?

With this general statement in mind, the four issues noted above will now be considered.

The nature of the threats

There are three elements to this issue, namely the source of the threats, the content of them, and the object of them. As to the first element, it is accepted that they must, as has already been noted, come from a third party (X). Pressure arising from other sources is not within the scope of duress. The D who pushes the V out of the way (that is, commits battery) in an attempt to leave a sinking ship, cannot plead duress, even if his life was in danger. The only possible defence here is 'necessity'. As to the nature of the threats, it seems to be generally accepted that a threat of anything less than serious personal injury will be insufficient to raise the defence. This is implicit in the statement in *Graham*. All the reported cases in which the defence has been successful have involved threats of this kind. Moreover, in *Valderrama-Vega*[76] threats to destroy the D's reputation were held to be insufficient.[77] Although it would be possible to operate a defence of duress where the level of the threat was balanced against the seriousness of the offence, English law seems to have largely rejected this, and a very high lower threshold is imposed before there is any possibility of the threat succeeding. Of course, the D who acts in response to threats which fall below this threshold may have this factor taken into account in sentencing, but it is not relevant to guilt or innocence.

The final consideration under this heading is whether the threats must be directed against the D himself. Although there is no clear English authority on the point, it is nevertheless generally agreed that the answer to this question is no: threats to others, in particular members of the D's family, will be sufficient to give rise to the possibility of a plea of duress. This was the view taken in the

---

75 [1982] 1 All ER 801, p 806, *per* Lord Lane CJ.

76 [1985] Crim LR 220.

77 Though in fact, in that case, there were also threats of violence, which could amount to 'duress'.

Australian case of *Hurley and Murray*,[78] where the threats were directed to the D's wife. There seems no reason to doubt that the same approach would be taken by the English courts, particularly since the development of the case law relating to 'duress of circumstances' (discussed below under 'Necessity', p 194) in which a number of the cases involve fears for the safety of people other than the D.

Effect on the D

This is the central issue for the operation of the defence. In fact, as will be seen from a careful reading of the quotation from Lord Lane in *Graham* set out above, the focus is not so much on the effect on the D personally, but the effect on a 'reasonable man'. In other words, the operation of the test is essentially 'objective' rather than 'subjective'. Thus, in relation to the D's perception of what X was threatening, the test is what the D '*reasonably* believed' X to have said or done. Whereas in self-defence, as we have seen,[79] the D who makes an unreasonable mistake is still entitled to be judged on the facts as he believed them to be, in respect of duress the D's belief must be reasonable. The law does not go so far as to require that X was actually threatening death or personal injury, but the D's belief that he was doing so must be one that a reasonable person would have held in the circumstances. This requirement of reasonableness has been criticised,[80] and it does appear inconsistent with the approach taken to unreasonable mistakes in other areas. It might, however, be argued that there is a distinction between self-defence, for example, and duress in that self-defence is 'justificatory' whereas duress is only 'excusatory'. It may be more acceptable to use an objective approach in relation to excuses, as opposed to justifications.[81]

Once it is established that the D reasonably believed that he, or possibly a third party, was being threatened with death or serious violence, attention turns to his reaction to the threats. The question is whether the D responded in a way that a person 'of reasonable firmness, sharing the characteristics of the' D would have done. Would such a person, faced with the threats, have committed the offence which the threatener was telling him to commit? Again, the test is objective. The D who has submitted to the threat because he is weak-willed, or easily terrified, will be unlikely to be able to rely on the defence.[82] As pointed out by Lord Lane in *Graham*, there is a close analogy

78 [1967] VR 526, Supreme Court of Victoria.

79 See above, p 174.

80 See, eg, Smith, JC and Hogan, B, *Criminal Law Cases and Materials*, 6th edn, 1996, London: Butterworths, p 245.

81 Cf, eg, the arguments of Slater, J, in 'Making sense of self-defence' (1996) 5 Nott LJ 140.

82 See, eg, *Horne* [1994] Crim LR 585.

here with the defence of provocation in relation to murder.[83] Just as in that case a D cannot rely on the fact that he is exceptionally hot-tempered, but is expected to show 'the self-control reasonably to be expected of the ordinary citizen', so in relation to duress the law requires the D 'to have the steadfastness reasonably to be expected of the ordinary citizen in his situation'.[84] Nevertheless, the test also refers to a reasonable person who 'sharing the characteristics' of the D. What characteristics can be considered? The comparison with provocation arises again in this context. As was noted in Chapter 4,[85] in relation to provocation, it is now accepted that, apart from age and sex, only those characteristics which affect the gravity of the provocation may be relied on. A similar approach in relation to duress would limit the relevant characteristics to age, sex, and those which affect the gravity of the threat. In practice, there would seem to be few characteristics which would meet this test. Mental instability, affecting the D's ability to withstand threats was rejected in *Hegarty*.[86] One possibility, however, is physical health. For example, a threat to wound the D is obviously more serious if the D is a haemophiliac. That characteristic is therefore one that should be taken into account if the threat is of that kind. Similarly, if the D suffers from heart disease, a threat to punch him in the chest (or indeed, more generally, to 'beat him up') may be more serious than the same threat uttered against a D who is in perfect health. It is difficult to envisage, however, other types of characteristic which could be relevant. The role for modification of the 'reasonable person' appears to be even more limited here than it is in relation to provocation.

A final point to be noted under this heading is that the D who has voluntarily put himself in a situation which is likely to lead to pressure being put on him to commit offences is unlikely to be able to rely on duress. Thus, the D who joins a terrorist group and is then told to commit offences, with the threat that if he does not he will himself suffer physical punishment (for example, 'knee-capping'), will have no defence of duress. As Lowry LCJ put it in the Northern Irish case of *Fitzpatrick*:[87]

> If a person behaves immorally by, for example, committing himself to an unlawful conspiracy, he ought not to be able to take advantage of the pressure exercised on him by his fellow criminals in order to put on when it suits him the breastplate of righteousness.

In *Sharp*,[88] the same approach was taken by the Court of Appeal in relation to a D who had joined a criminal gang and had joined in the commission of

83 See Chapter 4, pp 68–82.

84 [1982] 1 All ER 801, p 806.

85 See Chapter 4, p 74 *et seq*.

86 [1994] Crim LR 353.

87 [1977] NI 20.

88 [1987] QB 853.

offences where guns were carried. He said that he had wished to withdraw, but was threatened with violence. The court held that duress is not available to a D who voluntarily joins a gang 'which he knows might bring pressure on him to commit an offence and was an active member when he was put under such pressure'.[89] Simply being involved in criminal activity, however, will not necessarily lose the D the right to use the defence:[90] it must be shown that when he joined the enterprise he realised that he might be subject to pressure of this kind.

The immediacy of the threat

The nature of the defence is that the D is forced to act by the threat, and has no reasonable alternative. If, then, there is a gap between the issue of the threat and the time at which the D is to commit the offence, this may well result in the defence being lost. The D will be expected to take any reasonable opportunity to go to the authorities, or in some other way to attempt to nullify the effect of the threats. The requirement is not an absolute one, in that it is based on 'reasonableness'. If, looking at the circumstances overall, the escape route, while possible, might well not have been taken by a reasonable person in the D's situation, then the defence of duress will still be available. Thus, in the Australian case of *Hurley*,[91] it was held that the fact that the D's wife was being held as a hostage meant that he was not necessarily obliged to take a clear opportunity to go to the police. The main English authority is *Hudson and Taylor*.[92] The Ds in this case were two teenage girls, who were witnesses in a case of unlawful wounding. They were found to have given false evidence at the trial, and were charged with perjury. Their defence was that they had been threatened with being 'cut up' prior to the trial if they gave evidence which was unfavourable. The judge refused to allow this defence to go to the jury, because the threat was not immediate (that is, it preceded the perjury by some time). On appeal, the prosecution suggested that, in addition, the Ds could have sought police protection prior to the trial. Lord Widgery CJ stated the following general principle:[93]

> In the opinion of this court, it is always open to the Crown to prove that the accused failed to avail himself of some opportunity which was reasonably open to him to render the threat ineffective, and that on this being established the threat in question can no longer be relied on by the defence. In deciding whether such an opportunity was reasonably open to the accused the jury

89 [1987] QB 853, p 861.

90 *Shepherd* (1988) 86 Cr App R 47; *Lewis* (1992) 96 Cr App R 412.

91 [1967] VR 526, Supreme Court of Victoria.

92 [1971] 2 All ER 244.

93 *Ibid*, p 247.

> should have regard to his age and circumstances, and to any risks to him which may be involved in the course of action relied on.

Applying this approach to the facts of the case, it was clearly relevant that the man who was the source of the threats was in court when the Ds came to give evidence. His presence amounted to a reiteration of the threat, and thus could be regarded as dealing with the issue of immediacy. Secondly, it did not necessarily matter that the threats could not have been acted upon immediately after the Ds had given evidence:

> When ... there is no opportunity for delaying tactics, and the person threatened must make up his mind whether he is to commit the criminal act or not, the existence at that moment of threats sufficient to destroy his will ought to provide him with a defence even though the threatened injury may not follow instantly, but after an interval ... In the present case, the threats of Farrell were likely to be no less compelling, because their execution could not be effected in the court room, if they could be carried out in the streets of Salford the same night.

The defence of duress ought, therefore, to have been left to the jury.

The test of immediacy, as interpreted in *Hudson and Taylor* seems in effect to merge with the more general requirement that the D's response must be 'reasonable' if the defence is to be accepted. There is no rule of law that the threat must immediately precede the D's actions, not that the D must take any possible escape route: both matters are issues which the jury should decide on in all the circumstances, assessing the D's behaviour against the standard of the reasonable person.

Offences in respect of which duress can operate

This is the final issue to be discussed in relation to duress. There is no doubt that the defence can be raised in relation to all the non-fatal and sexual offences discussed in Chapters 5 and 6. The only area where there has been any doubt about the availability of the defence has been in relation to offences involving homicide. The House of Lords has taken differing views on this issue over the past twenty years, but the governing authority is now *Howe*.[94] The House there decided that duress is not, as a matter of law, available as a defence to a person charged with murder, either as principal or accessory. This decision involved the overruling of its earlier decision in *Lynch v DPP for Northern Ireland*,[95] where it had held that an accessory to murder could rely on duress. The case concerned the liability of a D who had acted as the driver for a terrorist gang. The gang had carried out the murder of a policeman. The House agreed that the D should have the possibility of being able to plead

94 [1987] 1 All ER 771.

95 [1975] 1 All ER 913.

duress. Doubts were, however, cast on the correctness of this decision by the subsequent Privy Council case of *Abbott v R*.[96] This also involved a D who had assisted in a murder, but on this occasion to an extent which made him a principal rather than an accessory. *Lynch* was therefore distinguishable. However, Lord Salmon commented that:

> Whilst their Lordships feel bound to accept the decision of the House of Lords in *Lynch v Director of Public Prosecutions for Northern Ireland*, they find themselves constrained to say that had they considered (which they do not) that that decision was an authority which required the extension of the doctrine to cover cases like the present, they would not have accepted it.[97]

The language used clearly indicated an unhappiness with the decision in *Lynch*, and it was therefore not altogether surprising that in *Howe* the view was taken that *Lynch* should be overruled. In a number of lengthy speeches, their lordships indicated that in their view the law prior to *Lynch* pointed to duress being unavailable in relation to murder. Moreover, they could find no clear or logical basis for distinguishing between principal and accessory in this context. It was by no means always the case that the greater moral responsibility attached to the principal. Lord Griffiths, for example, refers to 'contract killings' where:

> ... the murder would never have taken place if a contract had not been placed to take the life of the victim. Another example would be an intelligent man goading a weak-minded individual into a killing he would not otherwise commit.[98]

As a result, it was neither 'rational nor fair to make the defence dependent on whether the accused is the actual killer or took some other part in the murder'. Since the House of Lords was unanimous in its view that the actual killer ought not to have the defence of duress, it followed from that conclusion that an accessory ought also to be unable to use the defence. The law has thus returned to the position stated in *Blackstone's Commentaries*,[99] to the effect that a person under duress 'ought rather to die himself than escape by the murder of an innocent'.

The *Howe* approach has subsequently been applied to attempted murder, in *Gotts*,[100] though in this case the House of Lords split (3:2) on the issue. The view of the majority was expressed by Lord Jauncey in the following way:

> I can therefore see no justification in logic, morality or law in affording to an attempted murderer the defence which is withheld from a murderer. The intent required of an attempted murderer is more evil than that required of a

96 [1976] 3 All ER 140.

97 [1976] 3 All ER 140, p 143.

98 [1987] 1 All ER 771, p 789.

99 Blackstone, W (Sir), *Commentaries on the Laws of England (1765–69)*, Chicago: Chicago UP, Book iv, p 30.

100 [1992] 1 All ER 832.

> murderer[101] and the line which divides the two offences is seldom, if ever, of the deliberate making of the criminal. A man shooting to kill but missing a vital organ by a hair's breadth can justify his action no more than can the man who hits that organ. It is pure chance that the attempted murderer is not a murderer and I entirely agree with what Lord Lane CJ said [in the Court of Appeal]: '... the fact that the attempt failed to kill should not make any difference.'[102]

The defence is therefore unavailable to murder or attempted murder, whether the D is principal or accessory. It seems, however, that it will be available to a charge of conspiracy or incitement to murder, as well as to all other non-fatal offences against the person.

Before leaving this defence, we should also note the survival of the somewhat archaic defence of 'coercion'. This applies to a wife who can prove that the offence was committed in the presence of her husband and under his coercion.[103] It seems that this does not require specific threats, but simply the domination of the wife by her husband. The defence has been little used in practice, and is an anomaly which could well be abolished.[104]

Necessity

Until quite recently (that is, about 10 years ago), the view was generally held that English law did not recognise a general defence of necessity, though it might be available in relation to particular statutory offences, by means of a defence of 'lawful excuse'.[105] The authority for this was generally taken to be the famous 19th century case of *Dudley and Stephens*.[106] The Ds in this case had been cast adrift in boat, together with the V, who was a 17 year old cabin boy. After going for eight days without food, and six days without water, the Ds killed the V, and survived by eating his flesh and drinking his blood. Four days later they were picked up by a passing ship. The Ds were charged with murder. The jury found, in a special verdict, that the V would probably have died anyway within the four days, and that the Ds had had no reasonable prospect of survival if they had not killed and eaten the V. On the other hand, the jury also held that there was no greater necessity to kill the V as opposed

101 Ie, attempted murder requires proof of an intent to kill; murder may be found on the basis of an intention merely to cause serious bodily harm.

102 [1992] 1 All ER 832, p 840.

103 Criminal Justice Act 1925, s 47 – abolishing the previous presumption of coercion.

104 As has been recommended by the Avory Committee, Cmd 1677, and the Law Commission (Report No 83 (1977)).

105 See, eg, the Criminal Damage Act 1971.

106 (1884) 14 QBD 273.

to one of the other occupants of the boat.[107] The jury's verdict was referred to the QBD for a decision as to whether, on these facts, the Ds should be found guilty of murder. The judgment of the court, delivered by Lord Coleridge CJ was that they did not have a defence to the charge. There was some uncertainty as to whether this was genuinely a situation of necessity, but even if it was Lord Coleridge was clear that it would provide no defence to a charge of murder. He quoted the following passage from Lord Hale's treatise on the criminal law, where Lord Hale considers the view of some European jurists that theft is not theft in cases of extreme necessity, for example, of hunger or clothing. Lord Hale comments:[108]

> I take it that here in England that rule, at least by the laws of England, is false, and, therefore, if a person, being under necessity for want of victuals or clothes, shall upon the account clandestinely and *animo furandi* steal another man's goods, it is a felony and a crime by the laws of England ...

Thus, Lord Coleridge concludes, if 'Lord Hale is clear, as he is, that extreme necessity of hunger does not justify larceny, what would he have said to the doctrine that it justified murder'?[109] It was held that, on the facts found by the jury, the defendants should be convicted of murder.[110]

Although *Dudley and Stephens* was concerned with murder, the general hostility to the idea of a defence of necessity evident in the case led, as has been noticed, to a general reluctance to allow it in any area. The position has, however, changed somewhat in the last 10 years. Two cases involving reckless driving, *Willer*[111] and *Conway*,[112] considered the situation where the driver acted, not because he was *ordered* to drive recklessly (which would be a standard case of duress), but because he *chose* that way to escape from people who were threatening[113] either the driver himself, or a passenger in his car, with violence. The Court of Appeal in both cases was prepared to regard this as raising a possible defence of 'duress of circumstances', which as Woolf J noted in *Conway* could be regarded as a type of 'necessity':

> Whether 'duress of circumstances' is called 'duress' or 'necessity' does not matter. What is important is that, whatever it is called, it is subject to the same limitations as the 'do this or else' species of duress.[114]

107 In addition to the V and the Ds, there was one other occupant of the boat, who took no part in the killing.

108 I Hale PC 54.

109 (1884) 14 QBD 273, p 283.

110 Though the death sentence was later commuted to six months imprisonment.

111 (1986) 83 Cr App Rep 225.

112 [1988] 3 All ER 1025.

113 Or who he thought were threatening.

114 [1988] 3 All ER 1025, p 1029.

This area was further developed in *Martin*,[115] where the D argued that he had only driven his car while disqualified from driving because his wife had threatened to commit suicide unless the D drove his stepson to work. The judge refused to allow this defence to be put to the jury. The Court of Appeal held that he was in error in this ruling. Although the court was somewhat sceptical as to whether the D's story would have been believed by the jury, he was entitled to have it considered. In coming to this conclusion, Simon Brown J confirmed that 'English law does in extreme circumstances recognise a defence of necessity'. This may arise from wrongful threats to the D (when it is know as 'duress') or 'from other objective dangers threatening the [D] or others'. Since 'duress of circumstances' is so closely linked to duress by threats, the question to be put to the jury is essentially the same in both cases. Where duress of circumstances is raised, therefore, the jury should be instructed to consider:

> First, was the accused, or may he have been, impelled to act as he did because as a result of what he reasonably believed to be the situation he had good cause to fear that otherwise death or serious physical injury would result; secondly, if so, would a sober person of reasonable firmness, sharing the characteristics of the accused, have responded to that situation by acting as the accused acted?[116]

One difference between this type of necessity and duress by threats, is that here there need be no threat of illegality involved. The threat by the D's wife to commit suicide was not unlawful. Similarly, Simon Brown J gives the example of the situation of 'a disqualified driver being driven by his wife, she suffering a heart attack in remote countryside and he needing instantly to get her to hospital'.[117]

The defence is generally only going to be available where the unlawful action is a 'spur of the moment' reaction to a crisis. Thus, a D who decides to commit robberies because of threats of violence to him and his family from creditors will be unlikely to be able to use the defence: *Cole*.[118] Similarly, the defence will cease to be available if the D commits, or continues to commit, the offence after the threat has disappeared. This was one of the reasons for the failure of the defence in relation to a charge of driving with excess alcohol in both *Davis*[119] and *Pittaway*.[120]

115 (1989) 88 Cr App R 343.

116 *Ibid*, p 346.

117 *Ibid*, p 346.

118 [1994] Crim LR 582.

119 [1994] Crim LR 601. Cf *Bell* [1992] RTR 335, where the defence was successfully used in relation to such a charge.

120 For *Pittaway* [1994] Crim LR 601, the defences were also rejected by the Divisional Court because the magistrates had applied a subjective rather than an objective test to the existence of grounds for the D's fears.

It should be noted that none of the reported examples of the successful use of this defence involve a charge of assault, or other offence against the person. The most recent reported case, *Pommell*,[121] concerned the offence of possession of a firearm under s 5(1)(a) of the Firearms Act 1968. There is no reason to suppose, however, in appropriate circumstances the defence would not be available, like duress by threats, in respect of all offences against the person other than murder or attempted murder.

LAWFUL CORRECTION

It is well established in the common law that 'lawful correction' or 'lawful chastisement' is a defence to an assault charge. The principle is that a parent, or a person acting in the place of, or on behalf of, a parent, can administer reasonable physical punishment to a child in his or her care. Only if what is done is 'immoderate or excessive'[122] will the defence be lost.

The common law position has, however, been affected by several rulings of the European Court of Human Rights, to the effect that corporal punishment of children can in some circumstances amount to inhuman or degrading treatment.[123] This has led to the outlawing of corporal punishment in schools (both State and private) and children's homes.[124] The most recent ruling of the European Court of Human Rights, in the case of *A and B v United Kingdom*, was delivered in September 1998, found that the caning of a nine year old boy by his step-father constituted a breach of the Convention. The step-father had been prosecuted for assault, but had been acquitted. It is likely that the government will now act to amend the defence of lawful chastisement, and limit further what is permissible for parents to do by way of punishment of their children.

INSANITY

Insanity may be relevant at two stages in the criminal trial. First, there may be a question as to whether the D is fit to stand trial – the 'fitness to plead' issue. Secondly, where the D is fit to plead, a defence may be raised on the basis that at the time when the alleged offence was committed the D was suffering from 'insanity', and so should not be held responsible in the same way as an

121 (1995) 2 Cr App R 607.

122 *Hopley* (1860) 2 F & F 202, *per* Cockburn CJ, p 206.

123 Ie, under Art 3 of the European Convention on Human Rights. For discussion of these decisions, see Stone, R, *Textbook on Civil Liberties*, 2nd edn, 1997, London: Blackstone, pp 23–29.

124 See, eg, Education Act 1996, ss 548 and 549.

ordinary criminal. This section of this chapter is almost exclusively concerned with the second issue – that is, the defence of insanity at the time of the commission of the offence. The issue of fitness to plead is currently dealt with by the Criminal Procedure (Insanity) Act 1964, as amended by the Criminal Procedure (Insanity and Unfitness to Plead) Act 1991.[125] In general terms, the issue is whether the D is capable of understanding and participating in the proceedings, and will be decided by a jury (not usually the same one which hears the case if the plea is unsuccessful). This procedure is not discussed further here, however, and we now turn to the way in which insanity may provide the D with a defence at the trial.

The defence of insanity is defined primarily by the common law, although certain procedural issues are governed by statute. The 'special verdict' of 'not guilty by reason of insanity' is available to all offences tried on indictment, by virtue of s 2 of the Trial of Lunatics Act 1883.[126] The defence of insanity will not, therefore, operate in the same way in a summary trial – though evidence that a person is 'insane' under the *M'Naghten* rules (as discussed below) may be relevant to issues of *mens rea* or automatism. The powers of disposal available under the Mental Health Act 1983 will, however, mean that the magistrates will be able to make, for example, a hospital order if that is appropriate.[127] The rest of this section will concentrate on the position in relation to trials on indictment.

Prior to the Criminal Procedure (Insanity and Unfitness to Plead) Act 1991, a verdict of not guilty by reason of insanity compelled the judge (whatever the offence of which the D had been convicted) to order the D to be detained indefinitely in a secure hospital. Release was at the discretion of the Home Secretary. This meant that the verdict was generally unattractive except as a means of avoiding the mandatory sentence for murder. Even this became less of an attraction following the abolition of the death penalty. Defendants would generally prefer to argue for non-insane automatism (particularly in relation to non-fatal offences), or else, in relation to murder, that it should be reduced to manslaughter on grounds of diminished responsibility.[128] The 1991 Act, however, amended s 5 of the Criminal Procedure (Insanity) Act 1964, so that in relation to offences other than murder, the judge may make either:

(a) an order that the D be admitted to hospital; or

(b) a guardianship order, a supervision and treatment order, or an order of absolute discharge.

---

125 See, in particular, the 1964 Act, s 4.

126 As amended by the Criminal Procedure (Insanity) Act 1964.

127 See, eg, Mental Health Act, s 37.

128 See Chapter 4, p 82.

For non-fatal offences, therefore, a successful plea of insanity followed by an order of the above kind may be preferable to a conviction followed by imprisonment. In relation to a murder charge, however, the judge must make a hospital order subject to restrictions on discharge, and without limit of time. This means that the D who escapes conviction for murder by reason of insanity will, even under the revised rules, still be detained at the discretion of the Home Secretary. A conviction for manslaughter on the grounds of diminished responsibility may therefore remain the more attractive option in these circumstances.

The operation of the defence

The D who raises insanity as a defence must prove it on the balance of probabilities. This was established by the *M'Naghten* rules laid down by the House of Lords in *M'Naghten's* case,[129] which is still the governing authority on the defence. The rules state that a D is presumed to be sane, but that presumption can be rebutted if the D shows that he was insane according to the House of Lords definition (which is discussed below). It is also possible for the prosecution, if the D has put his state of mind in issue (for example, by claiming to have acted as an automaton), to seek to prove (presumably beyond reasonable doubt) that he was in fact insane.[130]

M'Naghten's case arose out of the trial of the D for the murder of the Secretary to the Prime Minister, Sir Robert Peel. The D was found not guilty by reason of insanity. Unhappiness with this decision led to the whole issue of the insanity being debated by the House of Lords. Following this, five questions were put to the judges, two of which were:

> What are the proper questions to be submitted to the jury, where a person alleged to be afflicted with insane delusion respecting one or more particular subjects or persons, is charged with the commission of a crime (murder, for example), and insanity is set up as a defence?

and

> In what terms ought the question to be left to the jury as to the prisoner's state of mind at the time when the act was committed?

The judges felt that these two questions could most conveniently be answered together, and their response was formulated by Lord Tindal CJ in these terms:

> The jurors ought to be told in all cases that every man is to be presumed to be sane, and to possess a sufficient degree of reason to be responsible for his crimes, until the contrary be proved to their satisfaction; and that to establish a defence on the ground of insanity, it must clearly be proved that, at the time of

129 (1843) 10 Cl & Fin 200.

130 *Bratty v Attorney General for Northern Ireland* [1963] AC 386.

> the committing of the act, the party accused was labouring under such a defect of reason, from disease of the mind, as not to know the nature and quality of the act he was doing; or, if he did know it, that he did not know he was doing what was wrong.

This passage from Lord Tindal continues to provide the definition of insanity which operates in this area of the criminal law – despite the fact that in many ways it would be regarded as outdated (particularly by medical opinion), and has led to some surprising results in certain situations. As we shall see, diabetics, for example, may in some circumstances be treated as 'insane' under the *M'Naghten* rules, despite the fact that this condition would not normally be regarded as being an illness affecting the mind.

The first part of the quotation, concerning the burden of proof in relation to insanity has already been dealt with. The second part divides into four issues which will be considered in turn, namely: what is a 'defect of reason'; what is a 'disease of the mind'; when will a D be adjudged 'not to know the nature and quality of his act'; when will the D be adjudged not to 'know that what he was doing was wrong'

Defect of reason

This means an inability to reason, not a failure to do so. As Ackner J put it in *Clarke*,[131] the *M'Naghten* rules 'do not apply and never have applied to those who retain the power of reasoning but who in moments of confusion or absent-mindedness fail to use their powers to the full'. Thus, the driver of a car who, as a result of illness, temporarily loses concentration and causes an accident, cannot claim to have been insane at the time. In *Clarke* itself the D was a woman who was found to have placed some items in a supermarket into her own bag, and failed to present them at the checkout. The trial judge ruled that the evidence presented on her behalf by her doctor and psychiatrist, which was intended to show that she had no intention to steal, in fact indicated that she was insane under the *M'Naghten* rules. The Court of Appeal reversed the trial judge's ruling, holding, for the reasons outlined above, that this was an inappropriate application of the insanity rules.

Disease of the mind

The D's inability to reason must be caused by a 'disease of the mind'. This does not necessarily mean a 'mental illness', or some physical problem with the brain; simply a disease which has as one of its effects an impact on the functioning of the D's mental powers. Thus, in *Kemp*,[132] the D suffered from

131 [1972] 1 All ER 219.
132 [1957] 1 QB 399.

arteriosclerosis, which affects the flow of blood to the brain. It was held that this was capable of being a 'disease of the mind'. As Devlin J commented:

> It does not matter, for the purposes of the law, whether the defect of reasoning is due to a degeneration of the brain or to some other form of mental derangement.[133]

The function of the phrase 'disease of the mind' is primarily, therefore, to limit the scope of 'defect of reason' – it is not intended that the insanity defence 'should apply to defects of reason which were caused simply by brutish stupidity without rational power'.[134]

Although it is an effect on the 'mind' which is the primary requirement, the use of the word 'disease' means that such an effect which arises from an external factor will not give rise to a defence of insanity. Thus, in *Quick*,[135] the D, who was a nurse in a mental hospital, was convicted of causing actual bodily harm to a disabled patient. The D's defence at trial was based on the assertion that he was diabetic, and had been suffering from a hypoglycaemic episode at the time of the assault. This meant that he did not know what he was doing. The hypoglycaemia was caused by an excess of the insulin which he had taken to control his diabetes. A failure to eat properly following the insulin dose, combined with the consumption of alcohol, had led to the loss of awareness of his actions. The trial judge ruled that the D's defence amounted to a plea of insanity. The Court of Appeal, however, did not agree. It felt that the D's:

> ... alleged mental condition, if it ever existed, was not caused by his diabetes but by his use of the insulin prescribed by his doctor. Such malfunctioning of his mind as there was, was caused by an external factor and not by a bodily disorder in the nature of a disease which disturbed the working of his mind.[136]

This established the principle, therefore, that a disease of the mind must result from a 'bodily disorder' as opposed to an 'external factor'. The implication from *Quick* is that a *hyper*glycaemic (as opposed to *hypo*glycaemic) episode, caused by diabetes uncorrected by insulin, might properly be classified as 'insanity' within the *M'Naghten* rules. This was confirmed by the Court of Appeal in *Hennessy*,[137] a case on driving while disqualified.

It can also be inferred from the diabetes cases that the 'disease' does not need to have a permanent or continuing effect on the brain. There can be temporary insanity within the *M'Naghten* rules, so that a diabetic who is not in a hyperglycaemic or hypoglycaemic state is not to be categorised as 'insane'.

---

133 [1957] 1 QB 399, p 407.

134 *Ibid*, p 408.

135 [1973] 3 All ER 347.

136 *Ibid*, p 356.

137 [1989] 2 All ER 9.

The principle was established by the House of Lords in *Sullivan*,[138] where the disease under consideration was epilepsy. The D had been observed kicking the V about the head and body. It seemed that this was likely to have occurred while the D was in the post-ictal stage of a seizure caused by psychomotor epilepsy. At this stage of the seizure, the person can:

> ... make movements which he is not conscious that he is making, including, and this was characteristic of previous seizures which the appellant had suffered, automatic movements of resistance to anyone trying to come to his aid. These movements of resistance might, though in practice they very rarely would, involve violence.[139]

Expert medical evidence was given to the effect that a 'disease of the mind' required a prolonged 'disorder of the brain functions', lasting at least a day. The House of Lords rejected this. The purpose of the legislation relating to the defence of insanity was 'to protect society against the recurrence of the dangerous conduct'.[140] The duration of the mental state during which such conduct occurred was therefore irrelevant. If the effect of the disease was to impair the mental faculties of reason, memory and understanding:

> ... it matters not whether the aetiology of the impairment is organic, as in epilepsy, or functional, or whether the impairment itself is permanent or is transient and intermittent, provided that it subsisted at the time of the commission of the act.[141]

'Disease of the mind' therefore includes any illness, mental or physical, which causes a 'defect of reason' in the D, whether it be temporary or permanent. 'Defects of reason', however, which result from the treatment of such an illness will not be regarded as being caused by a disease of the mind.

The D did not know the nature and quality of his act

The defect of reason caused by a disease of the mind must have one or two consequences if the D is to be treated as 'insane' under the *M'Naghten* rules. The second is that the D did not know that what he was doing was wrong, and that is considered below. The first possibility is that the D, as a result of his defect of reason was not aware of the 'nature and quality of his act'. This covers three main possibilities. The first is that the D was totally unaware of what he was doing – he was effectively acting unconsciously, or as an automaton. This was the position of the D in *Bratty v Attorney General for Northern Ireland*.[142] He had killed a girl, but claimed to have done so while in an automatous state. Since, however, the only explanation for his automatism

138 [1983] 2 All ER 673.

139 *Ibid*, p 675.

140 *Ibid*, pp 667–68.

141 *Ibid*, p 677.

142 [1963] AC 386.

was that it resulted from psychomotor epilepsy the House of Lords confirmed the judge's ruling that this amounted to a defence of insanity, rather than non-insane automatism (which would have led to a complete acquittal). Similarly, in *Burgess*,[143] the Court of Appeal ruled that a sleep-walker who committed acts of violence while in that automatous state should be categorised as insane under the *M'Naghten* rules.

The second state of mind which is encompassed by ignorance of the 'nature and quality of the act' is where the D is in effect hallucinating, or misinterpreting what he is doing. The D in *Lipman*,[144] who thought he was fighting with snakes when in fact he was stuffing bed sheets down his girlfriend's throat, would have been treated as insane if his state of mind had resulted from a disease, rather than taking LSD.

The third possibility is where as a result of his state of mind the D does not appreciate that what he is doing is dangerous. For example, he might believe that stabbing a person with a knife will cause them no harm. Once again, he will not understand the 'nature and quality of his act'.

The D did not know that what he was doing was wrong

There is clearly a potential overlap here with the previous category in that if the D has misunderstood the nature and quality of his act, he probably also does not realise that he is doing anything wrong. This category also covers, however, the situation where the D is fully aware of what he is doing, and its consequences, but his mental illness causes him to believe that this is not 'wrong'. The main question which has arisen for discussion here is the issue of what is meant by 'wrong'? What is the position of the D who thinks his actions are illegal but morally justified, or immoral but not against the law? The distinction between moral and legal wrongs for this purpose was considered in *Windle*.[145] The D had killed his wife who was herself mentally disturbed, and had frequently talked of committing suicide. There was some evidence that the D was suffering from a 'defect of reason'. It was argued on his behalf at the trial that the word 'wrong' in the *M'Naghten* rules means 'morally wrong', and that the D, although he knew his actions were contrary to law, thought that morally he was justified in committing 'a kindly act to put her out of her real or imagined sufferings'.[146] The trial judge refused to allow the defence of insanity to go to the jury, and the Court of Appeal confirmed that this decision was correct. As Lord Goddard explained:[147]

143 [1991] 2 All ER 769.

144 [1969] 3 All ER 410.

145 [1952] 2 All ER 1; see, also, *Codere* (1916) 12 Cr App R 21.

146 [1952] 2 All ER 1, p 2.

147 *Ibid*, p 2.

> A man may be suffering from a defect of reason, but, if he knows that what he is doing is wrong – and by 'wrong' is meant contrary to law – he is responsible.

The result is that the D who thinks, as a result of a defect of reason caused by disease of the mind, that his actions are morally justified although illegal cannot use the insanity defence; the D who thinks, for the same reason, that his actions are legal can do so (whether or not he thinks he is acting immorally).[148]

INTOXICATION

It is widely recognised that the consumption of alcohol can increase the belligerence of some people, and lower inhibitions. It can therefore give rise to a greater risk that such people will commit assaults of one kind or another. Because alcohol, however, affects a person's perception of the world, it may be argued that a person who is intoxicated did not form, or was not capable of forming, the *mens rea* of an offence with which he has been charged. The suggestion will be that the D did not intend or foresee the consequences of his actions. The same arguments may apply in relation to some 'recreational' drugs – or indeed to prescribed medication. To what extent can the D who has committed the *actus reus* of an offence use as a defence the fact that he was intoxicated by alcohol or drugs at the relevant time? The rules relating to this area are not altogether logical or consistent, but they are reasonably clear. First, it is clear that the D who deliberately takes alcohol or drugs in order to get up the courage to commit an offence cannot rely on his intoxicated state of mind to claim that he lacked *mens rea*.[149] This was confirmed by *Attorney General for Northern Ireland v Gallagher*,[150] though the point was not necessarily at issue in the case. It has, however, been accepted ever since. What of the D who becomes intoxicated without any initial idea of committing an offence? The starting point is the House of Lords decision in *DPP v Majewski*.[151] It was this case that confirmed the test which has dominated this area ever since,[152] namely that of whether the offence of which the D is charged is an offence of 'specific' or 'basic' intent. If it is a specific intent offence, then the D's self-induced intoxication may in some circumstances provide a defence; it if is a

148 This argument is not accepted by the editors of *Blackstone's Criminal Practice*. See 1998 edn, para A3.18, where it is suggested that 'the better view' is that 'in the case of an accused who does not appreciate that his act is legally wrong but who does realise that it is morally wrong, the defence would not be made out'.

149 This is often referred to as the 'Dutch Courage rule.'

150 [1963] AC 349.

151 [1977] AC 443.

152 The test is derived, as is clear from the speeches in *Majewski* from the earlier House of Lords decision in *DPP v Beard* [1920] AC 479.

basic intent offence then intoxication will not provide a defence. The position is different where the D has taken prescribed medication, or has taken the alcohol or drugs unwittingly (for example, through having his drink 'spiked'). The issues raised by these circumstances will be considered below. The discussion will initially focus on the situation where the D has knowingly taken alcohol, or drugs which have not been prescribed by a doctor. This is what is meant by 'self-induced' or 'voluntary' intoxication.

Self-induced or voluntary intoxication

The D in *Majewski* was charged with assault occasioning actual bodily harm and assault on a constable. The offences took place in a pub. The D was a drug addict who had also been drinking before the offences took place. He was involved in a fight with the police during which he shouted at them: 'You pigs, I'll kill you all, you fucking pigs, you bastards.' His defence was that at the time of the assaults he had 'completely blanked out', and was therefore unaware of what he was doing. On this basis, he alleged that he should be found not guilty, because at the relevant time he was incapable of forming the *mens rea* for the charges which he was facing. The trial judge, however, directed the jury to 'ignore the subject of drink and drugs as being in any way a defence to the assaults' and the D was convicted. The House of Lords dismissed his appeal.

The reasons for the House of Lords decision were clearly based on considerations of policy rather than a strict analysis of the requirements of the proof *mens rea* and whether they had been met in the circumstances alleged by the D. This is indicated by the way in which Lord Elwyn-Jones, for example, formulated the issue before the House:[153]

> If a man consciously and deliberately takes alcohol and drugs not on medical prescription, but in order to escape from reality, to go 'on a trip', to become hallucinated ... and thereby disables himself from taking the care he might otherwise take and as a result by his subsequent actions causes injury to another – does our criminal law enable him to say that because he did not know what he was doing he lacked both intention and recklessness and accordingly is entitled to an acquittal?

The way the question is framed clearly expects the answer 'no'. The policy that a person who has 'consciously and deliberately' got themselves into a particular state of mind should remain responsible for their actions notwithstanding the inability of the prosecution to prove intention or recklessness is decided. The law must then be 'interpreted' to fit with that policy. The process is even more explicit in the speech of Lord Salmon, in rejecting the arguments of academic commentators that, 'as a matter of logic'

153 [1977] AC 443, p 471.

if intoxication can provide a defence to some offences (for example, murder) on the basis of 'lack of *mens rea*', it must be capable of providing a defence to all defences requiring proof of a mental element. Yet, the law apparently takes the view that a distinction can be drawn between different offences. Lord Salmon comments:[154]

> The answer is that in strict logic this view cannot be justified. But, this is the view that has been adopted by the common law of England, which is founded on common sense and experience rather than strict logic. There is no case in the 19th century when the courts were relaxing the harshness of the law in relation to the effect of drunkenness on criminal liability in which the courts ever went so far as to exculpate a man from any offence other than one which required some special or specific intent to be proved ...

The caveat at the end of this quotation, referring to 'special or specific intent' indicates that there is a limit to the policy which says that voluntary intoxication should be ignored. As indicated above, there are certain offences, 'specific intent' offences, where the D who did not form the relevant *mens rea* because of his intoxication will be entitled to be found not guilty. 'Basic intent' offences, however, are treated differently, with the intoxication being ignored. The difficulty is to find any logical and consistent basis for categorising offences as falling into the 'specific intent' or 'basic intent' category. Early case law, including *Majewski*, put the emphasis on defining 'specific intent' – for example, by suggesting that offences requiring a 'purposive' intent were specific intent offences.[155] This is unsatisfactory, however, in that the courts have consistently held that 'intent' is not to be equated with 'purpose'. Nor is it possible to define specific intent offences as those where the *mens rea* requirement goes beyond the *actus reus* – as for example in s 18 of the OAPA 1861, where the *mens rea* requires an intention to cause grievous bodily harm or resist arrest, but the *actus reus* is satisfied by proof that the D recklessly (that is, not 'intentionally') caused a wound or grievous bodily harm.[156] Such an additional intention may be sufficient to put an offence into the specific intent category, but it is not a necessary requirement, since the offence of murder has always been regarded as an offence of specific intent. In relation to murder, far from the *mens rea* exceeding the *actus reus*, as we have seen,[157] the *mens rea* is satisfied by an intention to cause grievous bodily harm, whereas the *actus reus* requires the death of the V. Attempts to isolate the characteristics of the 'specific intent' offence have therefore not been very successful. In more recent years, and particularly following the House of Lords decision in *Caldwell*,[158] the focus has shifted to defining basic intent offences, by using the test that

154 [1977] AC 443, p 482.

155 See, eg, Lord Simon, *ibid*, p 479.

156 See Chapter 5, p 125.

157 Chapter 4, p 62.

158 [1982] AC 341; see Chapter 2, p 34.

any offence for which the prosecution only need to prove 'recklessness' on the part of the D is a basic intent offence. *Caldwell* itself was concerned with the effect of intoxication on a D charged with criminal damage. Lord Diplock stated that:[159]

> ... classification into offences of 'specific' and 'basic' intent is irrelevant where being reckless as to whether a particular harmful consequence will result from one's act is a sufficient alternative *mens rea*.

Despite Lord Diplock's attempt to downgrade the significance of the labels 'basic' and 'specific', they have continued to be used as a convenient method of distinguishing between those offences where evidence of intoxication is relevant and those where it is not. The focus on 'recklessness', however, highlights the fact that the courts often treat the D's action in becoming intoxicated as in some way supplying the mental element of the offence: the D has acted 'recklessly' in becoming intoxicated (though this, of course, ignores the normal rule that *actus reus* and *mens rea* should coincide in time).[160] This aspect of the courts' approach may also be regarded as being exemplified by the decisions in *Bailey*[161] and *Hardie*.[162] In *Bailey*, the court was concerned with a D who had committed offences after taking insulin to control his diabetes, but then failing to eat sufficiently. In *Hardie*, the D had committed violent offences after taking the anti-depressant drug, valium.[163] In both cases, the view was taken that a D who was unaware that the effect of the insulin (combined with the failure to eat), or the valium, could be to encourage violent behaviour, should be able to use the fact that they were under the influence of these substances as evidence that they had not formed the relevant *mens rea* even in relation to a basic intent. In effect, the courts were saying that in such circumstances the taking of the substance was not 'reckless'. The result of these decisions seems to be that intoxicants must be divided into two categories. First, there are those which the court will assume everyone knows are likely to lead to an increase in the likelihood of offending. Alcohol and controlled drugs will certainly fall into this category. It will not be open to a D in relation to these substances to claim that he was unaware of their effect. The second category consists of substances about which there is not general knowledge of their likely effects. Here, it will be open to the D to claim that he did not realise what might happen when he took the substance. Even in relation to this category, however, it would presumably be open to the prosecution to try to prove that a particular D was aware of the likely effect on his behaviour – perhaps because such an effect had occurred on a previous occasion when the substance was taken. There is no direct authority to

159 See Chapter 2, p 356; [1982] AC 341.

160 See Chapter 2, p 22.

161 [1983] 1 WLR 760.

162 [1985] 1 WLR 64.

163 The valium had not been prescribed for the D.

support this proposition, but it would seem to follow from the basis on which *Hardie* and *Bailey* were decided.

Applying all this to the offences with which this book is concerned, there is only one which can definitely be said to be in all circumstances a 'specific intent' offence, and that is murder. The other main contender is s 18 of the OAPA 1861, but, as has been pointed out by Smith and Hogan,[164] this may depend on the precise offence charged. There is no doubt that a D charged with causing grievous bodily harm with intent to do so will be able to use intoxication as evidence of lack of the relevant *mens rea*. A D charged with wounding with intent to resist arrest, however, might raise his intoxication as evidence that he did not foresee that the V would suffer a wound as a result of the his (D's) attempt to evade arrest. It is by no means clear, however, that the evidence should be regarded as being relevant to this part of the offence, for which recklessness is all that the prosecution has to prove. Generally, however, s 18 is regarded as falling into the specific intent category. Apart from these two offences there does not appear to be any authority which suggests that any other offence against the person is a specific intent offence. Professor Smith, however, has suggested that in relation to indecent assault, if the assault is one which is ambiguous as to its indecency, and therefore the purpose of the D needs to be proved,[165] the offence should be treated as being of specific intent.[166] In most cases, however, where there is no doubt as to the indecency of the D's actions, the offence will be one of basic intent.[167]

Effect of requirement of 'specific intent'

Where an offence is of specific intent, this means that the jury will be allowed to consider evidence of the D's intoxication in deciding whether or not he had the required *mens rea* at the relevant time. It is not necessary for the defence to be successful for it to be found that the D was totally incapable of forming the *mens rea*: it is enough that he did not in fact form it.[168] It is, of course, perfectly open to the jury to find that the D, though intoxicated, still knew what he was doing and intended the consequences of his actions. Even if the jury think that the D's state of mind was sufficiently affected by the intoxication to mean that he should not be convicted of the specific intent offence this will be unlikely to result in an acquittal. In relation to murder, the D may be (and probably should be) convicted of manslaughter, which is a basic intent offence. Similarly a successful use of intoxication in relation to a s 18 charge will not

164 *Op cit*, Smith and Hogan, fn 80, p 230.

165 See Chapter 6, p 160.

166 *C* [1992] Crim LR 642, and commentary thereon.

167 As was held to be the case in *C*.

168 *Pordage* [1975] Crim LR 575.

prevent a conviction under s 20.[169] And, if indecent assault is treated as a specific intent offence, the D will still be liable to be convicted of an assault occasioning actual bodily harm,[170] or common assault.

Effect of intoxication on basic intent offences

Where the offence is one of basic intent, there is no point in the D raising intoxication as part of his defence. The jury or magistrates will simply have to ignore it. Moreover, if the D, in claiming to have been intoxicated is admitting (as he almost certainly will be) that he committed the *actus reus*, then it may actually be a disadvantage to raise the issue. As we have seen, the courts may well then treat the voluntary intoxication as itself supplying the element of recklessness necessary for the offence, thus relieving the prosecution of proving that the D had the relevant state of mind at the time of the offence. A conviction thus becomes more likely than if the D had not raised the issue at all. A D who is charged with a basic intent offence for which he committed the *actus reus* at a time when he was voluntarily under the influence of drugs or alcohol will often be best advised to plead guilty.

Involuntary or 'prescribed' intoxication

What is the position where the D claims that his intoxication was involuntary, or the result of taking prescribed drugs? First, it must be considered what is meant by 'involuntary' in this context. It covers, for example, the D drinking orange juice which has been laced with vodka without his knowledge. It will also cover the D who is taking drugs prescribed by a medical practitioner. It does not, however, cover the D who mistakes the strength of the alcoholic drink which he is voluntarily drinking.[171] Once the D has started to consume alcohol voluntarily, he loses the opportunity of raising intoxication in his defence to a basic intent offence. It is not clear, however, whether the same rule would apply where the D unknowingly has his weak alcoholic drink laced with something much stronger. It is difficult to see that the D has been reckless in such a situation unless what he knowingly consumed would have been likely to render him so intoxicated as to significantly raise the likelihood of his committing offences.

Secondly, although evidence of involuntary intoxication will be relevant even in relation to basic intent offences, the jury or magistrates will still have to be convinced that the D did not form the relevant *mens rea*. It is open to them here, as it is with voluntary intoxication in relation to specific intent

169 See Chapter 5, p 119.

170 Ie, under the OAPA, s 47; see Chapter 5, p 114.

171 *Allen* [1988] Crim LR 698.

offences to decide that notwithstanding the intoxication the prosecution has proved that the D did have the relevant *mens rea*. As was made clear by the House of Lords in *Kingston*,[172] if the D claims that he only formed the intention to commit the offence because of the fact that his inhibitions had been lowered by virtue of the involuntary intoxication, this is no defence. The D had committed an indecent assault on a 15 year old boy, after his drink had been 'spiked' by another person. It was clear that he knew what he was doing at the relevant time, and that he was rightly convicted of the offence.[173] The involuntary intoxication was relevant to only to sentence, and not to guilt.

If, however, it is decided that the D did not, as result of his involuntary intoxication, act intentionally or recklessly, then he is entitled to be acquitted.

172 [1994] 3 All ER 353.

173 The Court of Appeal ([1993] 3 WLR 676) had taken a different view; a view which was firmly rejected by the House of Lords.

CHAPTER 8

PROPOSALS FOR REFORM

Many of the areas covered in this book have been the subject of reform proposals during the past 20 years. Most of these proposals have not, however, as yet been acted on. They have generally emanated from reports by the Law Commission. One such report, *Offences Against the Person and General Principles*,[1] has now formed the basis of a consultation paper and draft Bill issued by the Home Office in February 1998 (*Violence: Reforming the Offences Against the Person Act 1861*). The paper and the Bill deal with non-fatal and non-sexual offences against the person. Since it seems likely that this will be the first area on which there is likely to be legislation, this chapter will start with a discussion of the draft Bill, and will then look at some other areas where the Law Commission has proposed reform. Subject to this, the order of treatment in this chapter follows that for the book as a whole.

HOME OFFICE PROPOSALS ON NON-FATAL OFFENCES

Mens rea

The Bill deals with the mental element of the offences which it creates in cl 14, under the heading 'fault terms'. 'Intention' is defined in cl 14(1) in the following way:

> A person acts intentionally with respect to a result if:
>
> (a) it is his purpose to cause it; or
>
> (b) although it is not his purpose to cause it, he knows that it would occur in the ordinary course of events if he were to succeed in his purpose of causing some other result.

This definition of intention is based on that recommended by the Law Commission.[2] Insofar as it allows proof of intention to be established by proof of the D's purpose, it is noncontroversial and simply reproduces existing law. Paragraph (b) is designed to deal with the broader definition of intention recognised in current law in the decisions of *Moloney*, *Hancock*, *Nedrick* and *Woollin*.[3] It does not do so in terms of an inference from foresight of a probability, or 'virtual certainty', however, but in terms of the D's knowledge

1 Report No 218, 1993.

2 *Ibid*, cl 1.

3 See Chapter 2, pp 26–32.

as to what will happen 'in the ordinary course of events' as a result achieving his purpose. The test is subjective – it is what the D actually 'knows', not what he 'ought to know' that is important. Consider, for example, the D who, like the D in *Lamb*,[4] thinks that pulling the trigger on a revolver will not discharge a bullet if the chamber in front of the hammer is empty when he starts to pull. He will not be regarded as having intended to fire the gun (or therefore to injure anyone standing in the line of fire), even though it might be argued that he ought to have known that the chamber would rotate, bringing a bullet in front of the hammer. He did not know that the result (firing a bullet from the gun) would follow 'in the ordinary course of events' from success in achieving his 'purpose' (pulling the trigger). Similarly, this formulation ensures that a D who makes a mistake of fact will, as under the present law, be protected from the consequences of his actions. Thus, the D who throws the contents of a flask over the V, thinking that the flask contains water, whereas in fact it contains acid, will not be held to have intended to cause injury to the V. Once again, he did not know that the result (injury to the V) would follow in the ordinary course of events from achieving his purpose (giving the V a soaking).

The overall effect of the clause is probably to provide a slightly narrower scope for intention than under the current common law approach. The difference is marginal, however, and the vast majority of cases will fall to be decided the same way whichever approach to proving intention is used.

Clause 14(3) deals specifically with the issue of intentional omissions. It is in parallel terms to cl 14(1), and provides that:

> A person intends an omission to have a result if:
>
> (a) it is his purpose that the result will occur; or
>
> (b) although it is not his purpose that the result will occur he knows that it would occur in the ordinary course of events if he were to succeed in his purpose that some other result will occur.

This does not, of course, establish any general liability for intentional omissions. Whether an omission is a sufficient *actus reus* for an offence will be determined by the particular formulation of that offence. Some clauses of the Act, as we shall see, make specific reference to 'omission' as a means of committing an offence; in relation to other offences it is assumed that the current common law approach to liability for omissions will apply.[5]

Clause 14 also includes a definition of recklessness, in sub-para (2):

> A person acts recklessly with respect to a result if he is aware of a risk that it will occur and it is unreasonable to take that risk having regard to the circumstances as he knows or believes them to be.

This puts into statutory language the 'subjective' *Cunningham* test of recklessness, which, as we have seen is currently used in almost all offences

4 See Chapter 4, p 91.

5 See Chapter 2, p 16 *et seq*.

against the person.[6] The government has explicitly accepted that this is the appropriate approach for such offences.[7] Clause 14(4) applies this test to reckless omissions.

Clause 16 deals with the issue of the coincidence (or lack of coincidence) of *mens rea* and *actus reus*. Where a person lacks the fault element of an offence at a time when his act or omission may or does cause a result, he may nevertheless commit the offence if, having later become aware of the act or omission and the likely or actual result of it, and having the required fault element, he fails to take reasonable steps to prevent the result occurring or continuing. This would deal with a situation such as *Fagan v MPC*,[8] where the D stopped his car on a policeman's foot. He was not aware at the time that he had done this, and so did not have the *mens rea* for an assault at that moment. It was only by regarding the D's failure to move the car as being part of a continuing act capable of amounting to assault that he could be found to have committed an offence. Clause 16 would remove any doubt as to there being liability in such a situation.

Clause 17 deals with 'transferred malice',[9] and would put this concept on to a statutory basis as regards both acts and omissions.

THE NEW OFFENCES

The Bill contains a redefinition of 'assault', and a number of new offences to replace the those currently contained in the OAPA 1861. These are set out in the first part of the Bill, for the most part in descending order of seriousness.

Intentional serious injury

Clause 1 of the Bill sets out an offence of intentionally causing serious injury to another. This is intended to replace, in part, s 18 of the OAPA. It is the most serious offence included in the Bill, as is reflected in the fact that it carries a maximum sentence of life imprisonment. Paragraph (2) of the clause makes it clear that a person who is under a common law duty to act may commit this offence by omission.

The meaning of 'injury' is dealt with by cl 15. This states that it means '(a) physical injury, or (b) mental injury'. Physical injury includes 'pain, unconsciousness and any other impairment of a person's physical condition'.

6 See Chapter 2, p 33.

7 Home Office Consultation Document, *Violence: Reforming the Offences Against the Person Act 1861* (1998) para 3.11.

8 [1968] 3 All ER 442; see Chapter 2, p 20.

9 See Chapter 2, p 23.

Similarly, mental injury includes 'any impairment of person's mental health'. In relation to the offence under cl 1, though not any other offence in the Bill, injury can include 'injury' caused by disease. Deliberately infecting someone with a serious illness (either physical or mental) can therefore fall within this offence. The D who is HIV positive and has intercourse with a V with the intention (not merely being reckless) of infecting him or her with the virus can therefore be liable under this provision. Similarly, to feed someone with food infected with E-coli, or BSE, could also fall within this offence, provided that the relevant intention could be proved.

It should be noted that the Bill does not, either here or in any other offence, make any separate reference to 'wounding'. This type of injury is to be dealt with in the same way as any other.

The Bill does not attempt to identify what constitutes a 'serious' injury. This is presumably because this is regarded as a question of fact.[10] In this context, the case law on s 18 and s 20 of the OAPA may still be of use in providing guidance as to the types of injury which are appropriately categorised as 'serious'.

Clause 1 does not deal with the version of the s 18 of the OAPA offence which is based on the D's intention to resist arrest. The Bill deals with this situation in cl 6, which is discussed below.

Reckless serious injury

This offence, set out in cl 2, runs parallel to the cl 1 offence, but with the substitution of 'recklessly' causing injury, for 'intentionally' doing so. Other differences from cl 1 are that there is here no liability for omissions, and that injury does not include 'disease'.[11] The offence is broadly speaking a replacement for s 20 of the OAPA. It is triable either way, with the maximum penalty on indictment being seven years imprisonment.

Intentional or reckless injury

Clause 3 sets out the offence which would replace to a large extent s 47 of the OAPA. It simply makes it an offence where the D 'intentionally or recklessly causes injury to another'. Injury is defined in the same way as for the offence under cl 2. The Bill has therefore abandoned the distinction between 'grievous' and 'actual' bodily harm, replacing it simply with 'serious injury', and 'injury'. The other major difference from s 47 is that this offence is not dependent on the prosecution being able to prove that the D 'assaulted' the V. It is enough that the injury is 'caused' by the D.

10 See *op cit*, Consultation Document, fn 7, para 3.12.

11 *Ibid*, cl 15(2) and (3).

The offence, which would be triable either way, carries the same maximum penalty on indictment as s 47, that is, imprisonment for a maximum of five years.

Assault

This offence is the only one which carries the same name as an existing offence against the person. It is defined as being committed where a person:

(a) ... intentionally or recklessly applies force to or causes an impact on the body of another; or

(b) ... intentionally or recklessly causes the other to believe that such force or impact is imminent.

As will be seen, this defines assault in a way which incorporates the current offence of battery, thus giving it its wider meaning under the current law. More specifically, para (a) is the replacement for battery, and para (b) is the replacement for *assault*.

The offence are defined in terms of the application of force to, or the causing of an impact on the body of another. Clause 4(2) excludes any such impact or force which is 'generally acceptable in the ordinary conduct of daily life', provided that the D 'does not know or believe that it is in fact unacceptable to the other person'. Beyond this, the type of force or impact covered is not defined, and so it is likely that the old case law on assault and battery will still have some relevance in this area, for example in relation to the issue of whether the application of force to the V's clothing constitutes application of force to her body.[12]

In relation to the offence under (b), the use of the general word 'cause' means that it is irrelevant what behaviour of the D leads to the specified result. In other words, it can be words, actions, any combination of the two, or even silence.[13] The definition uses 'imminence' as the test of how quickly the application of the force or impact should be anticipated to follow whatever behaviour has led to the fear of it. This is different from the current phrase which refers to 'immediate' unlawful violence. It is not thought, however, that this should lead to any difference in practice as to the situations covered by the offence.

The *mens rea* of these offences is noncontroversial, requiring proof of intention or subjective recklessness.

The offence of assault is summary only, with a maximum penalty of six months imprisonment or a fine at level 5, or both.

12 See Chapter 5, p 111.

13 See Chapter 5, p 104 *et seq*.

It is the intention that the definition of assault contained in cl 4 should apply throughout the criminal law, wherever an offence includes assault as one of its elements, as for example is the case with indecent assault.[14] Schedule 1 to the Bill sets out the necessary amendments to existing statutes needed to achieve this objective. The Bill itself contains two offences which use 'assault' as part of the definition. These are discussed below.

Resisting arrest and other assault offences

Clauses 5–7 contain three offences which come into the category of what would currently be described as aggravated assaults.[15] Clause 5 sets out the offence of assaulting a constable who is acting in the execution of his duty, or assaulting a person assisting a constable who is so acting. This is basically a straightforward replacement for the existing offence under s 89 of the Police Act 1996. The only difference is the incorporation of the statutory definition of 'assault' (cl 5(2)). As noted by the Consultation Paper, the offence requires *mens rea* only as regards the assault, and not as regards the fact that the V, or the person the V is assisting, is a constable.[16] In taking this line, the Bill does not follow the Law Commission's recommendations, but the intention is to simply re-enact the current law in relation to this offence.[17]

Clauses 6 and 7 deal specifically with resisting arrest. Clause 6 is the equivalent of the relevant part of s 18 of the OAPA (that is, causing GBH with intent to resist or prevent lawful apprehension). The offence is committed where the D 'causes serious injury to another intending to resist, prevent or terminate the lawful arrest or detention of himself or a third person'. The drafting is unfortunate here in that it does not appear to require any *mens rea* in relation to the causing of injury, whereas s 18 requires intention or recklessness as to this part of the offence (through the use of word 'maliciously'). It leaves open the possibility of a D who, trying to escape arrest, accidentally causes serious injury, being liable for this offence, which carries a possible maximum sentence of life imprisonment. This surely cannot be what was intended by the drafter, and it is to be hoped that the point will be clarified before the Bill is put before parliament.

Clause 7 is a straight replacement for the offence under s 38 of the OAPA (assault with intent to resist or prevent lawful apprehension), using the new statutory definition of assault. The D is guilty of an offence under cl 7 'if he assaults another intending to resist, prevent or terminate the lawful arrest of

14 See *op cit*, Consultation Document, fn 7, paras 3.5–3.6.

15 See Chapter 5, p 118.

16 See *op cit*, Consultation Document, fn 7, para 3.8.

17 See *op cit*, Consultation Document, fn 7, para 3.8.

detention of himself or a third person'. It is triable either way, with a maximum penalty on indictment of two years imprisonment.

In relation to both cll 6 and 7, 'the question whether the defendant believes the arrest or detention is lawful must be determined according to the circumstances as he believes them to be'.[18] This puts into statutory form the rule as regards mistake of fact derived from *Williams (Gladstone)*.[19]

Dangerous substances

Clauses 8 and 9 contain two offences relating to causing injury, or the risk of injury, by the use of explosives or dangerous substances. These constitute a reworking of the relevant provisions of the OAPA.

The *actus reus* of the offence under either cl 8 or cl 9 is set out in cl 8(2), and is committed where the D:

(a) causes and explosive substance to explode;

(b) places a dangerous substance in any place;

(c) delivers or sends a dangerous substance to a person;

(d) throws a dangerous substance at a person; or

(e) applies a dangerous substance to a person.

An explosive substance is as defined by the Explosive Substances Act 1883,[20] and is therefore:

> ... deemed to include any materials for making any explosive substance; also any apparatus, machine, implement or materials used, or intended to be used, or adapted for causing, or aiding in causing any explosion in or with any explosive substance; also any part of any such apparatus, machine or implement.[21]

Clause 8(3) states that 'a dangerous substance is an explosive substance or any other dangerous substance'. 'Dangerous substance' is not further defined.

The offence under cl 8 is committed where the D commits one of the above acts with the intention of causing serious injury, or being reckless whether serious injury is caused. The offence under cl 9 is committed where the D commits one of the acts with the intention of causing or risking injury, or being reckless whether injury is caused. 'Injury' is to be defined as in cl 15, which has been discussed above.

18 Report No 218, cll 6(2), 7(2).

19 See Chapter 7, p 174.

20 *Op cit*, Consultation Document, fn 7, cl 8(4).

21 Explosives Substances Act 1883, s 9(1).

Both offences are triable on indictment only. That under cl 8 carries a maximum of life imprisonment; under cl 9 the maximum is 14 years imprisonment.

Other offences

Clauses 10–13 contain various miscellaneous offences, which are generally revisions of existing OAPA offences.

Clause 10 makes it an offence to make to any person 'a threat to cause the death of, or cause serious injury' to that person, or another, intending that the person to whom the threat is made should believe that it will be carried out. This extends the current offence under s 16 of the OAPA to include threats of serious injury.

Clause 11 is intended to replace the existing 'poisoning' offences under ss 23–25 of the OAPA . It makes it an offence for a D to administer a substance to, or cause it to be taken by, another either intentionally or recklessly, where the D knows the substance is capable of causing injury, and 'it is unreasonable to administer the substance or cause it to be taken having regard to the circumstances as he knows them to be'.

Clause 12 (taken together with the defence of 'lawful justification or excuse' in cl 18) restates the offence of torture currently contained in s 134 of the Criminal Justice Act 1988. The restatement makes no substantive change to the current law, apart from specifically including omissions in breach of a common law duty to act within the scope of the *actus reus*.

Finally, cl 13 makes it an offence intentionally or recklessly to cause danger to a person who is on a railway or is being carried on a railway. Clause 13(2) brings omissions in breach of common law duty to act within the scope of the *actus reus* of this offence. This general offence is intended to replace the more specific offences currently contained in ss 32–34 of the OAPA.

Defences

Clause 18 of the Bill provides that it will have effect subject to any enactment or rule of law providing:

(a) a defence; or

(b) lawful authority, justification or excuse for an act or omission.

All the general defences discussed in Chapter 7 will therefore be available, as appropriate. In addition, the Bill puts into statutory form the rules relating to the effect of involuntary intoxication on liability. The relevant provisions are contained in cl 19. They are intended to be more straightforward that the Law

Commission's current proposals for this area,[22] which are discussed later in this chapter.[23]

An 'intoxicant' for the purposes of cl 19 is 'any alcohol, drug or other thing which, when taken into the body, may impair the awareness or understanding of the person taking it'.[24] A person will be regarded as being 'voluntarily intoxicated' in three situations, namely, if:

(a) he takes an intoxicant otherwise than properly for a medicinal purpose;

(b) he is aware that it is or may be an intoxicant; and

(c) he takes it in such a quantity as impairs his awareness and understanding.[25]

The use of the word 'properly' in (a) means that the person will be regarded as being voluntarily intoxicated even though he takes the intoxicant for a medicinal purpose if either (i) he does not take it on medical advice, and is aware that taking it 'may result in his doing an act or making an omission capable of constituting an offence of the kind in question', or (ii) he does take it on medical advice, but then fails to comply with a 'condition forming part of the advice', being aware that this failure 'may result in his doing an act or making an omission capable of constituting an offence of the kind in question'.[26]

Where a person is 'voluntarily intoxicated' under these rules cl 19(1) states that he must be treated:

(a) as having been aware of any risk of which he would have been aware had he not been intoxicated; and

(b) as having known or believed in any circumstances which he would have known or believed in had he not been intoxicated.

The clause does not make any reference to 'specific intent' or to different types of offence, but the wording of cl 19(1) makes it clear that it only applies to those offences which can be committed 'recklessly'. The provision will have no relevance to offences that can only be committed intentionally, therefore, such as the offence of causing serious injury under cl 1. Where an offence has different elements, some of which can be committed recklessly and others requiring intention (as with cl 6 or 7 (resisting arrest)) the provision will only apply to the *mens rea* elements based on recklessness.

22 See *op cit*, Consultation Document, fn 7, para 3.23.

23 See below, p 232.

24 *Op cit*, Consultation Document, fn 7, cl 19(7).

25 *Op cit*, Consultation Document, fn 7, cl 19(3).

26 *Op cit*, Consultation Document, fn 7, cl 19(4).

OTHER PROPOSALS

Manslaughter

The Law Commission's current proposals in relation to the reform of the law of manslaughter are contained in Report No 237, *Legislating the Criminal Code: Involuntary Manslaughter*.[27] As well as proposing replacement offences for the current offence of involuntary manslaughter, the Report also contains specific proposals relating to the liability of corporations for deaths arising in the course of their activities.

Involuntary manslaughter

The Report recommends that the two existing categories of involuntary manslaughter, that is, 'unlawful act manslaughter' and 'manslaughter by gross negligence',[28] should be abolished. The offence of manslaughter would then only exist in relation to those situations where what would otherwise be murder is mitigated to manslaughter through provocation, diminished responsibility or a suicide pact.[29] In other words, 'voluntary manslaughter' would be the only type of manslaughter recognised by English law. One of the main reasons for making this change is that the current offence of manslaughter is seen as being too broad, and giving rise to difficulties in particular as regards sentencing.[30]

In place of the offence of involuntary manslaughter, the Report recommends the creation of two specific offences of 'reckless killing' and 'killing by gross carelessness'. The elements of these two offences are set out in a draft Bill attached to the Report.

Reckless killing

Clause 1 of the Bill provides that a person will be guilty of reckless killing, if 'his conduct causes the death of another' and 'he is aware of the risk that his conduct will cause death or serious injury' and 'it is unreasonable for him to take that risk having regard to the circumstances as he knows or believes them to be'.

The test is thus one of subjective, *Cunningham*, recklessness,[31] with the prosecution having to prove that the D was aware of the risk he was running.

27 The Report was published in March 1996.

28 See Chapter 4.

29 Chapter 4, p 68 *et seq*.; Homicide Act 1957, ss 2–4.

30 Report, paras 3.2–3.4.

31 See Chapter 2, p 33.

The test of whether it was reasonable to take the risk, however, is objective, though based on the D's perception of the circumstances.

'Injury' is defined in cl 8 as meaning:

(a) physical injury, including pain, unconsciousness or other impairment of a person's physical condition; or

(b) impairment of a person's mental health.

There is no definition of 'serious injury'. The Commission took the view[32] that no satisfactory definition was possible, since so much depended on the individual circumstances.

An example of the kind of behaviour which would fall within this offence would be that of the D's in *Hyam*, or *Nedrick*, who set fire to property intending to scare the occupants, but not intending to cause them death or serious injury. It could also cover, however, the surgeon who carries out a life-endangering operation in circumstances where it is unreasonable to do so. The consent of the patient to the procedure would not necessarily prevent it from being unreasonable to take the risk.[33]

The maximum penalty for this offence would be life imprisonment.[34]

Killing by gross carelessness

This is the second offence created by the Bill. It obviously has some links with the current offence of manslaughter by gross negligence, but is not identical to it.

Clause 2 of the Bill provides that a person will be guilty of this offence if he causes the death of another, and the following three conditions are satisfied. First, it would have been obvious to a reasonable person in the position of the D that there was a risk that his conduct would cause death or serious injury. Secondly, the D must have been capable of appreciating that risk at the material time. Thirdly, either the D's conduct fell far below what could reasonably be expected of him in the circumstances; or the D intended to cause some injury; or the D was aware of a risk that injury might be caused, and unreasonably took that risk. In the last two situations (intention to cause, or awareness of the risk of causing, injury), the D's conduct which caused or was intended to cause the injury must constitute an offence.[35] Thus, the D who acts in legitimate self-defence will not be caught by this provision.[36]

32 Agreeing with the conclusion of the CLRC in its 14th Report, *Offences Against the Person*, 1980, Cmnd 7844, London: HMSO, para 154.

33 See Report No 237, para 5.12.

34 Draft Bill, cl 1(2).

35 *Ibid*, cl 2(4).

36 See Report No 237, p 52, footnote 62. But is this provision necessary given that cl 8(2) specifically states that the Act has effect 'subject to any enactment or rule of law providing a defence, or providing lawful authority, justification or excuse'?

In assessing whether the risk should have been obvious to the D, account must be taken of '(a) knowledge of any relevant facts which the [D] is shown to have at the material time; and (b) any skill or experience professed by him'.[37] The test of obviousness is to this extent subjective. This is further emphasised by cl 2(3) which state that the D must have been 'capable of appreciating' the relevant risk at the material time. As the Report explains,[38] this formulation is designed to avoid the kind of situation which arose in *Elliott v C*,[39] where a court in applying the *Caldwell* test of recklessness[40] felt obliged to ignore evidence that the D, a 14 year old girl, probably lacked the intelligence to appreciate the risks involved in her actions. She had to be judged by the standard of the reasonable adult. The wording of cl 2(2) ensures that those who are incapable of appreciating a risk, through illness or mental deficiency, for example, will not be found liable.[41]

As regards what can reasonably be expected of a D, for the purpose of deciding whether his conduct falls 'far below' that standard under cl 2(1)(c)(i):

> ... regard shall be had to the circumstances of which he can be expected to be aware, to any circumstances shown to be within his knowledge and to any other matter relevant for assessing his conduct at the material time.[42]

The 'far below' test is adapted from that applying to dangerous driving,[43] which the Commission regarded as having operated without serious problems. It is intended to avoid the circularity of the current 'gross negligence' test in manslaughter, which effectively requires the jury to decide that the D's behaviour constitutes an offence if it is so negligent as to be criminal.[44]

The Commission gives, in paras 5.36 and 5.37, two examples of how it thinks that this offence might apply in practice:

> *Example 1: D, a climbing instructor, took a group of inexperienced climbers out with inadequate equipment in very bad weather. They got trapped and one of them died*
>
> In order to convict the D, the jury would have to answer 'yes' to all the following questions: (1) Would it have been *obvious* to a reasonable experienced climbing instructor in D's place that taking a group of inexperienced climbers out in the prevailing conditions would create a risk of

37 Draft Bill, cl 2(2).

38 Paras 4.20–4.22.

39 [1983] 1 WLR 939.

40 See Chapter 2, p 34.

41 Incapacity as a result of voluntary intoxication should be ignored, however: cl 8(3).

42 Draft Bill, cl 2(3).

43 See Road Traffic Act 1988, s 2A.

44 See Chapter 4, p 97.

causing death or serious injury to one of them?; (2) Was the D *capable* of appreciating this risk?; and (3) Did his conduct fall far below what could reasonably be expected of him in all the circumstances?

Example 2: The D caused the V's death by punching him in the head, not realising that serious injury might result; the impact of the blow caused a blood clot in the brain

The jury would have to decide whether it would have been obvious to a reasonable person in the D's position that punching the V as hard as he did would create a risk of causing death or serious injury, and whether the D was *capable* of appreciating the risk at the time in question (unless he was incapable due to voluntary intoxication). If the answer to both of these questions in 'yes', and if it is satisfied that the D intended to cause *some* injury to the V, or was reckless as to doing so, the jury must convict. If not, the accused may be convicted of the appropriate non-fatal offence in the alternative.

As regards the penalty for this type of offence, the Law Commission does not make a firm recommendation. It regards it as a less serious offence than reckless killing, and therefore is clear that the maximum penalty should be a determinate prison sentence, rather than life imprisonment. The discussion in paras 5.47–5.52 reveals that the Commission sees some attraction in equating the penalty to that which attaches to causing death by dangerous driving, that is, 10 years. On the other hand, it recognises the anomaly which might then arise whereby an unintentional killing in the course of rape, arson or robbery might attract a lesser sentence than the non-fatal offence. It seems likely that the penalty should be fixed at some point between 10 and 15 years.

Finally, it should be noted that in relation to both the new offences, liability for an omission which has led to death should only fall within their scope where the omission involves a breach of a duty at common law.[45]

Corporate killing

Changes in the law of manslaughter to make it more possible for a corporation to be found guilty of this offence have followed a number of recent 'accidents' which involved the death of significant numbers of people. The first of these was the sinking of the cross-channel ferry, the *Herald of Free Enterprise* in March 1987. This was followed by the King's Cross underground station fire (November 1987), the Piper Alpha oil platform disaster (July 1988) and the Clapham rail crash (December 1988). In all these cases, the corporation responsible for the operation concerned was the subject of criticism. A prosecution of P & O European Ferries in relation to the *Herald of Free Enterprise* was started, following an inquest verdict of 'unlawful killing', but fell foul of the traditional approach of English law that to render a company

45 Cf Chapter 2, p 16, for consideration of the current position as regards omissions.

criminally liable for anything other than a regulatory offence, it is generally necessary to find that one or more individuals representing the 'directing mind and will' of the company themselves had the *mens rea* necessary for the offence.[46] Since this could not be established, the judge directed an acquittal. There has, in fact, only been one successful prosecution of a company for manslaughter. This involved a 'one-man' company which had run adventure holidays for children, and had organised a canoeing trip at sea which led to the death of several participants.[47] The managing director of the company was also found liable, and in that context it was obviously easy to attach liability to the company. The success of the prosecution in this case, however, probably served only to emphasise that in relation to large corporations the current law makes such success very unlikely. This being the case, it could be argued that English law is failing to meet its obligation to protect the right to life of the victims of such events.[48] The Law Commission's proposals try to remedy the position by making 'management failure' rather than failures by particular individuals, the test of liability. This attempts to meet the argument that in some of the cases mentioned above it seemed that corporate policies might have led to the safety of the public being put at greater risk than was justifiable.

The offence is set out in cl 4 of the draft Bill. It states that a corporation will be guilty of 'corporate killing' if two conditions are satisfied.[49] First, 'management failure by the corporation' must be the cause, or one of the causes of someone's death. Secondly, that failure must constitute 'conduct falling far below what can be reasonably be expected of the corporation in the circumstances'. The standard is thus similar to that being proposed for one of the versions of killing by gross carelessness, discussed above.

The meaning of 'management failure' is developed in cl 4(2). This states there is such a failure by a corporation:

> ... if the way in which its activities are managed or organised fails to ensure the health and safety of persons employed in or affected by those activities.

The question of whether there has been such a failure is a question of fact to be determined by the jury. The Law Commission attempts, however, in paras 8.21–8.33 of its Report to give some examples of how it might work in practice. There would be no need to show that any particular individual was at fault, though this might be the case,[50] and might contribute to a finding of

46 *P & O European Ferries (Dover) Ltd* (1991) 93 Cr App R 72.

47 *Kite and OLL Ltd* (1994) unreported, Winchester Crown Court.

48 See Chapter 4, p 55.

49 Draft Bill, cl 4(1).

50 See draft Bill, cl 4(2)(b), which states that a management failure may be found to have caused a death 'notwithstanding that the immediate cause is the act or omission of an individual'.

'management failure'. The Commission uses as a simple hypothetical example of a lorry driver employed by a company who causes death by dangerous driving while on the company's business. It explains that:[51]

> ... this act would not *of itself* involve a management failure so as to incur corporate liability; nor would the company be *vicariously* liable for the driver's negligence. The company might be liable, however, if the incident occurred because the driver was overtired at the material time in consequence of a requirement to work excessively long hours, or because she consistently worked very long hours in her desire to earn overtime, and the company had no adequate system of monitoring to ensure that this did not happen.

A management failure may thus arise from either an act (requirement to work long hours) or an omission (lack of an adequate system of monitoring). There are obviously clear links to the obligations imposed on employers' to provide a 'safe system of work'.[52] The proposed offence would not exist, however, solely for the protection of employees, but for anyone affected by the corporation's activities.

Clause 4(4) rules out accessorial liability in relation to this offence. As the Commission explains, the new offence is intended to deal with the special case of corporations, so that the 'indirect extension of an individual's liability, by means of the new corporate offence, would be entirely contrary to our purpose'.[53]

The primary penalty for the new offence would be a fine. The Bill also makes provision, however, for 'remedial orders' against a convicted corporation to be made by the court.[54] These may specify the steps needed for the corporation to remedy the failure that has led to the conviction. Such an order would in its turn be backed up by specific criminal offences in the event of non-compliance.[55]

DURESS

The Law Commission's proposals in relation to the defence of duress are contained in Report No 218, *Legislating the Criminal Code: Offences against the Person and General Principles*.[56] They are set out in cll 25 and 26 of the draft Bill attached to the report, and deal separately with duress by threats, and duress of circumstances.

51 Report No 237, para 8.21.

52 *Ibid*, para 8.10.

53 *Ibid*, para 8.58.

54 Draft Bill, cl 5(1).

55 *Ibid*, cl 5(5).

56 1993, Cm 2370, London: HMSO.

Duress by threats

The defence of duress by threats as set out in cl 25 of the Bill largely follows the principles of the current common law defence.[57] Thus, the threat must be, or be believed to be, of death or serious injury to the D or another;[58] the D must believe that 'the threat will be carried out immediately if he does not do the act or, if not immediately, before he' or the other person threatened can obtain effective official protection;[59] and the D must believe 'that there is no other way of preventing the threat being carried out'.[60]

In three important ways, however, the Law Commission's recommendations, and the draft Bill, differ from the current position. First, the Law Commission recommends that the defence should be available to all offences, including murder. As we have seen in Chapter 7, following *Howe*[61] and *Gotts*,[62] the current position is that duress is not a defence to murder or attempted murder.[63] The Law Commission, and the majority of those with whom it consulted, felt that it was requiring an unrealistic standard of the D to expect him to sacrifice his own life for the sake of another. As the Law Commission puts it:[64]

> In our view, it is not only futile, but also wrong, for the *criminal* law to demand heroic behaviour. The attainment of a heroic standard of behaviour will always count for great merit; but failure to achieve the standard should not be met with punishment by the State.

Moreover, where the threat is towards a third party, the simple moral equation involved in the D killing to save his own life does not arise.

The second way in which the proposed statutory defence differs from the common law is that the test of whether the D should have resisted the threat is stated more subjectively. Under the common law, the test is whether a sober person of reasonable firmness would have resisted the threat.[65] Thus, the unusually timid or weak-willed may not be able to rely on the defence. The Law Commission rejects this position, and states in the Bill simply that the threat must be one:

> ... which, in all the circumstances (including any of his personal characteristics that affect its gravity), [the D] cannot reasonably be expected to resist.[66]

57 See Chapter 7, p 187.

58 Report No 218, draft Bill, cl 25(2)(a).

59 *Ibid*, cl 25(2)(b).

60 *Ibid*, cl 25(2)(c).

61 [1987] AC 417.

62 [1992] 2 AC 412.

63 See p 192.

64 Report No 218, para 30.11.

65 See Chapter 7, p 189.

66 Report No 218, draft Bill, cl 25(2).

Although the D would not be able to upon intoxication as a relevant circumstance,[67] other relevant aspects of his character may be taken into account as one the circumstances affecting the decision as to whether he could 'reasonably' have been expected to resist the threat.

The third difference from the common law is less favourable to the D. This is that the burden of proof in relation to duress is to be placed on the D. The D would be required to prove, on the balance of probabilities, that the alleged threats were made. The Law Commission considers that this change is reasonable because it feels that the defence:

> ... is much more likely than any other defence to depend on assertions which are particularly difficult for the prosecution to investigate or subsequently disprove.[68]

This reversal of the burden would also extend to the limitation of the offence, present in the current law as well, that it should not be available to a person:

> ... who knowingly and without reasonable excuse exposed himself to the risk of the threat made or believed to have been made.[69]

This applies, for example, to the D who has voluntarily joined a terrorist organisation. He cannot then use the defence of duress to escape liability for offences committed as a result of this membership. The Law Commission's proposal would mean that:

> If the question arises whether a person knowingly and without reasonable excuse exposed himself to such a risk, it is for him to show that he did not.[70]

Duress of circumstances

The Bill would put into statutory form the common law the defence of duress of circumstances, or necessity,[71] that has developed in recent years.[72] As with duress by threats the statutory defence, unlike the common law one, would be available in relation to any offence, including murder.

Duress of circumstances is defined by cl 26(2) as arising where the D does an act and:

> (a) he does it because he knows or believes that it is immediately necessary to avoid death or serious injury to himself or another; and

67 Report No 218, draft Bill, cl 33(1).

68 Report No 218, para 33.6.

69 *Ibid*, draft Bill, cl 25(4).

70 *Ibid*, cl 25(4).

71 It should be noted that the Law Commission distinguishes duress of circumstances from necessity – Report No 218, paras 35.4–35.6.

72 See Chapter 7, p 194.

(b) the danger that he knows or believes to exist is such that in all the circumstances (including any of his personal characteristics that affect its gravity) he cannot reasonably be expected to act otherwise.

From this it can be seen that the wording of this defence mirrors that of duress by threats. It is very broad, and could be interpreted to cover threats, or situations of self-defence or prevention of crime. The use of the duress of circumstances where these other offences are applicable is specifically excluded by cl 26(5).

As with duress by threats, the burden of proof is placed on the D. Similarly, the D cannot rely on a danger to which he has voluntarily exposed himself, with the burden of proof again falling on the D.

SELF-DEFENCE, PREVENTION OF CRIME

The common law defences of self-defence and the statutory defence of prevention of crime are brought together in cl 27 of the Bill attached to the Law Commission's Report No 218, *Legislating the Criminal Code: Offences against the Person and General Principles*.[73] The clause lists various purposes for which the use of force will not constitute an offence. The force must be only such as is reasonable in the circumstances as the D believes them to be. Thus far the clause exactly matches the common law. The list of purposes, however, does contain some degree of extension or clarification of the current position. There are five purposes listed in cl 27(1), as follows:

(a) to protect himself or another from injury, assault or detention caused by a criminal act;

(b) to protect himself or (with the authority of that other) another from trespass to the person;

(c) to protect property belonging to another from appropriation, destruction or damage caused by a criminal act or (with the authority of the other) from trespass or infringement; or

(d) to prevent crime or a breach of the peace.

This list makes it clear that it is possible for what would otherwise constitute an offence against the person to be justified by the desire to protect property, or to protect another from a non-criminal trespass to the person, provided that the force used is reasonable in the circumstances believed to exist. This probably extends the present law.[74]

The meaning of 'use of force' is defined in cl 29. This states that in addition to the direct application of force, it includes: causing an impact on another;

73 1993, Cm 2370, London: HMSO.

74 Cf Chapter 7, pp 172–73.

threatening to use force; and detaining a person without actually using force. The same clause also provides that behaviour which would constitute an attempt to commit an offence is protected by this defence, in addition to behaviour which would otherwise amount to the offence itself.[75]

Clause 27 contains provisions clarifying that an act may for the purposes of the defence be a 'crime' or 'criminal' notwithstanding the fact that the person committing it may not be liable on the grounds of, for example, lack of capacity, automatism, insanity, duress or intoxication. It also limits the 'subjective' approach which applies generally to the D's view of the circumstances in the situation where the D is using force against a constable or a person assisting a constable. Here, the question of whether the constable is acting in the execution of duty is to be determined as a matter of fact,[76] and not as question of what the D believed.[77]

Finally, cl 28 provides that the use of force in effecting or assisting in a lawful arrest does not constitute an offence, provided that it is only such force as is reasonable in the circumstances as the person using the force believed them to be. This seems simply to be a re-enactment of the relevant part of s 3 of the Criminal Law Act 1967, and does not amend the law on this issue.

CONSENT

The Law Commission issued a consultation paper on the issue of *Consent and Offences against the Person* in 1994.[78] The decision of the House of Lords in *Brown*,[79] in the same year, prompted it to carry out further consideration, and a longer consultation paper was issued in 1995 – that is, Consultation Paper No 139, *Consent in the Criminal Law*. The Commission has not yet issued firm proposals as result of this consultation. What follows is therefore concerned with its preliminary views, as expressed in the 1995 consultation paper. The paper was issued prior the decision of the European Court of Human Rights which found that the convictions in *Brown* did not constitute an infringement of any of the provisions of the European Convention on Human Rights.

Given the preliminary nature of the views, and the fact that no specific proposals for reform are in the pipeline, these suggestions will be dealt with relatively briefly.

The Law Commissions current suggestions for this area of the law are contained in paras 4.47–4.53.

75 Report No 218, draft Bill, cl 29(2).

76 Or possibly law?

77 Report No 218, draft Bill, cl 27(6). For discussion of the current law on this issue, see Chapter 7, p 174.

78 Consultation Paper No 134.

79 [1994] 1 AC 212 – discussed in Chapter 7, p 178 *et seq*.

Serious disabling injury

There are certain types of offences to which the Commission suggests consent should never be a defence. These are those which involve the D in inflicting 'serious disabling injury' either intentionally, or recklessly.[80] Implicit in this is that the a person who intentionally or recklessly causes fatal injuries cannot plead consent.

'Serious disabling injury' is defined in para 4.51 as an injury or injuries which:

(a) cause serious distress; and

(b) involve the loss of a bodily member or organ or permanent bodily injury or permanent functional impairment, or serious or permanent disfigurement, or severe and prolonged pain, or serious impairment of mental health, or prolonged unconsciousness.

This definition, which was originally put forward by Professor Glanville Williams in a different context,[81] clearly has a considerable degree of overlap with the concept of 'grievous bodily harm' under s 18 or 20 of the OAPA 1861.[82] Not all injuries which would be classified as GBH would fall within the Law Commission's proposal, however. A fractured skull, for example, would clearly be GBH, but would not necessarily have the effects to bring it within the scope of 'serious disabling injury'.

Other injuries

In relation to the causing of injuries which fall short of a seriously disabling injury, the Commission's suggestion that a defence of consent should generally be available, irrespective of whether the injuries were caused intentionally or recklessly.[83]

Exceptions

Age

Although it will be possible, under the Commission's proposals, for people under the age of 18 to give a valid consent to injuries which are not seriously disabling, this will only be the case where the particular individual is able 'by

80 Consultation Paper No 134, para 4.48.

81 Williams, G, 'Force, injury and serious injury' (1990) 140 NLJ 1227, p 1229.

82 See Chapter 5, p 120.

83 Consultation Papers, paras 4.49 and 4.50.

reason of age and maturity to make a decision for himself or herself on the matter in question'.[84] Moreover, in relation to injuries caused intentionally for sexual, religious or spiritual purposes no consent by a person under 18 should be regarded as valid.[85]

Medical treatment or research

Injuries, of whatever degree of seriousness, arising during 'proper medical treatment or care' or 'properly approved medical research' should not give rise to criminal liability if the V has consented to the treatment, care or participation in the research.[86]

Recognised sport

A person should not be guilty of an offence of causing injury which occurs 'in the course of playing or practising a recognised sport in accordance with its rules'.[87] A recognised sport should mean:

> ... all such sports, martial arts activities and other activities of a recreational nature as may be set out from time to time in a list to be kept and published by the UK Sports Council in accordance with a scheme approved by the appropriate minister for the recognition of sports, and the rules of a recognised sport should mean the rules of that sport as approved in accordance with the provisions of such a scheme.[88]

Fighting and horseplay

A person who intentionally or recklessly causes injury of any type in the course of fighting[89] should not be able to use the defence of consent. This should not apply, however, to an injury falling short of a serious disabling injury, which is caused in the course of 'undisciplined consensual horseplay'.

Conclusions

The overall effect of these recommendations would be to extend the current scope of the defence of consent. In particular, the participation in consensual sado-masochistic activities which involved the causing of more than transient or trifling bodily harm would no longer be an offence, provided that the

84 Consultation Paper No 134, para 5.19–5.21.

85 *Ibid*, paras 10.52–10.55.

86 *Ibid*, paras 8.1–8.51.

87 *Ibid*, para 12.68

88 *Ibid*, para 13.19.

89 Other than as part of a recognised sport.

participants were all over the age of 18, and the injuries fell short of being seriously disabling. In other words, the House of Lords decision in *Brown*[90] would be substantially reversed.

INTOXICATION

As we have seen earlier in this chapter, the Home Office proposals in relation to the reform of non-fatal offences contain provisions relating to the effect of voluntary intoxication on liability.[91] More comprehensive proposals were contained in the Law Commission's Report No 229, *Legislating the Criminal Code: Intoxication and Criminal Liability*, published in 1995. The proposals contain a draft Bill, and what follows refers to the clauses of that Bill.

The meaning of an 'intoxicant' is dealt with in cl 4. It means 'alcohol, a drug or other substance (of whatever nature) which, once taken into the body, has the capacity to impair awareness, understanding or control'. A person is 'intoxicated' if his awareness, understanding or control is affected by an intoxicant. The fact that a person is particularly susceptible to being affected by the substance is irrelevant for these purposes.[92]

The provisions as regards the liability of those who are intoxicated are contained in cl 1. These state that if a person's intoxication is 'voluntary',[93] and it is alleged that he had the mental element of an offence in that he:

(a) acted intentionally with respect to a particular result;

(b) had a particular purpose in acting in a particular way;

(c) had any particular knowledge or belief; or

(d) acted fraudulently or dishonestly,

then evidence of his intoxication may be taken into account in assessing his state of mind at the relevant time. If, however, the prosecution does not need to prove any of (a) to (d), then the person is to be treated as 'having been aware at the material time of anything of which he would have been aware but for his intoxication'.[94]

Clause 1(4) provides that where the person's intoxication was involuntary then evidence of his intoxication may always be taken into account in determining whether the alleged mental element has been proved.

90 [1994] 1 AC 212. See Chapter 7, p 181.

91 See above, p 218.

92 Report No 229, draft Bill, cl 4(1).

93 The meaning of 'voluntary' and 'involuntary' is discussed further below.

94 Report No 229, draft Bill, cl 1(3).

The effect of these provisions is by and large to replicate the current common law position whereby in relation to offences where liability is based on recklessness evidence of voluntary intoxication is irrelevant. Where, on the other hand, the prosecution is required to prove a specific mental state going beyond recklessness, such evidence can be considered in deciding whether the D did in fact have that mental state at the relevant time.

The distinction between 'voluntary' and 'involuntary' intoxication is dealt with by cl 5. It deals with it by defining 'involuntary' intoxication and then providing that a person who is intoxicated other than involuntarily is intoxicated voluntarily. A person is involuntarily intoxicated under the clause if one of four conditions is satisfied, namely:

(a) at the time he took the intoxicant he was not aware that it was or might be an intoxicant; or

(b) he took the intoxicant solely for medicinal purposes; or

(c) the intoxicant was administered to him without his consent; or

(d) he took the intoxicant in such circumstances as would, in relation to a criminal charge, afford the defence of duress by threats or any other defence recognised by law.

Condition (b) (intoxicant taken for medicinal purposes) is further dealt with by cl 5(2). If the D was aware that the intoxicant might give rise to 'aggressive or uncontrollable behaviour on his part', or failed to take reasonable precautions to counter such an effect, being aware that it might occur, then he will be regarded as being voluntarily intoxicated unless the intoxicant was taken on medical advice, and in accordance with any directions given by the person providing the medical advice.

A person who is particularly susceptible to being affected by an intoxicant (either because of a physical or mental condition, or because of something done or omitted to be done by him) then he will be regarded as being involuntarily intoxicated, unless he was aware of the susceptibility.[95] This would apply, for example, to the diabetic D who fails to understand the effects of failing to eat after taking insulin.[96]

Clause 6 contains some complex special rules to deal with the D who has taken a combination of intoxicants, but was not aware that one or more of them was an intoxicant. The clause provides that if the D would not have been intoxicated but for the unrecognised intoxicant (the clause refers to it as the 'undetected substance'), then he will be regarded as being involuntarily intoxicated. Further, if his lack of awareness is solely due to the undetected substance, then he will not be regarded as having been aware for the purposes of cl 1(3). Similarly, if he is in an automatous state which is solely attributable

95 Report No 229, draft Bill, cl 5(3).

96 *Bailey* [1983] 2 All ER 503.

to the undetected substance he is to be regarded as involuntarily intoxicated for the purposes of cl 2 (discussed below).

The final provisions of the Bill to be considered are with the effect of intoxication on states of mind concerned with defences. Clause 2 concerns automatism. Where the automatism was caused wholly or in part by voluntary intoxication, then the D can rely on the automatism to rebut the presence of the specific states of mind listed in cl 1(2) (above). If the prosecution does not need to prove one of these states of mind, however, the automatism will be disregarded, and the D will be treated as having been aware of anything which he would have been aware had he not been intoxicated.[97]

Clause 3 deals with the effect of intoxication on beliefs which would otherwise negative liability. The clause follows the same general principle as is applied by cl 1. Thus, where the offence requires the proof of one the specific states of mind listed in cl 1(2), then the D who holds a belief that would negative liability can rely on this, even though his intoxication is voluntary. The D, for example, who kills in the mistaken belief that he is being attacked, could use his belief as a defence to a charge of murder. He could still be convicted of manslaughter, however, since this does not require proof of one of the specific states of mind.[98] Similarly, he could use the belief as a defence to a charge under s 18 of the OAPA, but not under s 20.[99]

As regards voluntary manslaughter cl 3(3) provides that where an intoxicated D kills, but holds:

> ... a particular belief which, had he not been intoxicated, would have operated to reduced the homicide to manslaughter, that belief shall so operate whether the intoxication was voluntary or involuntary.

So the D who mistakenly, as a result of intoxication, thinks that the V has acted in a way which would amount to provocation, can nevertheless rely on this in defence to a charge of murder, even if the intoxication was voluntary.

Overall, the proposals contained in the Law Commission's Report would substantially reproduce the current law, but with some anomalies being addressed. There is little to criticise in the proposals, but the form and structure of the draft Bill seems unduly complex. The simpler approach taken in the Home Office proposals is probably to be preferred.

---

97 Ie, under Report No 229, draft Bill, cl 1(3).

98 See *ibid*, para 7.13.

99 See Chapter 5, pp 114–27.

BIBLIOGRAPHY

Archbold, *Criminal Evidence, Pleading and Practice*, 1998, London: Sweet & Maxwell

Ashworth, A, *Principles of Criminal Law*, 2nd edn, 1995, Oxford: Clarendon

Ashworth, A, 'The doctrine of provocation' [1976] CLJ 292

Blackstone, W (Sir), *Commentaries on the Laws of England (1765–69)*, Chicago: Chicago UP

Card, Cross and Jones, *Criminal Law*, 14th edn, 1998, London: Butterworths

Clarkson, CMV and Keating, HM, *Criminal Law: Text and Materials*, 4th edn, 1998, London: Sweet & Maxwell

CLRC, 14th Report, *Offences Against the Person* (1980), Cmnd 7844, London: HMSO

Fletcher, G, *Rethinking Criminal Law*, 1978, New York: Little, Brown

Gardner, S, 'Appreciating *Olugboja*' (1996) 16 Legal Studies 275

Griew, E, 'The future of diminished responsibility' [1988] Crim LR 75

Harris, D, O'Boyle, K and Warbrick, C, *Law of the European Convention on Human Rights*, 1995, London: Butterworths

Kennedy, I, *Treat Me Right, Essays in Medical Law and Ethics*, 1988, Oxford: Clarendon

Kennedy, I, and Grubb, A, *Medical Law*, 2nd edn, 1994, London: Butterworths

Kenny, CS, *Outlines of Criminal Law*, 16th edn, 1952, Cambridge: Cambridge UP

Lacey, N, Wells, C and Meure, D, *Reconstructing Criminal Law*, 2nd edn, 1998, London: Butterworths

Mackay (Lord), 'The consequences of killing very young children' [1993] Crim LR 21

Slater, J, 'Making sense of self-defence' (1996) 5 Nott LJ 140

Smith, JC, 'Commentary on the Court of Appeal's decision in *Parmenter*' [1991] Crim LR 43.

Smith, JC and Hogan, B, *Criminal Law Cases and Materials*, 6th edn, 1996, London: Butterworths

Stephen, JF, *Digest of the Criminal Law*, 4th edn, 1887, London: Macmillan

Stone, R, *Principles of Contract Law*, 3rd edn, 1997, London: Cavendish Publishing

Stone, R, 'Reckless assaults after *Savage and Parmenter*' (1992) 12 OJLS 578

Stone, R, *Textbook on Civil Liberties*, 2nd edn, 1997, London: Blackstone

Stone, R, *Law of Agency*, 1996, London: Cavendish Publishing

Stone, R, *Textbook on Civil Liberties*, 2nd edn, 1997, London: Blackstone

INDEX